Sebastian Lohsse | Reiner Schulze
Dirk Staudenmayer (Eds.)

Smart Products

Münster Colloquia on EU Law and the Digital Economy VI

HART

Nomos

The Deutsche Nationalbibliothek lists this publication in the Deutsche Nationalbibliografie; detailed bibliographic data are available on the Internet at http://dnb.d-nb.de

ISBN: HB (Nomos) 978-3-8487-8556-8
ePDF (Nomos) 978-3-7489-2977-2

British Library Cataloguing-in-Publication Data
A catalogue record for this book is available from the British Library.

ISBN: HB (Hart) 978-1-5099-5675-3

Library of Congress Cataloging-in-Publication Data
Lohsse, Sebastian | Schulze, Reiner | Staudenmayer, Dirk
Smart Products
Münster Colloquia on EU Law and the Digital Economy VI
Sebastian Lohsse | Reiner Schulze | Dirk Staudenmayer (Eds.)
246 pp.
Includes bibliographic references.

ISBN 978-1-5099-5675-3 (hardcover Hart)

Onlineversion
Nomos eLibrary

1st Edition 2022

Contents

An Introduction

'Smart Products' – A Focal Point for Legal Developments in the Digital Economy

Sebastian Lohsse, Reiner Schulze & Dirk Staudenmayer[*]

As smart products become increasingly common, EU law faces new challenges. In this phase of the transition to the digital economy, the sale of such products and other contracts relating to such products pose new questions. Whereas certain questions have already been addressed by the 'Digital Contract Directives' – the Sale of Goods Directive (SGD) and the Digital Content Directive (DCD)[1] – these Directives arguably do not cover all aspects to be dealt with even at present. Moreover, especially with the increasing integration of artificial intelligence (AI), smart products will remain a focal point for legal developments in the digital economy. This is true not only for contract law but also for tort law when taking into account the perspective of smart products becoming able to act autonomously. This article shall serve as an introduction both to current and future aspects of the legal developments in these two fields.

I. What are 'smart products'?

In a nutshell, smart products are goods which are equipped with digital content, whether embedded in the goods or not, or which are connected with digital services.

---

* Sebastian Lohsse und Reiner Schulze are Professors of Law, Centre for European Private Law, University of Münster. Dirk Staudenmayer is Head of Unit Contract Law, DG Justice and Consumers, European Commission and Honorary Professor at the University of Münster. The present contribution expresses only the personal opinion of the authors and does not bind in any way the European Commission.

1 Directives 2019/770 on certain aspects concerning contracts for the supply of digital content and digital services (DCD) and 2019/771 on certain aspects concerning contracts for the sale of goods (SGD), OJ 22.5.2019, L 136/1 and L 136/28; on both Directives see *Staudenmayer*, The Directives on Digital Contracts: First Steps Towards the Private Law of the Digital Economy (2020), ERPL, 219 et seq.; for a more detailed analysis of the DCD see the article-by-article commentary, Schulze/Staudenmayer (eds.), EU Digital Law (2020).

1. *Definition in EU law*

Smart products are already indirectly defined in the EU *acquis*. The legislator of the 'Digital Contracts Directives' wanted to include (not all, but) some smart products into the scope of the SGD. It calls this sub-category 'goods with digital elements' and defines them as 'any tangible movable items that incorporate or are inter-connected with digital content or a digital service in such a way that the absence of that digital content or digital service would prevent the goods from performing their functions'.[2] The digital content or digital service incorporated in or interconnected with such goods with digital elements are included in the scope[3] of the SGD if they are provided with the goods under the sales contract.[4] In this context it is irrelevant whether digital content is already installed at the time of the conclusion of the contract of sale or whether it is, according to the contract, installed only later.[5]

The effect of this is that the consumer-buyer of such goods would have remedies for a lack of conformity of the goods themselves and of the digital content or digital service incorporated in or interconnected with them. If, however, the criteria of the definition of goods with digital elements (or of the SGD scope requiring the supply under the sales contract) are not fulfilled, but the conformity of the digital content or digital service incorporated in or interconnected with goods is at stake, the consumer remedies would be determined according to the DCD.[6] It was the intention of the legislator that the two Directives be complementary;[7] this is manifested in the drafting of the respective articles and recitals.[8]

2 Article 2 No 5 (b) SGD and Article 2 No 3 DCD.

3 And consequently excluded from the scope of the DCD, see Articles 3 (4) and 2 No 3 DCD.

4 Article 3 (3) SGD. Whether goods are provided under the sales contract with digital elements, is to be determined either by express provision in the contract or as the result of an interpretation of the sales contract, see Recitals 15 SGD and 21 DCD, which also contain an example for such an interpretation. Both Directives contain the same presumption, namely that in cases of doubt, the sales contract covers these digital elements, see Articles 3 (3) 2 SGD, 3 (4) 2 DCD. Whether the consumer has also concluded a license agreement with the third party which supplies the digital content is not pertinent, see Recitals 15 and 21 SGD.

5 Recitals 14 SGD and 21 DCD; see also examples in Recitals 21 DCD and 15 SGD.

6 Articles 3 (1), (3) DCD; Recital 22 DCD and 16 SGD with examples.

7 Recitals 20 DCD, 13 SGD.

8 Recitals 20 – 22 DCD, 13 – 16 SGD.

Therefore, the basic element of the definitions and scope provisions of the 'Digital Contracts Directives' can be used to define smart products, namely 'any tangible movable items that incorporate or are inter-connected with digital content or a digital service'.

2. *Why are smart products important for the Digital Economy?*

The importance of smart products is firstly linked to the rise of the Internet of Things (IoT) as such. The number of IoT devices has evolved very rapidly and the increase over recent years was even considerably stronger.[9] If one takes one of the estimates – 46 billion IoT devices by the end of 2021 – as an example, one could say statistically that in 2021 every human on this planet had around 6 IoT devices. In reality, this saturation level is obviously unevenly spread; the average number of connected devices per household in the US in 2020 for instance, was 10.[10]

Within this overall development of the IoT, the increasing number of smart homes has a strong impact on the use of smart products. The number of smart homes in Europe and North America was estimated to have reached 102.6 million in 2020.[11] North America is the more advanced smart home market, with an estimate of 51.2 million smart homes, i.e. 35.6 % of all homes. The strong market growth of 18.7 % in 2019 and 2020 is expected to continue and to reach close to 78 million homes by 2024. This would mean that more than half (53 %) of all homes have smart products. In Europe there was a total of 51.4 million smart homes estimated at the end of 2020. This is forecasted to exceed 100 million homes at the end of 2024, representing a market penetration of 42 %.

---

9 Obviously there are different figures, but all statistics agree on a very strong growth rate; see for instance How Many IoT Devices Are There in 2021? More than Ever! (techjury.net) (last accessed on 22.08.2021) which point out, referring to Juniper Research, that the number of IoT devices in 2021 will reach 46 billion, constituting a 200 % increase compared to 2016; see also Number of IoT devices 2015–2025 (statista.com) (last accessed on 22.08.2021) which forecast that the number of IoT connected devices installed worldwide will grow from 15, 41 in 2015 to 75, 44 in 2025 (in billions).

10 See How Many IoT Devices Are There in 2021? More than Ever! (techjury.net) (last accessed on 22.08.2021), referring to Statista.

11 See for this and the following figures IoT News – The number of smart homes in Europe and North America will reach 179 million in 2024 (Iotbbusiness-news.com) (last accessed on 22.08.2021), referring to a research report from the IoT analyst firm Berg Insight.

In parallel with this, the sale of smart products is a fast-growing trend in many retail sectors. Amazon's Echo Dot already became the best-sold article on amazon.com for three Christmas sales in a row (2016, 2017 and 2018)[12]. Among the most sold product categories in 2021 were digital assistants like the ones produced by Google and Amazon, which can be used for shopping but also controlling smart homes, and other smart products dealing with different aspects of security in a smart home (e.g. smart door cameras, bells and locks; air quality monitors and smoke alarms; IT-security) or used to switch on and off lights, household appliances, media, heating etc.[13]

II. Smart products in present contract law

1. New dimensions for European contract law

From a contract law perspective, smart products are a key element of the SGD and the DCD, with each furthering the development of European contract law, adding a new dimension in the form of the supply of digital content and of the sale of goods with digital elements. Both Directives primarily concern consumer contracts (B2C), albeit with an impact on commercial contracts (B2B) due to the trader's redress against earlier links in the chain of contracts (Article 18 SGD; Article 20 DCD).

The SGD extends beyond the 1999 Consumer Sales Directive[14] by responding to challenges posed by digitalisation, especially through its provisions on goods with digital elements. The SGD covers many different types of smart products – from smartphones and laptops to autonomous household appliances and vehicles. The DCD concerns core aspects of contract law regarding the supply of digital content and digital services, but does not draw fine distinctions between the contract model applicable to the supply. This includes, as in the SGD for sales contracts, particularly the

12 https://voicebot.ai/2018/12/26/amazon-echo-device-sales-break-new-records-alexa-tops-free-app-downloads-for-ios-and-android-and-alexa-down-in-europe-on-christmas-morning (last accessed on 22.08.2021).

13 For the list of list of the most sold IoT Devices in 2021, see 18 Most Popular IoT Devices in 2021 (Only Noteworthy IoT Products) (softwaretestinghelp.com) (last accessed 22.08.2021).

14 Directive 1999/44/EC of the European Parliament and of the Council of 25 May 1999 on certain aspects of the sale of consumer goods and associated guarantees [1999] OJ L 171/12.

conformity of such products and the consumer's remedies (including the respective obligations following the termination of contract) as well as the possibility for the trader to modify the performance rendered. The DCD covers the 'physical' smart products where the tangible medium merely serves to carry the digital content (Article 3 (3) DCD), such as a USB-Stick. Furthermore, taking into account the above mentioned determination of the scope of this Directive, it extends to a much wider spectrum of smart products. Regardless of the manner of supply, the Directive not only covers simple applications in the 'smart home' but also complex forms of AI.

Through the provisions of these 'Digital Contract Directives', the sale of goods with digital elements and the supply of digital products, with the different elements of smart products, are integrated into the structures and concepts of European contract law which have emerged over the past decades, particularly through the Consumer Sales Directive. Nonetheless, the Directives also develop these concepts and structures to take account of the changes resulting from digitalisation, including the importance and characteristics of smart products.[15] The combination of continuity and innovation is readily apparent in the notion of conformity, which serves as a basic conceptual framework for both Directives, albeit with some differences.[16] Both Directives have not only adopted the central notion of conformity from the Consumer Sales Directive but have also made further additions (such as 'reasonable expectations'). Whereas the SGD adopts these concepts for the sale of goods, the DCD applies them beyond the sale of goods in principle to all different types of contracts concerning digital content or digital services. In this respect, a concept that was originally at home in sales law now provides a conceptual framework for general contract law.[17] Furthermore, both Directives have developed the concept in two respects. With regard to their approach in general, the relationship between the subjective and objective criteria for conformity have changed vis-à-vis the Consumer Sales Directive to favour an objective standpoint. For the specific requirements for digital products, a significant innovation with extensive consequences for contract practice can be seen in particular in the trader's update obligations and (under the Digital Content Directive) the ability to modify the digital content or digital service.

---

15 *Schulze/Zoll*, European Contract Law (3rd edn, 2021), § 1 para. 65 et seq.; *Staudenmayer*, Die Richtlinien zu den digitalen Verträgen (2019), ZEuP, 663.

16 *Schulze*, Die Digitale-Inhalte Richtlinie (2019), ZEuP, 665 (709).

17 *Schulze/Zoll*, European Contract Law (3rd edn, 2021), § 5 para. 37 et seq.

2. *Update obligations*

a) *An innovative approach*

The update obligations form a central aspect of the provisions on conformity under the 'Digital Contract Directives'. Such obligations are included both in the subjective (Article 6 (d) SGD; Article 7 (d) DCD) as well as in the objective requirements (Article 7 (3), (4) SGD; Article 8 (2), (3) DCD). The need for such rules was highlighted in particular in relation to the importance of security updates.[18] However, the update obligations are by no means limited to such type of updates. According to the wording of the legislation, the trader is obliged to supply the consumer with updates as stipulated in the contract (Article 6 (d) SGD; Article 7 (d) DCD) and updates that are necessary to keep the good or digital product in conformity (Article 7 (3) SGD; Article 8 (2) DCD).

Accordingly, the update obligations have a dual link to the notion of conformity. On the one hand, from an objective perspective the obligation itself, its scope and content are measured against what is necessary to maintain all other subjective and objective requirements regarding conformity. For example, for the conformity of goods with digital elements or of a digital product, the suitability for purposes for which the goods/digital product would normally be used may be necessary (Article 7 (1) (a) SGD; Article 8 (1) (a) DCD). An update obligation may arise for the trader if, due to a change in the technology, this suitability can only be maintained via an update. On the other hand, the correct performance of the update obligation is itself part of conformity. There is thus a non-conformity if the trader does not supply an update although this is provided in the contract itself or is necessary for the objective conformity with the contract. The same applies where the trader supplies an update, but this does not satisfy the requirements under Article 7 (3) SGD or Article 8 (2) DCD. In such cases the remedies for non-conformity under Article 13 et seq. SGD or Article 11, 14 et seq. DCD are available to the consumer (in principle, bringing into conformity, price reduction or termination).

Furthermore, the new provisions on updates are characterised by a two-pronged approach. Whereas they oblige the trader to supply digital content in the form of updates, this supply obligation is also combined with an information duty regarding the update itself. The trader is to inform the consumer of the availability of the update and of the consequences of

18 Recitals 30 und 31 SGD; Recital 47 DCD.

the failure to install it (Article 7 (4) (a) SGD; Article 8 (3) (a) DCD).[19] The consumer can then decide whether to install the update. However, this not only provides an informed basis for the consumer's decision (not) to take action but also limits the scope of the trader's responsibility: the trader is not liable for any lack of conformity resulting solely from the lack of the relevant update if he has complied with the aforementioned information duty, yet the consumer has failed to install the update within a reasonable time.

The provisions on update obligations are especially innovative as they provide for further performance as requirement for conformity in contracts that are primarily structured around the single exchange of performances.[20] They therefore deviate from the traditional approach in sales law (and also in European consumer sales law), namely that the relevant point in time for conformity is at the passing of risk or at the time of delivery. In many cases the update obligation therefore extends the trader's responsibility for conformity beyond such point in time. The duration is determined by what the consumer may reasonably expect given the type and purpose of the goods and the digital elements or of the digital product, and taking into account the circumstances and nature of the contract (Article 7 (3) (a) SGD; Article 8 (2) (b) DCD). Depending on these reasonable expectations, the update obligation can even extend beyond the period of liability for non-conformity.[21]

This innovative approach is also linked with a new distinction regarding the temporal dimension. For contracts for the single act of supply or for a series of such individual acts of supply, the performance of the primary obligation is to be at a particular point in time (e.g. supplying a game via downloading to a smart device or sending each week a link to the next module in an online course). For such contracts the digital product typically remains in the sphere of the consumer, who has the possibility to access and use the digital product for an indefinite period.[22] As just mentioned, the duration of the update obligations is determined by what the consumer may reasonably expect. This is distinguished from contracts for the continuous supply over a period of time (e.g. a subscription contract for music or for cloud-storage). The supply can either be for a defined

19 For details see EU Digital Law/*Staudenmayer*, Article 8 DCD para. 125 et seq.; HK-BGB/*Schulze*, § 327f BGB para. 6.

20 *Schulze/Zoll*, European Contract Law (3rd edn, 2021), § 5 para. 47 et seq.

21 Recital 47 DCD. For details, EU Digital Law/*Staudenmayer*, Article 8 DCD para. 129 et seq.; HK-BGB/*Schulze*, § 327f BGB para. 7 et seq.

22 Recital 56 DCD.

period of time (e.g. a fixed two-year subscription contract) or for an indefinite period (e.g. a subscription contract which continues to run until the consumer decides to cancel). The decisive feature is the obligation for the trader to continue to supply the digital product to the consumer throughout this period. In such cases the periods of time for the primary obligation to supply (supply period) and for the update obligation overlap, assuming of course that the DCD applies. For contracts for goods with digital elements (such as the pre-installed operating system on a tablet-PC), however, the SGD provides an approach that is tailored to sales law (on the basis of a two-year liability and update period, with extensions for supply periods longer than two years and with the possibility for Member States to extend such time limits (Article 7 (3) (b) in conjunction with Article 10 (2), (5) SGD).

This distinction in the 'Digital Contract Directives' between single supply (or a series of individual acts of supply) and continuous supply over a period of time introduces a new structural element into European contract law. Its significance is not limited to the provisions on conformity; it also concerns the time periods and duration for liability, the burden of proof, price reduction and the reimbursement following termination (Articles 10 (2), (5), 11 (3) SGD; Articles 11 (2), (3), 12 (2) and (3), 14 (5), 16 (1) DCD). In each instance the new concept within the 'Digital Contract Directives' divides the spectrum of contracts falling within their scope using an approach differing from the distinction between sales and service contracts or the traditional classification of contract types under national laws.[23]

b) *Problems and regulatory gaps*

It is to be expected that a number of questions arise from new technologies in the form of smart products and from a new legal approach, such as the update obligations. Such questions require clarification through legal doctrine and case law. Some of these questions can only be outlined here, but others are covered in more depth in the contributions to this volume. The legal nature of update obligations requires particular attention from a doctrinal perspective, requiring consideration that the update obligations

---

23 *Schulze*, Die Digitale-Inhalte Richtlinie (2019), ZEuP, 665 (714 et seq.), also on the differences in relation to German law; *Wendland*, Sonderprivatrecht für Digitale GüterInhalt (2019), ZVglRWiss, 191 (210 et seq.)

take the form of individual measures (i.e. through the supply of the individual update for the smart product during the relevant time period), yet such acts do not signal the end of the performance obligation. It will often rather be necessary for the trader to constantly monitor the technological developments surrounding the smart product in order to determine whether there is the need for an update and, if so, the suitable content thereof. In this respect the update obligation may be considered a 'continuous obligation'.[24]

Likewise, the relationship between the update obligations and the corresponding information duties also needs to be considered. Here the duty to inform the consumer of the necessary update (Article 7 (3) SGD; Article 8 (2) DCD) may need to be viewed as being ancillary to the primary obligation (supplying the update).[25] Contrastingly, an 'obligation' for the trader to inform the consumer not only about the availability of the update but also of the consequences of failing to install it (Article 7 (4) (a) SGD; Article 8 (3) (a) DCD) is rather to be understood as an *Obliegenheit*, to use the German legal term: in the event of breach the consumer does not have a claim to demand performance (or damages), but performance is merely in the trader's interest.[26] Similarly, it is also necessary to determine the legal nature of the installation of the supplied update by the consumer (Article 7 (4) SGD; Article 8 (3) DCD).[27] The consumer is free to decide whether to install the update, but from a legal perspective the installation is in the consumer's own interest as otherwise he would exclude the trader's liability.

Further consideration will also be needed with regard to determining the duration of the update obligation for smart products in cases of single supply or a series of individual acts of supply. In light of the various different circumstances surrounding supply the legislator refrained from setting a strict time period to subject the duration of the update obligations to a uniform period. This gain in flexibility is, however, offset by the loss of legal certainty for the parties. Developing 'case groups' (first through legal

---

24 *Wendehorst*, Aktualisierungen und andere digitale Dauerleistungen, in: Stabentheiner/Wendehorst/Zöchling-Jud (eds.), Das neue Gewährleistungsrecht für Waren, digitale Inhalte und digitale Dienstleistungen (2019), p. 111 (118); *Schulze/Zoll*, European Contract Law (3rd edn, 2021), § 5 para. 47.

25 HK-BGB/*Schulze*, § 327f BGB para. 6; see for the classification as a primary obligation, however, *Schneider*, Impulse und Probleme der Digitale-Inhalte-Richtlinie und deren Umsetzung im BGB (2021), ITRB, 182 (189).

26 On *Obliegenheit* see German Civil Code/*Schulze*, § 242 BGB para. 26.

27 See the contribution by *Janssen*, in this volume.

doctrine but then increasingly by the courts) could contribute to affording greater clarity to Article 7 (3) (a) SGD and Article 8 (2) (b) DCD, especially in contract practice, and increase legal certainty.

However, it may be doubted whether the law *de lege lata* overcomes the highlighted weaknesses of consumer protection concerning agreed deviations from the update obligations.[28]. According to Article 7 (5) SGD and Article 8 (5) DCD, there is no lack of conformity if, at the time of the conclusion of the sales contract, the consumer was specifically informed that a particular characteristic was deviating from the objective requirements for conformity and the consumer expressly and separately accepted that deviation when concluding the contract. In practice the trader therefore merely has to provide the consumer with a pre-formulated text on the deviations from the update obligation with an infamous 'I have read and agree to' box at the time of concluding the contract. In short, a simple tick of a box releases the trader from his update obligation. Recital 49 DCD expressly provides that the requirement of 'active and unequivocal conduct' by the consumer can be satisfied by 'ticking a box'. Even though the recitals to directives do not bind the courts,[29] it is questionable whether the ECJ will develop a stricter standard for 'active and unequivocal conduct' than is given in Recital 49 DCD.[30]

The question of damages – more precisely the harmonisation of damages for non-conformity – is a further problem surrounding the update obligations in relation to smart products and the conformity requirements in general. This is not addressed in the 'Digital Contract Directives' and as such is a matter for future European legislation. The proposal for the DCD did contain a rudimentary rule for damages,[31] but this was ultimately removed during the legislative process. Recital 73 DCD indeed acknowledges that a right to damages exists in all Member States, but the requirements, scope and content of the damage claims are certainly not the same across the Member States (e.g. the question of strict or objective

28 See e.g. *Spindler*, Umsetzung der Richtlinie über digitale Inhalte in das BGB (2021), MMR, 451 (456).

29 See C-162/97 *Nilsson* ECLI:EU:C:1998:554, para. 54.

30 On the question of the extent of the protection under the Unfair Terms Directive *Spindler*, Umsetzung der Richtlinie über digitale Inhalte in das BGB (2021), MMR, 451 (457 et seq.).

31 Article 14 COM(2015) 634 final. For detail see *Machnikowski*, Regulation of Damage on National or European Level, in: Schulze/Staudenmayer/Lohsse (eds.), Contracts for the Supply of Digital Content: Regulatory Challenges and Gaps (2017), p. 141.

liability, compensation of consequential losses,[32] evidence of the scope of loss and for future loss, etc.). This can have a considerable effect on the level of consumer protection in relation to smart products. Termination or price reduction will often offer no practical remedy where there is a failure to supply an update (especially as there will often not be a comparable alternative). Damages are also more effective to ensure conforming performance by the seller or supplier of smart products.[33] However, the lack of harmonisation is not only a disadvantage for the level of consumer protection but also for the objective of attaining a functioning internal market. In a cross-border respect the differing national rules concerning damage claims make it difficult for businesses to determine whether there is indeed a claim and, if so, the extent thereof. This is perhaps the greatest risk for a business in the event of non-conforming performance.

A particularly burdensome deficit in the provisions on update obligations may ultimately lie in the choice of addressee. According to the 'Digital Contract Directives' the update obligations are to be performed by the trader who concluded the sales or supply contract with the consumer. In fact, it is often a third party who is in the position to prepare and execute the update – this will often be the manufacturer, but could also include a licence holder or other provider. There is thus the question whether – and in any case how – the consumer shall be enabled to enforce claims against such third parties for an update of a smart product or for liability for failure to supply an update. Additionally, attention is also to be directed towards the legal framework surrounding the responsibility for the update between the various different links in the supply chain.[34]

3. *Modification of digital products*

a) *The trader's right to modify digital products*

The update obligations are closely linked to the provisions on the trader's unilateral contractual right to modify the digital content or digital service (Article 19 DCD). The trader may often deem it necessary (e.g. for security purposes or in light of new technologies or market developments) not on-

---

32 *Martens*, Contracts for the Supply of Digital Content – Consequential Loss, in ibid. p. 155.

33 *Schulze*, Die Digitale-Inhalte Richtlinie (2019), ZEuP, 665 (720 et seq.).

34 See the contributions by *H. Schulte-Nölke* and *C. Wendehorst*, in this volume.

ly to supply updates to maintain conformity but to make new versions of the digital product available ('upgrade'). Through such upgrades the trader modifies the contract with the consumer in relation to the characteristics of the product. However, in such circumstances the consumer may wish to continue to use the earlier version of the product (e.g. due to familiarity with the features). This would not accord with the trader's interest in only supplying one (or few) versions, for example to avoid the obligation to supply updates to older versions. The consumer would not be sufficiently protected in such a conflict of interests if freedom of contract allowed unrestricted contractual agreements on the trader's unilateral right to modify the digital product. Article 19 DCD therefore serves to balance the interests of the parties relating to upgrades.

The provision does not afford the trader with a comprehensive right to modify the digital product. It rather only covers cases in which the contract provides for such a right.[35] Article 19 DCD determines the permitted content and in particular the limitations and consequences of the right to modify. Its scope is restricted to modifications of the digital content (i.e. measures which maintain the essence of the product but do not in effect replace it with another).[36] Furthermore, it is limited to contracts for the continuous supply as per Article 8 (2) (a) DCD (in contrast to contracts for single supply or for a series of individual acts of supply). For such contracts the right to modify the digital contract extends beyond the contractually-owed updates under Article 7 (d) and Article 8 (2) (a) DCD and thus leads to a deviation from the performance due under the contract. Article 19 (1) DCD concerns all such changes, irrespective whether they are beneficial or detrimental (or neither) to the consumer. According to this provision, modifications of the digital product beyond what is necessary to maintain conformity are only permitted where certain requirements are satisfied. In contrast Article 19 (2) and (3) DCD afford the consumer the right to terminate the contract as a means to protect the consumer from modifications that limit the access or use of the product. The provision neither affects the role of the Unfair Terms Directive[37] in assessing the contract

---

35 For details see EU Digital Law/*Wendland*, Article 19 DCD para. 10; HK-BGB/*Schulze*, § 327r BGB para. 1 et seq.

36 *Spindler*, Umsetzung der Richtlinie über digitale Inhalte in das BGB (2021), MMR, 451 (528, 531).

37 Council Directive 93/13/EEC of 5 April 1993 on unfair terms in consumer contracts [1993] OJ L 95/29.

terms concerning modification rights nor the possibility for the parties to conclude a new contract for the supply of the digital product.[38]

b) Open questions

A number of questions and problems soon become apparent when looking at the effect of Article 19 DCD in practice. For example,[39] under Article 19 (1) (a) DCD the contract must allow and provide a valid reason for such a modification. The abstract nature of this condition means that there is a lack of detail surrounding whether and to what extent the condition is satisfied in particular circumstances. Article 19 (1) (b) DCD requires clarification whether the wording 'without additional cost to the consumer' also covers contracts in which the cost is not monetary but in fact the supply of personal data. Where the legal effects of Article 19 (1) are concerned, it remains to be considered how and with what restrictions the trader may make modifications (in particular whether he may independently engage with the consumer's digital environment[40]) and whether the consumer does not just need to tolerate the modification but is obliged to cooperate during the process. The contributions to this volume cover further questions surrounding the right to modify digital products. The scope covers the general problems of securing the consumer's power to freely consent to modifications (and the possible limitations thereof) to the question whether a corresponding right to modify also applies to goods with digital elements.[41] The effect of the new provisions on modification on contract design is of course especially important for contract practice.[42]

4. From transposition to transition

The update obligations and the right to modify digital products are prominent examples for the extensive development experienced by European contract law over recent years. There are of course other developments that cannot be discussed in detail here, yet their transposition can give national

38 Recital 75 DCD.
39 On the following examples, see HK-BGB/*Schulze*, § 327r BGB para. 4 et seq.
40 Against such possibility, *Möllnitz*, Änderungsbefugnis des Unternehmers bei digitalen Produkten (2021), MMR, 116 (120).
41 See the contribution by *K. Sein*, in this volume.
42 See the contribution by *I. Conrad*, in this volume.

law important new features. For instance, the DCD has completed the system of performance obligations and remedies for non-performance. The Directive regulates not just the obligation to perform in conformity and the consequences of non-conformity but also sets the obligation for the trader to perform (by supplying the digital product) and the corresponding consequences for non-performance (Articles 5 (1), 11, 13 DCD).[43] The 'Digital Contract Directives' provide that the consumer exercises the right to terminate the contract by making a corresponding statement to the trader (in accordance with the tendency in modern contract law, but deviating from the tradition in some Member States in which termination could only be effected by the court). Furthermore, the provisions on termination under the DCD cover contracts for single supply as well as 'long-term' contracts, including those contracts described in some legal systems as *Dauerschuldverhältnisse* ('contracts for the performance of a continuing obligation'). They therefore differ from the tradition in German law to provide separate rules for the *Rücktritt* in single supply contracts (§ 314 BGB; revocation) and the *Kündigung* in such *Dauerschuldverhältnisse* (§ 323 BGB; termination). Beyond this, the DCD now provides European consumer contract law with a system of the rights and obligations of the parties in the event of termination. This covers traditional obligations (such as reimbursement, Article 16 (1) DCD) as well as new types of rights and obligations tailored to the features of digital products (such as the prohibition on the use of data, the right to retrieve data, the obligation to refrain from using the digital product; Articles 16 (3)–(5), 17 (1) DCD).

The discussion of the further development of the concept of conformity by the new European legislation should also mention the other innovative approaches which concern smart products or digital products. This includes, for example, the provisions on the integration into the digital environment (Article 9 DCD) and on the installation of goods with digital elements (Article 8 (b) DCD) which expands on the model in Article 2 (5) Consumer Sales Directive. Even further, the provisions on conformity and the corresponding definitions in the 'Digital Contract Directives' feature numerous concepts that are of fundamental importance for a modern contract law that heeds the economic and social significance of smart products and digital products. For example, this concerns many of the definitions in Article 2 SGD and Article 2 DCD, such as 'digital content',

43 *Schulze/Zoll*, European Contract Law (3rd edn, 2021), § 5 para. 11 et seq.; on the controversial question whether the consumer has a corresponding claim, see § 6 para. 56.

'digital service', 'goods with digital elements', 'integration' and 'digital environment'. It also affects criteria, such as taking account of (personal) data as counter-performance (Article 3 (1) DCD) and technical standards (Article 7 (1) (a) SGD; Article 8 (1) (a) DCD), the inclusion of installation instructions (Articles 6 (c), 7 (1)(c) SGD; Articles 7 (c), 8 (1) (c) DCD), the provisions on the most recent version (Articles 8 (6) DCD) or the protection where third-party rights are violated (Article 9 SGD; Article 10 DCD).

These new approaches and concepts have now found their way into national law through the transposition of the Directives. They thereby belong to the core aspects of consumer law in all EU Member States. However, it is conceivable that the transposition into national law does not just mean a step towards further harmonisation of consumer law in the EU and adjustments to the digital age. It rather also appears feasible that in several cases the effects can extend beyond the scope of the Directives. For instance, it may be worthwhile for the national legislator and courts to use several of the aforementioned concepts and criteria in neighbouring fields of consumer law or indeed even in the B2B context. The latter is a distinct possibility because the application of the concepts covered in the Directives extends anyway to particular B2B legal relationships because of the provisions on redress (Article 18 SGD; Article 20 DCD). Applying different meanings to the notions of functionality, compatibility and interoperability (Article 8 (1) (b) in conjunction with Article 2 Nos 10–12 DCD) in cases falling outside the DCD would hardly be an ideal solution in practice. It therefore remains to be seen whether in the near future several of the new Directives' approaches and concepts provide a catalyst for further approximation of EU contract law in the digital age.

III. Prospects for future legal developments on smart products in both tort and contract law

1. Smart products in tort law

Whereas European contract law has already reacted, albeit somewhat incomplete, to the questions posed by smart products for the time being, the European legislator has not yet addressed tortious liability to a comparable extent, although it has not, of course escaped the attention of the European institutions. Challenges in this area are manifold and will become increasingly urgent with the future integration of elements of AI into smart products.

a) Multiplicity of actors

Most importantly, challenges result from the multiplicity of actors involved. While for decades we have been thinking in categories of fault and strict liability on the part of the tortfeasor being complemented by the producer's liability per the Product Liability Directive (PLD)[44], smart products blur the picture ever increasingly. With digital content or digital services being incorporated into or interconnected with physical goods not only the provider or 'manufacturer' of software comes into play. Rather, the necessity for updates as well as the dependency of smart products on the provision of data (be it from other smart products or the cloud) shifts the focus regarding liability. Instead of the user being the primary addressee of liability regimes, the focus will probably be directed more to those responsible for the operation of the 'smart element' of the object in question. Notably, this shift of liability has been addressed in the European Parliament's 'resolution of 20 October 2020 with recommendations to the Commission on a civil liability regime for artificial intelligence' and the corresponding proposal for a regulation[45]. At least with a view to systems incorporating AI, the proposal states that liability shall fall upon the 'operator' rather than on a mere user of the system. Moreover, the proposal suggests different standards of liability dependent upon the risk being connected with the particular AI-system. For the operator of a 'high-risk AI-system', for instance, there shall be strict liability (Article 4 of the proposed regulation).

b) Questions of user liability

While the balancing of liability between the different actors and the inclusion of operators into any sort of liability regime is probably one of the

---

44 Council Directive 85/374/EEC of 25 July 1985 on the approximation of the laws, regulations and administrative provisions of the Member States concerning liability for defective products, [1985] OJ L 210, p. 29 et seq.

45 European Parliament resolution of 20 October 2020 with recommendations to the Commission on a civil liability regime for artificial intelligence, P9_TA(2020)0276. – On this resolution, in more detail, *Wagner*, Haftung für Künstliche Intelligenz – Eine Gesetzesinitiative des Europäischen Parlaments (2021), ZEuP, 545 (572).

most challenging tasks,[46] smart products also raise questions with a view to the liability of the ordinary user of a smart product as such. With smart products incorporating AI-elements, these questions which already lay at the focus of one of the previous Münster Colloquia on EU Law and the Digital Economy[47], will become especially pressing. It goes without saying that the user himself will be responsible according to the ordinary regimes of fault liability existing in national laws. Just as standards of care for the operator have to be developed, it will become increasingly demanding also to determine standards of care to be observed by the user.[48] Under which circumstances would a user have acted negligently when employing a particular AI-system in a particular situation? At the same time, such standards of care of the operator and the user as well as other possible actors will have to be balanced amongst each other. For instance, to what extent is the user himself rather than any other actor obliged to make sure that the software is updated? What safety measures have to be taken by the user himself when employing smart products incorporating AI-systems? In how far can a user be held responsible for the safety of the product at all? Taking into account the complexity of AI-systems maybe a user, for example, cannot examine safety questions himself but would only have to react to warnings by the producer, supplier, or operator.[49]

Apart from that, questions of constructing liability for smart products incorporating AI-elements may reach even further. In particular, the unpredictability of the behaviour of such products and their ability to act autonomously gives rise to the question, whether – even in absence of strict liability regimes – a user can be held liable where there is no fault on the part of himself but merely a 'mistake' on the part of the AI system. According to the so-called *respondeat superior*-model, the primary actor could be held liable in such circumstances for his (human) assistant's fault. His assistant's negligent behaviour (i.e. a breach of duty and/or the negligence as such) would be attributed to him (cf. e.g. § 278 BGB – a provision which,

---

46 For an overview about the different aspects of allocation of liability as between the different actors, see *Wagner*, Verantwortlichkeit im Zeichen digitaler Techniken (2020), Versicherungsrecht, 717 et seq.

47 Lohsse/Schulze/Staudenmayer (eds.), Liability for Artificial Intelligence and the Internet of Things (2018).

48 Cf., e.g, *Karner*, Liability for Robotics: current rules, challenges, and the need for innovative concepts, in: Lohsse/Schulze/Staudenmayer (eds.), Liability for Artificial Intelligence and the Internet of Things (2018), p. 118.

49 Cf. *Spindler*, User Liability and Strict Liability in The Internet of Things and for Robots, in: Lohsse/Schulze/Staudenmayer (eds.), Liability for Artificial Intelligence and the Internet of Things (2018), p. 125 (132).

in German law however, does not apply in mere tort law cases which are governed by § 831 BGB instead). With AI being able to act independently just as an ordinary assistant, it seems almost natural to ask whether this model might also be adequately suited to construct liability for AI.

From a formal point of view, as AI has no legal personality it is not addressee of duties or standards of care. Strictly speaking, it can thus neither act illegally nor negligently. It also goes without saying that this does not call for legal personality to be ascribed to AI, although such personality has occasionally been called for.[50] Rather, as has already been frequently observed, the relevant provisions could be applied by analogy. More precisely, it has been argued they should indeed be applied. The main argument is that according to the *respondeat superior*-model the principal has to bear responsibility for the assistant's fault, because he profits from employing the assistant. Moreover, he would also be the cheapest cost avoider because he, rather than the other party, can influence how the assistant is acting. It is argued that both aspects would be equally true where the assistant is an AI system.[51]

The main question would then concern the construction of such analogous application. In principle there are two possible ways that have already been identified. On the one hand, there is the so-called anthropocentric approach: would the same mistake give rise to liability if this mistake had been made by a human being employed by the principal (or by the principal himself). At first glance, this approach might seem both feasible and useful as by applying the relevant provisions as if a human assistant had been chosen, it seems to perfectly implement the idea of an application by analogy. And indeed, some scholars have resorted to exactly this approach.[52] However, this approach does not come without obstacles. Most importantly, AI-systems and human beings may not be comparable at all. Moreover, the analogous application of the *respondeat superior*-model presupposes that the damage results from some sort of autonomous decision of the AI-system. However, we may not be able to find out why the AI-system acted in a manner that caused damage. As

50 Most prominently in the European Parliament's resolution of 16 February 2017 with recommendations to the Commission on Civil Law Rules on Robotics, P8_TA(2017)0051, para. 59 (f); see also *Teubner*, Digitale Rechtssubjekte? (2018), AcP, 155 et seq.

51 See e.g. *Hacker*, Verhaltens- und Wissenszurechnung beim Einsatz von Künstlicher Intelligenz (2018), Rechtswissenschaft, 243 (254).

52 *Hacker*, Verhaltens- und Wissenszurechnung beim Einsatz von Künstlicher Intelligenz (2018), Rechtswissenschaft, 243 (261 et seq.).

much as the damage might be due to an autonomous decision, it might also be due to a mere technical defect which would not give rise to liability under the *respondeat superior*-model. This problem might be addressed by a reversal of the burden of proof – but would such reversal not in fact result in a form of strict liability because the presumption of 'fault' could hardly ever be rebutted? Furthermore, the anthropocentric approach might also hinder technological development: if the user of an AI system was liable for behaviour comparable to human fault, developers of AI systems might be encouraged to develop systems that avoid exactly such behaviour but at the same time might fall short of the technical possibilities that could be realised.[53]

The obvious difficulties with the anthropocentric approach have called for an alternative approach relating to the characteristic features of AI systems. This approach is concerned with constructing AI-specific fault equivalents. Obviously, such approach overcomes the aforementioned difficulties, yet it raises other questions. Most importantly, technical standards to be followed by an AI system seem to relate to the producer's, seller's or 'backend operator's' liability rather than to a liability based on the attribution of 'negligent behaviour' to the user.[54] An AI-specific equivalent to fault would probably have to be something like a technical standard that has to be fulfilled by the AI system. It is difficult to see why a shortfall of such technical standards should fall upon the user rather than the producer. Constructing user-liability apart from ordinary fault liability and strict liability regimes therefore remains an open issue.

c) *Questions of product liability*

Smart products are also accompanied by challenges for product liability regimes. Several of these challenges are further elaborated upon in the contributions to this volume. To begin with, as is true for user liability, the liability of a manufacturer, stemming from the PLD, has to be balanced against possible new liability regimes of other actors, in particular operators. The European Parliament in its proposal has addressed this question by giving priority to the PLD if the manufacturer also acts as backend-op-

53 This is admitted also by *Hacker*, Verhaltens- und Wissenszurechnung beim Einsatz von Künstlicher Intelligenz (2018), Rechtswissenschaft, 243 (263).

54 Once again, see *Hacker* Verhaltens- und Wissenszurechnung beim Einsatz von Künstlicher Intelligenz (2018), Rechtswissenschaft, 243 (264).

erator (Article 11 of the proposed regulation). More important, however, seems to be the question upon whom – the manufacturer or the operator – liability for smart products should actually fall and what kind of liability regime would seem appropriate for these actors.[55] One may even think about more radical approaches in light of the complexity of smart products, the multiplicity of actors, and the interaction of smart products with other smart products as well as with the digital environment. For instance, it may therefore be argued that the classical concept of products could be supplemented by a more complex notion. Following this argument, a whole system of interconnected devices, a 'beyond-product ecosystem' with its combination of 'old-style' products and modern services of updating, upgrading, and operation, could be regarded as the relevant product in a product liability regime.[56]

Even without such radical approach, however, and leaving aside issues of balancing liability between different actors, smart products also pose questions with a view to the existing product liability regime as such. Most obviously, the incorporation of digital elements, and AI in particular, raises the question in how far such digital elements qualify as a product within the meaning of Article 2 PLD. While arguably such qualification is possible, it might become important to ensure that such qualification does not lead to an extension of product liability to mere services.[57]

Moreover, accepting the qualification of software or other digital elements as products as such, one has to bear in mind that the PLD refers to defects that are inherent to products at the time when they are put on the market. Smart products, however, are far from being inalterable after this moment: updates of their software may result in new defects, but with the integration of AI-elements the ability of smart products to learn and to adapt to their environment also raises the question whether defects resulting from such learning-processes may also give rise to liability under product liability regimes. Arguably, with a view to such developments of the product after it has been put on the market for the first time the existing product-liability regime is not without gaps.[58] And once more, it is unclear, who should be held responsible.

After all, while smart products are problematic with a view to several different aspects of the existing liability regimes, the most challenging

55 Cf. *Wagner*, Haftung für künstliche Intelligenz – Eine Gesetzesinitiative des Europäischen Parlaments (2021), ZEuP, 545 (555 et seq.).
56 See the contribution by *T. Rodríguez de las Heras Ballell*, in this volume.
57 On these questions, see the contribution by *G. Wagner*, in this volume.
58 See the contribution by *G. Borges*, in this volume.

questions arguably do not follow from isolated aspects of these regimes. It instead seems that it will hardly be possible to find convincing solutions without addressing the question of a proper allocation of liability as between the different actors in first place.

2. *Prospects for contract law: autonomous contracting*

As regards contract law, smart products being linked with AI will bring about new questions with a view to novel forms of contracting. The use of AI facilitates new business models in the digital economy, which in turn comes along with questions over whether, and to what extent, existing private law is adapted to those developments. The present introduction can raise, but not answer these questions.

a) *The legal novelty of autonomous contracting*

Novel forms of contracting could consist of autonomous contracting between a machine and a human or between machines, with at most an indirect and very limited human intervention, like using an AI system (and enabling or not disabling certain features). The legal issue discussed here is not automated contracting[59] where software is programmed, according to certain pre-defined settings, to take certain decisions when certain pre-determined conditions are fulfilled. Such cases have already been debated for quite some time and by and large existing contract law can handle them.[60] The term 'autonomous contracting' as used here, refers to AI systems which, in particular on the basis of advanced methods of machine learning, take decisions which are neither pre-defined nor foreseeable for humans, but where (in the etymological meaning of the word 'autonomous') the AI system itself provides the rules according to which it takes a certain decision.

Such novel forms of contracting can exist in both B2C and B2B contracts. An example in B2C transactions might be a smart fridge. Already

59 As regards this distinction cf. for instance *Specht/Herold*, Roboter als Vertragspartner? (2018), MMR, 40 et seq.

60 See for instance for German law *Cornelius*, Vertragsabschluss durch autonome elektronische Agenten (2002), MMR, 353 (354 et seq.); *Spindler*, in: Spindler/Schuster (eds.), Recht der elektronischen Medien (4th edn, 2019), Vor §§ 116 ff. BGB, para. 6.

today, around 70 years after the introduction of electric fridges in European households, consumers can buy smart fridges, which are able – with the help of sensors, a connection to the IoT and on the basis of simple AI – to identify which products are stored in it and make suggestions via an app to the householder regarding which foodstuffs to buy when they are in a supermarket. The next likely step is, that when the fridge detects that a particular product (for instance milk) has actually run out or based on previous consumption patterns will soon run out, it autonomously orders that product itself from the supermarket. This, however, is only the simplest variant of the example. The product order could be also more differentiated, depending on specificities of the owner. For instance, the fridge could order semi-skimmed milk for the adults in the family and full-fat milk for a small child. In addition, the fridge may also decide to order foodstuffs which are not regularly stocked in the fridge. For instance, it may know, based on consumption patterns of the previous year, that the owner likes regional organic asparagus and therefore it will order it again in the following year when it is again in season. The order could be sent to a pre-determined supplier, which could be a retailer, but also to a producer, who directly supplies to the fridge, for instance a local organic farmer in the example of the regional organic asparagus. The fridge could however also choose the supplier among those offering the relevant product. An additional dimension of the example could be where the smart fridge chooses the supplier or product based on what it has learned from the purchasing behaviour of the fridge owner from earlier transactions (e.g. a preference for the cheapest product, or the best quality or the best price/quality ratio product). Another possible scenario is the use of purchasing power. For instance, an individual smart fridge might place an order jointly with other smart fridges of the same or other producers in order to take advantage of a larger bargaining power thereby obtaining cheaper prices.

For comparable examples in a B2B environment, one could consider certain specialised transactions carried out by autonomous electronic agents acting as buyers and sellers in stock trading. Examples could also quite easily exist within industrial production. Due to the growth of IoT and the digitalisation of production processes, 'lot-size one production' will be possible. For instance, a machine on the production line of an automobile producer might know in advance that within a specific timeframe it has to produce a tailor-made car for which it needs specific components. It could contact the machines on the production line of several suppliers, check with them whether and under what conditions, e.g. price, technical specifications, time of delivery, the respective components could be delivered and then conclude the contract with the respective machines of one of those suppliers.

Fortunately, contract law is an area of law which provides considerable flexibility in approach. Simple variants of the above-mentioned examples can be arranged in contractual practice in form of, for instance a framework contract[61] between the buyer and one or several pre-determined suppliers. Such framework contracts could include the agreement on certain parameters, defining in a more or less general way the products to be ordered by the AI-equipped devices.

For more advanced variants of the above-mentioned examples, one would need to have a closer look at the interpretation and application of existing EU, international and national contract law to ascertain whether and under what conditions such novel forms of contracting are possible. Where requirements exist, one would need to examine whether in this context they are meaningful and have an added value; if not, they may need to be adapted. If there is a need for adaptation, such adaptations should try to facilitate the possibility of such novel forms of contracting. After all, if parties want to conclude such contracts where many features of the agreement are left to the decision of machines, why should they be prevented from doing it?

b) *Intention to be bound and sufficient agreement?*

aa) The European dimension

While general contract law aspects such as formation, validity, nullity, or effects of contracts are at present outside the scope of the 'Digital Contracts Directives',[62] all European private law systems and the major European restatements presume or take as their point of departure two elements for

61 *Spindler,* in: Spindler/Schuster (eds.), Recht der elektronischen Medien (4th edn, 2019), §§ 116 ff. BGB, para. 7; *Sester/Nitschke*, Software Agent mit Lizenz zum …? (2004), CR, 548 (554), (albeit with a critical view) see this as a possibility; however, it is doubtful how this option should work with more complicated scenarios, for instance in the fridge example the variants where the supplier is not predetermined.

62 Article 3 (6) SGD and recital 18 SGD, Article 3 (10) DCD and recital 12 DCD.

the conclusion of a contract, the parties' intention to bind themselves and a sufficient agreement.[63]

The first question arising for autonomous contracting (much discussed in legal doctrine) is whether the contract can be attributed to a party/the parties using a method of autonomous contracting, such that the party is bound by the terms of that contract. While in the case of automated contracting a party may not be aware of the declaration concluding the contract, such party is considered to be bound by the contract, because that party has used the relevant software.[64] Such attribution of the intention to be bound by the contract is justified, because the software in case of automated contracting acts in a classical consequential "If – then" situation. If certain conditions, which are pre-defined are fulfilled, the software launches a reaction, which is also pre-determined.

However, in the case of autonomous contracting this may be different, where the relevant AI operates at a higher level of autonomy.[65] At the present stage of technological development, AI still acts within pre-defined boundaries. These can result from technical limits; for instance, an autonomous vacuum cleaner or lawnmower will not be equipped to conclude contracts. They can also stem from the way AI is designed. However, one of the boundaries may simply be that AI is designed to do what the person behind the AI is supposed to want to do and is able to do this autonomously. One can compare this with the 'Quick Quotes Quill' of Rita Skeeter in Harry Potter, which picks up everything what has been said (or not said) in an interview and autonomously turns it into an article in the truth-distorting style and with the kind misleading content which

63 This is in the clearest way reflected in PECL 2:101 – Lando/Beale (eds.), Principles of European Contract Law Parts I and II (2000); see also ACQP 4:101- *Research Group on the Existing EC Private Law (Acquis Group)* (ed.), Principles of the Existing EC Contract Law Parts I (2007) and II (2009); DCFR II.-4:101- von Bar/Clive (eds.), Principles, Definitions and Model Rules of European Private Law – Draft Common Frame of Reference (DCFR) Volume I (2009), Article 30 CESL; as to national laws cf. also the DCFR II.-4:101 notes I. 1 et seq.; *Christandl*, in: Jansen/Zimmermann (eds.), Commentaries of European Contract Laws (2018), PECL 2:101, para. 7 et seq. with further references.

64 See for German law for instance *Spindler*, in: Spindler/Schuster (eds.), Recht der elektronischen Medien (4th edn, 2019), Vor §§ 116 ff. BGB, para. 6 with further references to legal doctrine and case law.

65 Cf. *Spindler*, in: Spindler/Schuster (eds.), Recht der elektronischen Medien (4th edn, 2019), Vor §§ 116 ff. BGB, para. 7; beckonline.GrossKommentar/*Möslein*, BGB § 145 para. 71; *Specht/Herold*, Roboter als Vertragspartner? (2018), MMR, 40 et seq.; *Sester/Nitschke*, Software Agent mit Lizenz zum …? (2004), CR, 548 (554).

this yellow press journalist would have used, had she written the article herself.[66] The more autonomous the decision of the AI is in implementing what the party or parties are assumed to require from the contract, the more doubtful it becomes whether the present legal justification used for automated contracting can still apply.

There are different approaches mentioned in the legal discussion. While some still want to attribute such autonomous contracting to the person using the AI,[67] others see the need for different solutions. For instance, it has been suggested to use an analogy to the legal construction when a blank document has been handed over which the recipient can fill out at will.[68] Some authors do not think that a solution can be found on the basis of existing law and therefore suggest the need for intervention by a legislator[69], for instance to use/adapt the rules on agency/representation.[70]

Another question which can arise in certain scenarios of autonomous contracting is whether there was a sufficient agreement between the parties for the contract to be valid. All European private law systems[71] and the

---

66 Harry Potter and the Goblet of Fire, 2000, p. 266 et seq.

67 For instance *Cornelius*, Vertragsabschluss durch autonome elektronische Agenten (2002), MMR, 353 (355 et seq.); *Wulf/Burgenmeister*, Industrie 4.0 in der Logistik – Rechtliche Hürden beim Einsatz neuer Vernetzungs-Technologien (2015), CR, 404 (406 et seq.); *Weingart*, Vertragsschluss durch Verhandlungsagenten (2002), CR, 701 (704 et seq.); this is seen critically by *Weitzenboeck*, Electronic agents and the formation of contracts (2001), IJLIT, 204 (214).

68 *Sester/Nitschke*, Software Agent mit Lizenz zum …? (2004), CR, 548 (550 et seq.); however, they admit themselves that with growing AI autonomy the basis for this analogy will become more doubtful.

69 See for instance *Loos*, Machine-to-Machine Contracting in the Age of the Internet of Things, in: Schulze/Staudenmayer/Lohsse (eds.), Contracts for the Supply of Digital Content: Regulatory Challenges and Gaps (2017), p. 59 (79); *Spindler*, in: Spindler/Schuster (eds.), Recht der elektronischen Medien (4th edn, 2019), Vor §§ 116 ff. BGB, para. 7.; *Sester/Nitschke*, Software Agent mit Lizenz zum …? (2004), CR, 548 (550, 554).

70 *Loos*, Machine-to-Machine Contracting in the Age of the Internet of Things, in: Schulze/Staudenmayer/Lohsse (eds.), Contracts for the Supply of Digital Content: Regulatory Challenges and Gaps (2017), p. 59 (74 et seq.); *Specht/Herold*, Roboter als Vertragspartner? (2018), MMR, 43 et seq.; *Sester/Nitschke*, Software Agent mit Lizenz zum …? (2004), CR, 548 (550, 554); this is also discussed by *Weitzenboeck*, Electronic agents and the formation of contracts (2001), IJLIT, 204 (215 et seq.).

71 See *Christandl*, in: Jansen/Zimmermann (eds.), Commentaries of European Contract Laws (2018), PECL 2:103, para. 4 with further references and the notes I. 1., IV. 9 – 23; DCFR II.-4:103 – von Bar/Clive (eds.), Principles, Definitions and Model Rules of European Private Law – Draft Common Frame of Reference (DCFR) Volume I (2009).

major European restatements[72] agree that a sufficient agreement between parties is a necessary condition for the conclusion of a contract. While it may not be necessary to agree on natural or accidental terms, agreement of the essential terms is generally considered necessary.[73] The choice of the seller, the nature and amount of the product to be bought and the way how the price is determined are likely to figure among the terms which are essential for the conclusion of a contract.[74] If the relevant case scenario of autonomous contracting between machines is such that agreement of the essential terms cannot be confirmed, one may need to think whether adaptations to the general doctrine are desirable.

Whatever solution ultimately chosen, the overall objective should be to allow the roll-out of the technology and the corresponding new business models, if they are accepted by the market. In order to facilitate such acceptance of novel forms of contracting[75], it would be useful on the one hand to ensure that the parties have an acceptable level of control and on the other hand, to safeguard the necessary legal certainty that parties can rely on the contracts agreed between machines.

Such acceptable level of control would consist firstly in the possibilities of the contracting parties to determine in advance the pre-settings of the contracting process. Secondly, one should also consider some minimum possibilities of correcting *a posteriori* if steps have been taken which do not correspond to the will of a contractual party. It needs to be seen whether correcting *a posteriori* a step which does not correspond to the will of a contractual party can be done with the existing legal tools and if not, whether and how they could be adapted or taken as a model for such corrections.

---

72 PECL 2:103 – Lando/Beale (eds.), Principles of European Contract Law Parts I and II (2000); DCFR II.-4:103 – von Bar/Clive (eds.), Principles, Definitions and Model Rules of European Private Law – Draft Common Frame of Reference (DCFR) Volume I (2009); Article 30 (1) (c) CESL.

73 As to the distinction between natural, accidental and essential terms, going back to Roman law (naturalia, accidentalia and essentialia negotii), see *Christandl*, in: Jansen/ Zimmermann (eds.), Commentaries of European Contract Laws (2018), PECL 2:103, para. 2 et seq. with further references.

74 See also Article 14 (1) 2 of the UN Convention on the International Sale of Goods (CISG) which requires to indicate the goods and expressly or implicitly fix or make provision for determining the quantity and the price.

75 While arguing for attributing the acts of an electronic agents to the party using it, *Weitzenboeck*, Electronic agents and the formation of contracts (2001), IJLIT, 204 (222 et seq., 232 et seq.) also emphasises that this is of little use if businesses and consumers feel uncomfortable with using electronic agents.

The rules on errors/mistakes and avoidance of contract come to mind if one considers that the smart product may make an autonomous 'error/mistake'. The fridge may for example order the wrong product (e.g. a decorative pumpkin instead of an edible pumpkin), order too much or not enough of a certain product (e.g. not enough semi-skimmed milk for the consumption of the adults but too much full-fat milk for the consumption of the child) or order a product which is no longer required (e.g. our fridge owner has lost his taste for asparagus, wishes to switch to purchasing a cheaper vegetable or decides he prefers green to white asparagus).

Rules in national laws and the major European restatements on errors/mistakes and avoidance of contract can be broadly divided in two groups, according to how they balance the interests at stake, i.e. looking primarily at the mistaken party and restricting the type of the relevant mistakes or asking whether the other party was responsible for the mistake.[76] Notwithstanding these differences, they all deal with situations where one contractual party has agreed to the contract while being in error/mistaken or misapprehending certain elements of fact or law or there was an error in expression or communication of the will of the relevant contractual party. In other words, the will the party intended to declare and the declared statement concluding the contract differ. However, in cases of autonomous contracting between a machine and a human or between machines there is no such error/mistake as there is no sufficiently concrete will of the contracting party from which the statement can diverge. Although there is a general will of the party using autonomous contracting that the AI[77] concludes contracts, the human party leaves it to the AI to take the specific concrete decisions. Therefore, there is an insufficiently concrete 'will' of the human user of AI which encompasses the specific contract concluded by the autonomously acting AI. In other words, there is nothing from which the contractual statement made by the autonomously deciding AI could differ. For the same reason, there could be no inaccuracy in communication either. There was no statement by

76 See *Lohsse*, in: Jansen/Zimmermann (eds.), Commentaries of European Contract Laws (2018), Introduction before PECL 4:101, para. 4 as regards this distinction, PECL 4:103, para. 2 et seq. as to the origins in legal history and para. 5 et seq. as to present laws and major restatements; for the different national laws see also the notes I. 1. et seq.; DCFR II.-7:203 in von Bar/Clive (eds.), Principles, Definitions and Model Rules of European Private Law – Draft Common Frame of Reference (DCFR) Volume I (2009).

77 Certainly there is no such will of the AI, see *Weitzenboeck*, Electronic agents and the formation of contracts (2001), IJLIT, 204 (221).

the human user of autonomously contracting AI which could be falsified when being expressed or being transferred by the AI to the recipient of the statement. The statement of the AI was not falsified either.

The other cluster of rules which might potentially be used to deal with the issue concerns representation/agency. However, a direct application of the rules on representation/agency does not seem possible, as these rules assume that the representative/agent has a legal personality.[78]

Attributing legal personality to autonomous AI[79] is however not a solution, it simply refers the problem. If autonomous AI is able to conclude contracts on its own behalf or on behalf of the principal, it could become debtor and creditor of contractual rights and obligations or possibly be liable to the principal or the third party. This would only be possible if it is able to control the necessary financial means to fulfil such obligations. Consequently, a party would have to attribute such means to the autonomous AI. Therefore, there is little point in using the legal construction of attributing legal personality to AI but rather place the obligations on the party behind the AI who in any event would have to make the necessary means available to fulfil obligations and remedy liabilities.

As neither set of rules would appear to fit the case, it may be a task for the future to see whether elements of these rules could be used as a basis or model to find adapted solutions for making novel forms of contracting practical.

bb) The international dimension

At the international level, only the UN Convention on the International Sale of Goods (CISG) contains substantive uniform international rules on contract formation. Article 14 (1) CISG stands on the grounds of the above-mentioned approach of the European private law systems and major European restatements. It requires for a sales contract offer that it is sufficiently definite and indicates the intention of the offeror to be bound in case of acceptance. As explained above, this is not obvious for autonomous contracting.

---

78 For the major restatements, see *Rademacher*, in: Jansen/Zimmermann (eds.), Commentaries of European Contract Laws (2018), Art 3:101, para. 1.

79 This is suggested by and discussed for instance by *Weitzenboeck*, Electronic agents and the formation of contracts (2001), IJLT, 204 (211 et seq.).

While providing hardly any substantive rules on contract formation,[80] the UN Convention on the Use of Electronic Communications in International Contracts (ECC)[81] might nevertheless become relevant for novel forms of contracting. However, for the purposes of the present discussion its potential utility is significantly reduced by the complete[82] exclusion of consumer contracts in its Article 2 (1) a).[83]

The ECC is based on an approach of functional equivalence between electronic and paper communication.[84] According to its Article 8, a communication or a contract shall not be denied validity on the sole ground that it is in the form of an electronic communication. This is expanded by Article 9 which states that, where the law requires a communication to be in writing, that requirement is met with an electronic communication. The most interesting provision in the present context is Article 12 which states that a contract between an automated message system and a natural person, or between automated message systems, shall not be denied validity on the sole ground that no natural person reviewed or intervened in the actions of the automated message system. However, the ECC falls short of attributing the relevant electronic communication to a specific person.[85] An automated message system is defined in Article 4 g) so widely that not only automated contracting but also autonomous contracting could fall under it. It seems however more likely from the explanatory note[86] that at the time of its adoption in 2005, the ECC did not want to change the paradigm whereby an automated message system is capable of performing only within the technical structures of its

80 See para. 4 of the explanatory note, https://uncitral.un.org/sites/uncitral.un.org/files/media-documents/uncitral/en/06-57452_ebook.pdf (last accessed 5. 9. 2021); this is also highlighted by *Gabriel*, The United Nations Convention on the Use of Electronic Communications in International Contracts: An Overview and Analysis (2006), 11 UNIF. L. REV. n.s., 285 (296).

81 For an overview of the ECC, see the explanatory note, ibid. and *Gabriel*, The United Nations Convention on the Use of Electronic Communications in International Contracts: An Overview and Analysis (2006), 11 UNIF. L. REV. n.s., 285 (296).

82 Compared to the different solution in Article 2 (a) CISG, which can lead to its application to consumer contracts.

83 As regards the reasoning underlying this exclusion linked to the insufficient level of consumer protection in the ECC see explanatory note, para. 71 et seq.

84 See explanatory note, para. 50 et seq.

85 *Gabriel*, The United Nations Convention on the Use of Electronic Communications in International Contracts: An Overview and Analysis (2006), 11 UNIF. L. REV. n.s., 285 (302).

86 Para. 211.

pre-set programming. This applies even more to Article 13 (2) (b) of the UNCITRAL Model Law on Electronic Commerce (MLEC). Going further than the ECC, this provision contains a rule attributing a data message to the originator if it was sent by an information system programmed by, or on behalf of, the originator to operate automatically. However, in the light of the adoption of the MLEC in 1996, this is likely to be meant as only to relate to automated contracting.

Nevertheless, the explanatory note of the ECC mentions that through future developments in AI, a computer may be able to learn through experience, modify the instructions in its own programs and even devise new instructions, as a result of which it would therefore have the ability to act autonomously and not just automatically.[87] Accordingly, UNCITRAL has already decided to launch preparatory work for taking into account AI-enabled forms of contracting in the context of the ECC and CISG.[88]

c) *Knowledge and control of the parties in autonomously concluded contracts*

Contracting parties may also need a sufficient degree of knowledge in advance regarding the level of control they will relinquish to the autonomously contracting AI before they engage into using it and an appreciation of what residual abilities they retain to influence or correct these decisions. Ideally, these should be translated into relevant requirements. Existing requirements which touch on these types of issues may well need to be adapted to the various types of autonomous technology used.

The EU acquis contains rules on what kind of information needs to be given to a contractual party, in particular where the party is a consumer,

---

87 It is interesting to note that this statement is a quote (albeit not marked as such in the ECC explanatory note) from *Allen/Widdison,* Can Computers Make Contracts, 9 HARV. J. L. & TECH. 25 (1996) 27; the same quote (while being marked as such) is used in the US Uniform Electronic Transactions Act (UETA) of 1999, see Section 3 UETA and Comment 1 to this Section; this is an example how the ECC draws on US legislation.

88 See report of the 54th UNCITRAL session 2021, A 76/17, para. 234 – 237 and preparatory documents A/CN.9/1064 para. 11 and 16, A/CN.9/1064/Add.1, para. 7 and 11 and A/CN.9/1065, para. 10, 18, 31, 35 as well as for the 53rd UNCITRAL session 2020 the preparatory documents A/CN.9/1012, para. 21 and A/CN.9/1012/Add.1, para. 34 et seq., 45.

and at which time and in what manner it is given. If consumer information is at stake, the respective requirements are of a mandatory nature.[89]

The E-Commerce Directive (ECD) contains some rules on pre-contractual information and the contracting process.[90] For contracts concluded by electronic means, Article 10 (1) ECD includes several pre-contractual information requirements, among which are the technical steps to conclude the contract and the technical means for identifying and correcting input errors. These requirements reflect the fact that that the ECD was conceived in the 1990s and adopted in 2000, when e-commerce consisted of buying from a website or via means like e-mails and that they are built on this state of technology.[91]

The Consumer Rights Directive (CRD)[92] contains the pre-contractual and contractual information obligations with the broadest scope[93] among the consumer contract directives (and is therefore here used as an example). Article 6 (1) CRD contains a long list of pre-contractual information requirements for distance contracts which, according to Article 6 (8) CRD are required in addition to the information requirements of the ECD. They need to be given at a stage where the consumer can still influence and change the transaction decision. According to Article 7 (8) (a) CRD the same information needs to be provided also after the conclusion of the contract.

The list of pre-contractual information requirements includes elements which would be decided by the autonomously acting AI (for instance the characteristics of the goods and services, the identity of the trader or the price).[94] The fact of requiring such information to be provided to

---

89 Article 10 (1) ECD and as regards the EU consumer contract acquis for instance Article 25 CRD.

90 Articles 10 et seq. of Directive 2000/31 on certain legal aspects of information society services in particular electronic commerce.

91 EU Digital Law/*Arroyo Amayuelas*, Introduction to Articles 10 – 11, para. 3 et seq.; critical also *Sester/Nitschke*, Software Agent mit Lizenz zum …? (2004), CR, 548 (553).

92 Directive 2011/83, OJ of 22. 11. 2011, L 304/64.

93 According to its Article 3 (1) it covers as a matter of principle all B2C contracts; *Sein*, Concluding Consumer Contracts via Smart Assistants (2018), EuCML, 179 (182), argues convincingly, that the possibly here relevant exemption of Article 3 (3) (j) CRD as regards "supply of foodstuffs, beverages or other goods intended for current consumption in the household, and which are physically supplied by a trader on frequent and regular rounds to the consumer's home, residence or workplace" needs to be interpreted narrowly.

94 Article 6 (1) (a), (b) and (e) CRD.

the consumer before the transaction decision raises the question whether the design and the content of present EU precontractual and contractual information requirements is sufficiently well adapted to autonomous contracting.

When the EU legislator modernised the CRD[95], among other matters it adapted its provisions to some extent to apply to platforms and automated decision-making (e.g. by including relevant precontractual information requirements[96] and deleting obsolete information like the fax number[97]). However, while it took into account the use of algorithms by platforms,[98] it did not deal with autonomous contracting.

Pre-contractual information obligations contained in EU consumer contract Directives are one way to remedy the structural imbalance between traders and consumers as regards the available information; the consumer is informed about all essential elements which are important for his transaction decision.[99] One may wonder if pre-contractual information requirements are the right tool for the contracts discussed here, because the purpose of using autonomous contracting is precisely to make contracting easy for the user. This includes ensuring that the consumer using it no longer has to consider pre-contractual information.[100]

Contractual information disclosure is designed to ensure that the other contractual party (in particular a consumer) has available and can retain information which may be relevant at a later stage for claims against the trader. This arises in particular for the consumer from the definition of 'durable medium' which has been used in a number of EU consumer contract directives.[101] This definition regulates the way the pre-contractual

95 Recitals 17 et seq. Directive 2019/2161 of 27 November 2019 as regards the better enforcement and modernisation of Union consumer protection rule.

96 See the new Article 6 (1) (ea) introduced by Directive 2019/2161.

97 Recital 46 Directive 2019/2161.

98 See for instance recitals 19 and 22 et seq. Directive 2019/2161.

99 *Staudenmayer*, Die Richtlinien des Verbraucherprivatrechts, in: Schulte-Nölke/Schulze (eds.), Europäische Rechtsangleichung und nationale Privatrechte (1999), p. 63 (73).

100 *Sester/Nitschke*, Software Agent mit Lizenz zum ...? (2004), CR, 548 (552) see therefore a conflict between the objective of consumer protection and the use of autonomous contracting.

101 "Durable medium means any instrument which enables the consumer to store information addressed personally to him in a way accessible for future reference for a period of time adequate for the purposes of the information and which allows the unchanged reproduction of the information stored"; this definition has been regulated for the first time in Article 2 (f) of the Distance Marketing of

and contractual information has to be provided. For all contracts, this purpose is reflected in the ECD obligation[102] to make the contract terms available in a way that they can be stored and reproduced. This purpose of contractual information remains valid even in cases of autonomous contracting.

It is worth considering whether certain pre-contractual information obligations, which would not provide added value in cases of autonomous contracting, might no longer be required in these cases, while those which are still relevant could be retained[103]. Alternatively, one may also consider whether such information is still required at a pre-contractual stage or whether it would be sufficient to provide it only as contractual information.[104] A relevant question may also be, whether there are ways how the consumer can renounce to provision of information, i.e. "stay uninformed", while still sticking to the mandatory nature of consumer law.[105]

In the context of this reflection, the right of withdrawal granted by EU consumer contract law[106] may also play a role. When designing a suitable toolbox of instruments for corrections which could be done *a posteriori* by the consumer, this right, possibly in an adapted format, should be kept in mind.

Another tool in this box could be the future AI Act.[107] For products classified in Article 9 as high-risk systems, Article 13 contains information obligations for users, including user instructions, allowing them to use AI-equipped systems appropriately. Article 14 requires a certain degree of human oversight. While the purpose of these duties is mainly aimed at preventing risks to health, safety and fundamental rights, these could

---

Consumer Financial Services Directive 2002/65, OJ of 9. 10. 2002, L 271/16; the most recent cases were Article 2 (13) DCD and 2 (11) SGD.

102 Article 10 (3) ECD.

103 In such case *Sester/Nitschke*, Software Agent mit Lizenz zum ...? (2004), CR, 548 (553) point to the need to 'translate' them into machine-readable information.

104 *Sein*, Concluding Consumer Contracts via Smart Assistants (2018), EuCML, 179 (185) points to the possibility how this can be done already under the present CRD through the use of its Article 10 (2) in order to avoid the extension of the period for the consumer's right of withdrawal, while also mentioning the disadvantage of Article 6 (6) CRD for such solution.

105 *Sein*, Concluding Consumer Contracts via Smart Assistants (2018), EuCML, 179 (184); the command ‚Shut up, Alexa' quoted by Sein for voice assistants is a similar case.

106 For instance in Article 9 CRD.

107 See the recently adopted Commission proposal, COM(2021) 206 final.

contribute to helping the parties become aware of the technical possibilities offered by those smart products equipped with AI that qualify as 'high-risk'.

IV. Conclusion

The importance of smart products for the digital economy is obvious. While the legislator has already taken steps to regulate certain aspects, future developments will probably require more radical supplements to the existing rules. Academic discussion and research on these future developments has already presented proposals some of which have been outlined above and are further elaborated upon in this volume. Undoubtedly, the importance of the roll-out of the enabling technology of AI for private law and the further emergence of the technology as such will lead to a continuous deepening of this discussion and research. In turn, such discussion and – eventually – regulation of the consequences of AI characteristics both for the application of liability rules and for contract law will facilitate the roll-out of AI.

The Update Obligation for smart products

Digital obligations of sellers of smart devices under the Sale of Goods Directive 771/2019*

Hans Schulte-Nölke[1]

I. Main thesis of this paper

This paper deals with the new obligations that sellers have when the subject matter of a sales contract is a smart device under the Sale of Goods Directive 771/2019 (hereinafter: the SGD). The main thesis is that the SGD's digital obligations theoretically improve the protection of consumers who purchase smart devices. However, the additional consumer protection does not go very far and does little to help consumers, since the SGD still adheres to the classic contract model, according to which only the seller is obliged towards the consumer. In cases where the functionality of the smart device depends on a third-party service provider that is not a party to the sales contract, the consumer's remedies against the seller are against the wrong debtor, because it is usually the third-party service provider that causes the smart device's lack of conformity, and the seller has little or no leverage to prompt the third-party service provider to remedy the situation.

II. A step by step farewell to the law of the Roman aediles

As is well known, the former Consumer Sales Directive 1999/44 granted the consumer as the buyer of a non-conforming good – in addition to the right to an appropriate price reduction or to rescind the contract – the right to have the goods brought into conformity with the contract by repair or replacement. This innovation was already the first farewell to the law of the Roman aediles, which was adopted in many civil codes, including the German BGB.

---

* A slightly expanded and revised version of the paper given on 10 June 2021, supplemented by some references to recent literature.

1 Professor of Civil Law, University of Osnabrück and Radboud University Nijmegen.

This classical law of sale was developed through the edicts of the curulian aediles, who acted in their capacity as overseers of the markets of Rome and of buying and selling in general. A large part of the provisions in the edicts of the aediles dealt with the buying and selling of slaves and beasts of burden. The edicts formed the basis for the *actiones aediliciae*, the most important of which were the *actio redhibitoria* (action to rescind the sale due to defects in the goods sold) and the *actio quanti minoris* (action to reduce the contract price).[2]

In this tradition, the central and fundamental obligations of the seller were to deliver the goods and transfer ownership. The law of sale was characterised by the principle that these obligations were limited to a single point in time, usually the time of delivery. If the seller transferred ownership at that time and the goods were in conformity with the contract, then the seller had fulfilled its obligations. Only this single point in time was decisive for the question of whether the seller had fulfilled its obligations.

Until recently, the consumer was likewise only entitled to rights under the former Consumer Sales Directive 1999/44 if the lack of conformity of the goods already existed by the time of delivery. This dependence of the buyer's rights on the condition of the goods at the moment of delivery also went back to classical Roman law.

The SGD changed this basic principle for smart devices, i.e. goods that contain a digital element or where the sales contract provides for a continuous supply of digital content or a digital service over a period of time.[3] Examples include a smartwatch, a fitness tracker or goods that are part of a smart home, such as a smart lock. For such items, the seller's obligations are no longer limited to a single point in time. Rather, the seller is subject to obligations that last for a period of time. The sales contract, which had been a one-time exchange contract since the times of Roman law, has now become a continuing obligation.[4] This paper sets out the reasons why the next step has yet to be taken, namely that in the case of goods with digital elements, not only the seller but also other persons involved in the digital elements should be liable to the consumer.

2 Dig. 21 tit. 1 (De Aedilicio Edicto).

3 *Weber*, EuCML 2017, 207, 209; *Seritti*, EuCML 2021, 180, 183.

4 *Carvalho*, EuCML 2019, 194, 198 et seq.

III. Obligation to update in the wording of the SGD

The basic provision on the liability of the seller is Article 10 (1) SGD, which reads as follows:

> (1) The seller shall be liable to the consumer for any lack of conformity which exists at the time when the goods were delivered and which becomes apparent within two years of that time. Without prejudice to Article 7 (3), this paragraph shall also apply to goods with digital elements.

This, as a legislative starting point, is still the basic rule of Roman law that does not differ from the Consumer Sales Directive 1999/44.[5] Only one moment matters, namely "the time when the goods were delivered."[6] The directive only provides for a punctual duty of performance on the part of the seller, not a continuing duty to provide a service or to make updates after delivery.[7] The innovation is hidden in the second sentence of Article 10 (1) SDG, which gives a clarifying reference to an exception set out in Article 7 (3) SGD. Article 7 (3) SGD reads:

> (3) In the case of goods with digital elements, the seller shall ensure that the consumer is informed of and supplied with updates, including security updates, that are necessary to keep those goods in conformity, for the period of time:
>
> (a) that the consumer may reasonably expect given the type and purpose of the goods and the digital elements, and taking into account the circumstances and nature of the contract, where the sales contract provides for a single act of supply of the digital content or digital service; or
> (b) indicated in Article 10 (2) or (5), as applicable, where the sales contract provides for a continuous supply of the digital content or digital service over a period of time.

5 Cf. Article 3 (1) Consumer Sales Directive 1999/44.

6 On the lack of a definition of „delivery“ in the SGD (and the lacking reference to Article 18 (1) of the Consumer Rights Directive 2011/83) cf. *Twigg-Flesner*, in: Arroyo Amayuelas / Cámara Lapuente (Eds), El Derecho privado en el nuevo paradigma digital (2020), <https://ssrn.com/abstract=3526228> accessed 20 Dec 2021, 9.

7 *van Gool/Michel*, EuCML 2021, 136, 141.

This provision only applies to goods with digital elements as defined in Article 2 SGD. Where such goods with digital elements are the subject matter of the contract is the basic principle of the seller's obligation to perform only at the moment of delivery modified.

The obligations of the seller after delivery are quite limited. The seller is not obliged to keep the goods in conformity with the contract. The seller is only obliged to "ensure" that the consumer is supplied with the updates that are necessary to keep the goods in conformity. The wording of this provision seems to take into account the frequent situation that the seller itself is not the provider of the digital element and usually not in a position to supply consumers with the necessary updates.[8] Too often, it would be impossible for the seller to actually perform the obligation placed on him to supply the necessary updates.[9]

In fact, this is not much different from when it comes only to the obligation to ensure that consumers are supplied with updates. Such an obligation also presupposes that the seller has the necessary means (including money) and/or can exert influence over a third party service provider who is actually able to provide updates. Thus, under the SGD, it is hard to imagine the consumer actually suing the seller to enforce the obligation to ensure the provision of a necessary update as part of the consumer's right to have the goods brought into conformity with the contract.[10] The enforcement of this obligation by the consumer is so unlikely that it will nearly always remain an empty law in the books. The practical relevance of this provision is limited to a stepping stone for the consumer's remedies at the second level of the hierarchy of remedies, i.e. the right to terminate the contract or reduce the price.[11] This is a surprising return to the classical buyer's rights of the Roman aediles, which were limited to rescission and price reduction.

Nevertheless, Article 7 (3) SGD expresses a fundamental change in the law of sale in another respect. The seller's obligations are no longer limited to a specific point in time.[12] The contract of sale becomes a continuing

---

8 Cf., on Article (2) 8 DCSD, which has a similar wording, *Staudenmayer*, in Schulze / Staudenmayer (Eds.), EU Digital Law (2020), Article 8 DCSD, No. 119.

9 *Staudenmayer*, NJW 2019, 2889, 2890 f.

10 Cf. Article 13 (2) SGD.

11 Cf. Article 13 (4) SGD.

12 The ground-breaking character of the update obligation in the SGD and the DCSD is acknowledged, e.g., by *Wendehorst*, in: Stabentheiner / Wendehorst / Zöchling-Jud (Eds.), Das neue europäische Gewährleistungsrecht (2019), 111; *Schulze*, ZEuP 2019, 695, 713; *Metzger*, JZ 2019, 577, 581.

obligation with regard to the obligation to supply updates for the digital element, and no longer an obligation that must and can be fulfilled at a specific moment.[13]

Of course, this then raises the question of how long the seller remains obliged to provide updates after delivery. This question is answered by Article 7 (3) SGD under letters a) and b); this matter is dealt with separately in another contribution to this volume and will therefore be left aside for the purposes of this paper.[14]

IV. Liability of the seller for the continuous supply of the digital content or digital service

An even further-reaching obligation of the seller to provide digital services to the buyer even after delivery is provided for in Article 10 (2) SGD. The provision reads as follows:

> (2) In the case of goods with digital elements, where the sales contract provides for a continuous supply of the digital content or digital service over a period of time, the seller shall also be liable for any lack of conformity of the digital content or digital service that occurs or becomes apparent within two years of the time when the goods with digital elements were delivered. Where the contract provides for a continuous supply for more than two years, the seller shall be liable for any lack of conformity of the digital content or digital service that occurs or becomes apparent within the period of time during which the digital content or digital service is to be supplied under the sales contract.

It becomes clear that this provision has a narrower scope than Article 7 (3) SGD. It not only requires that the subject matter of the contract are goods with digital elements, but also that the sales contract stipulates that digital content or a digital service will be supplied continuously over a period of time.[15]

However, this obligation of the seller is worded differently than in Article 7 (3). The provision does not express that the seller is obliged to do anything (e.g. to "ensure" the supply of updates). It only expresses that the

---

13 *Staudenmayer*, NJW 2019, 2889, 2893.

14 See *Janssen* (in this volume), 91.

15 *Kalamees*, 12 (2021) JIPITEC, 131, 135 et seq.

seller is liable for any lack of conformity of the digital content or service for a specified period of time, which is typically two years from delivery.[16] There is another difference between the two provisions. Article 10 (2) SGD obliges a permanent, continuous supply of the digital content or the digital service, while Article 7 (3) SGD only obliges the seller to ensure the necessary updates here and there, to the extent that such updates are necessary. Nevertheless, Article 10 (2) SGD also includes an obligation to update if such updates are necessary for the continuous supply of the digital content or digital service.

V. Categories of subject matters of sales contracts

A first interim result of reading the SGD's regarding digital obligations of the seller leads to a threefold distinction, namely:

(1) goods without digital elements,
(2) goods with digital elements and
(3) goods with digital elements, where the contract provides for a continuous supply of digital content or a digital service.

The first category – goods without digital elements – does not entail anything new. There is no digital obligation and also no obligation to physically "update" (e.g. by maintenance). The obligation of the seller is limited to a point performance at a certain moment in time, i.e. the delivery of the goods.

Secondly, if the subject matter of the contract is goods with digital elements, Article 7 (3) SGD, read in conjunction with Article 10 (1) SGD, obliges the seller to ensure the necessary updates even after delivery over the applicable period of time.

Thirdly, if the subject matter is goods with digital elements, where the contract provides for a continuous supply of digital content or a digital service over a period of time, Article 10 (2) SGD provides for an obligation to continuously provide that service over the applicable period of time. This includes an obligation to update the digital content or service in so far as it is necessary to keep it running.

For the purposes of a full picture, there is, fourthly, a contract for the provision of digital content and/or digital services that are not incorporated in, or are loosely interconnected with, goods. Such a contract does

16 *de Franchesci*, 12 (2021) JIPITEC, 143, 150; *Kalamees*, 12 (2021) JIPITEC, 131, 138.

not fall under the SGD at all, though it may fall under the Digital Content and Services Directive 770/2019 (hereinafter: the DCSD), which provides for rather similar remedies, including an obligation to update.[17]

VI. A practical example: Smart lock

A smart lock for a private house door might provide an example to illustrate the application of these provisions. Imagine a smart lock installed at your front door that can be opened and locked through an app on your mobile phone. This smart lock is certainly a good with digital elements in the sense of Article 7 (3) SGD. Whether it is also a good with digital elements where the sales contract provides for a continuous supply of digital content or a digital service over a period of time in the sense of Article 10 (2) SGD, depends on the technicalities of the smart lock. The more elaborate smart locks that are actually available on the market are usually connected to a service platform, which is also connected through an app on the user´s mobile phone. In such a setting, the operating of the service platform is crucial for the function of the smart lock. Such a case would fall under Article 10 (2) SGD. In connection with Article 7 (3) and 10 (1) SGD, the seller of such a smart lock has a full set of digital obligations. Firstly, the seller is obliged to ensure the necessary updates of the software built in the smart lock under Article 7 (3) and 10 (1) SGD. Moreover, the seller is also obliged to uphold the functioning of the service platform and the app installed on the user´s mobile phone und Article 10 (2) SGD. This obligation, of course, also includes providing the necessary updates to the software of the service platform and the app.

VII. Update obligations of the seller

The following focuses on the update obligations of the seller of such a smart lock. Article 6 and 7 SGD provide objective and subjective requirements for conformity, which apply in parallel.[18] Article 7 (3) SGD, which only applies to goods with digital elements (here: the smart lock), obliges the seller to provide updates, including security updates, that are necessary

---

17 *Meller-Hannich*, DAR 2021, 493, 494; *Staudenmayer*, ZEuP 2019, 663, 671 et seq; *Helmig*, IWRZ 2019, 200, 200 et seq.

18 *Vanherpe*, ERPL 2020, 251, 259 et seq.; *Seritti*, EuCML 2021, 180, 181.

to keep the goods in conformity. These updates must be provided for a period that the consumer may reasonably expect. How long such a period would be would have to be clarified by the courts. Since the consumer can reasonably expect to be able to use the smart lock for at least several years (say at least five), it is clear that the seller is under this obligation for a relatively long time. If the contract does not specify the obligation to update, only the objective requirements are applicable.

In the event that the contract stipulates that certain updates will be provided for a certain time, there may be a conflict between the subjective and the objective requirements.[19] It goes without saying that subjective requirements stipulated in the contract, which go beyond the objective requirements, would prevail if this happens. It is also rather clear that the seller may not, as a rule, stipulate update obligations that fall behind the objective requirements. The only, rather rare, exception to this may be the case where the seller very clearly states, thereby fulfilling the requirements of Article 7 (5) SGD and other provisions, that there will be no updates or that updates will fall short of the objective requirements.[20]

The basic underlining idea of this interplay between objective and subjective requirements with very strict information duties is that only a very well-informed consumer, who actually knows what he is contracting for, has to accept contractual stipulations regarding updates that fall behind the objective requirements.[21] Surprisingly enough, this rather sophisticated interplay between objective and subjective requirements applies, if one takes the wording literally, only for goods with digital elements, but not for the situation where the contract provides for the continuous supply of digital content or a digital service over a period of time according to Article 10 (2) SGD. However, it becomes clear from the reference to Article 7 (3) (b) SGD that the drafters of the SGD presumed that the same interplay of objective and subjective requirements should also apply for the seller´s obligations to continuously supply a digital service over a period of time under Article 10 (2) SGD.

---

19 For an overview of the individual criteria for subjective and objective conformity *Twigg-Flesner*, in: Arroyo Amayuelas / Cámara Lapuente (Eds), El Derecho privado en el nuevo paradigma digital (2020), <https://ssrn.com/abstract=3526228> accessed 20 Dec 2021, 8 et seq.

20 *Spindler/Sein*, MMR 2019, 488, 489.

21 *Seritti*, EuCML 2021, 180, 181.

VIII. Who is obliged to update?

A second look at the example of the smart lock reveals that there are actually several persons involved in the sale and the accompanying services. There is, firstly, the seller of the smart lock. Such smart locks can be obtained through a broad variety of distribution channels. Distributors include the big online sellers and highly specialised smart home equipment suppliers as well as small local brick and mortar shops that offer a broad range of consumer electronics, such as electrical household appliances, mobile phones and their accessories along with smart home products, including smart locks. It is fairly evident that only a few of these sellers, if any, are capable of actually providing any updates on their own. The seller is usually not the producer of the smart lock. Rather, the seller obtains the smart lock via a chain of contracts from other suppliers, which may include retailers, importers and, finally, the producer himself. It is not very likely that, in this chain of contracts, anyone other than the producer or a third-party service provider will actually be able to provide updates.

In a situation where the smartphone is not directly connected with the smart lock but where a service platform, which is connected with the smart lock and with the app on the user's mobile phone, forms the key element, it is most likely that the provider of this service platform is the only person who will be able to update the app on the consumer's mobile phone and, of course, its own service platform. It is also imaginable that the service platform provider can update the software of the smart lock via an internet connection.

On the market, there are situations where the producer of the smart lock itself also provides the service platform. In such a situation, this personal union of the producer and the service provider of the necessary platform is the key figure who is able to provide the necessary updates and maintain the operation of the platform and the app on the user's smartphone. There are also situations, however, where the producer and the service provider are different persons, which makes the legal situation even more complex.[22] It goes without saying that there are often even many further persons involved in the provision of such services. These are, in

22 On several models how the relationship between seller, third-party provider and consumer can be contructed, cf. *Wendehorst*, in: Stabentheiner / Wendehorst / Zöchling-Jud, Das neue europäische Gewährleistungsrecht (2019), 111, 118 et. seq.; Wendehorst (in this volume), 63, 83 et. seq.

particular, app developers and the app store, where the user downloaded the app, which may also be involved in providing updates.

The answer to the question of which person is obliged under the SGD to provide updates and maintain the service platform as necessary for the proper functioning of the smart lock, the answer is clear and simple. It is only the seller. The seller is the sole obligor under the SGD. This simple finding, however, does not give a solution, but it rather describes a problem. Technically, the seller will often be the least able person to provide the necessary updates and to ensure the operation of the platform on its own.[23]

It is therefore an interesting question whether other persons, in particular the producer and/or the third-party platform operator, are also obliged to provide updates and maintain the service platform. Looking into the SGD, the answer is, again, very clear. As already stated, the SGD only obliges the seller. If none of the other persons mentioned above also function as the seller under the contract concluded with the consumer, then they do not have any obligations towards the consumer.

However, full harmonisation by the SGD does not mean that no other persons than the seller can have any obligations towards the consumer, because the consumer's legal relations with other persons fall outside the scope of the SGD, and thus outside the area of law fully harmonised by the EU. There may be, in particular, further contracts concluded between the consumer and a third-party platform or app operator, for example. In practice, it will often be the case that the consumer, after downloading and installing the app on the mobile phone, has to open an "account" and, in the course of clicking through, accept the terms and conditions of the service platform operator or app developer.[24] This process may be construed under the rules of interpretation of legal conduct as the conclusion of a contract, usually a licensing agreement. Such a contract may give rise to obligations of the platform operator or the app operator towards the consumer, which may also include an obligation to keep the digital service running and to regularly update the necessary software. Such a contract between the consumer and a third-party platform operator or app

---

23 *Sein/Spindler*, ERCL 2019, 257, 270 et seq.

24 Cf. Recital (21) SGD which states that ascertaining a bilateral contractual relationship between the seller and the consumer, of which the supply of the incorporated or inter-connected digital content or digital service forms part, should not be affected by the mere fact that the consumer has to consent to a licensing agreement with a third party in order to benefit from the digital content or the digital service.

developer may even fall under the DCSD, if, for example, the consumer provides data in exchange for the service.[25] However, it is not very likely that this contract between the consumer and the platform operator or app developer will contain terms that include an obligation to maintain the service for a certain period of time and to regularly update.

It is also imaginable that contracts concluded in the chain of distribution give rise to an obligation of the producer and/or the platform operator to maintain the platform service and to provide updates. It is even imaginable that such a contract forms a contract in favour of a third party, which would give the consumer a direct claim for updates against the producer and/or platform operator. In the present day, however, such consumer-friendly contracts with third parties, who are not sellers, do not seem to exist in practice.

The most frequent situation seems to be that the seller is the only person that is under any obligation to maintain the digital service and to provide all necessary updates of the software built into the smart lock, the app and the service platform itself.[26] It is most likely that the producer, the platform operator and other persons involved are not under any obligation towards the consumer. It will, however, at least sometimes be the case that the producer or other persons are obliged towards the seller to provide updates to the consumer and to maintain the platform service.

IX. Digital "servitisation" of sales contracts and risk allocation to sellers

For goods with digital elements and, even more so, for sales contracts that provide for a continuous supply of a digital service, such as a smart lock, the SGD introduces a service element into the contract of sale. The SGD imposes digital obligations on sellers, including necessary updates, the maintenance and continuation of a promised digital service, and even a potential obligation to repair the digital element of a good under Article 13 (2) SGD. This does not exactly lead to a problematic situation whereby sellers are burdened with obligations they cannot fulfil themselves. Many sellers of classical physical goods without any digital elements are not capable of fulfilling their obligation to repair either. The law nevertheless places such obligations on them because it is usually feasible for sellers

25 On the rather complex demarcation issues cf. Article 3 (4) and Recital (21) SGD; *Vanherpe*, ERPL 2020, 251, 254–255.

26 *Staudenmayer*, ZEuP 2019, 663, 672 et seq.

to organise a repair by third parties, often the producer of the goods or a service organisation set up by the producer.

Regarding the digital obligations of sellers, it is, however, much more likely that sellers are actually not capable of finding a third-party provider to fulfil their digital obligations. The reasons are both practical and due to a lack of licences or other rights that may be necessary for updates. This is certainly true where sellers sell a broad variety of digital goods stemming from producers from all over the world, which are completely outside of their reach. In such situations, the law placing digital obligations on sellers, results in a pure allocation of risks. If this risk manifests, for example in the case that the seller has to pay back the price to a consumer, then there is only a rather weak right of redress against prior steps in the distribution chain provided in Article 18 SGD.[27] So what looks at first glance like a "servitisation" of the sales contract is in reality often a mere allocation of risk to the seller.

X. *Effects for consumer protection*

In theory, the new digital obligations in the SGD, in particular the update obligations, improve the level of consumer protection for contracts covered by this directive. The consumer now has rights against the seller to receive updates for the digital element and the accompanying digital service. However, in practice, this right may often not be enforceable because the seller is often not factually or legally able to provide the updates it is obliged to provide.[28] Moreover, the seller is not in a sufficiently strong position to force other persons involved in the production of the goods, the development of the software or the provision of the digital service to provide necessary updates. The consumer will, in such cases, be left only with the other remedies for lack of conformity under the SGD, in particular the right to terminate the contract or to reduce the price.

The new update obligation in the SGD may nevertheless have an indirect effect on better information of consumers who buy goods with digital elements or goods where the sales contract provides for continuous supply of a digital service. This effect is due to Article 7 (5) SGD, which may

27 *Kalamees*, 12 (2021) JIPITEC, 131, 140, who argues that Member States should design their national rules on right of redress as extensively mandatory.

28 *Firsching*, ZUM 2021, 210, 219.

force sellers, in order to avoid liability for lack of conformity, to inform consumers that no updates will be provided.

There may even be further indirect effects of the update obligation. For example, the distribution of a good with digital elements or goods that need the continuous supply of a digital service, without ensuring that necessary updates will be provided for a sufficiently long period of time, may cause an unfair commercial practice. Therefore, the update obligation introduced by the SGD may make it easier for consumer authorities or consumer associations to take action against producers or distributors that do not ensure that necessary updates are provided. The update obligation in the SGD may also help to shape consumers' expectations regarding updates, which then indirectly influences market participants who are not sellers, in particular producers, distributors or service platform providers. The SGD creates a baseline for consumers' legitimate expectations of which updates they will receive, and for how long. In this way, the SGD could help to place indirect pressure on all suppliers in the market to provide the updates that consumers can reasonably expect.

XI. Market effects of the update obligations

As said, it is at least imaginable that the update obligations, which are only imposed on sellers under the SGD, will contribute to a general market pressure on producers, distributers, software developers and others to provide the necessary updates. However, since the capability for providing updates may exclusively be in the hands of one individual market participant (e.g., the producer), the obligation on the seller to ensure that necessary updates are being provided may create vertical distribution restraints. Moreover, SMEs might find themselves at a disadvantage since very big sellers with strong market power may actually be able to ensure, due to their market power, that updates are actually provided. Weaker market participants, such as small local dealers in brick and mortar shops, do not have the power to bring any pressure to bear on producers or third-party platform operators. If they sell goods with digital elements that require updates or goods that require the continuous supply of a digital service, they simply have to take the risk that updates will be provided by third parties completely outside of their control. This might hinder them in selling such goods. The update obligation may also have disadvantages for innovation if it prevents producers from providing Application Programming Interfaces (APIs) that would allow parties to develop and distribute their own apps for the smart device that the producer puts into circulation.

It must be hoped that competition laws will effectively fight such adverse defects on the competitiveness of markets.

XII. Conclusions

The SGD introduces the right of the consumer to receive updates to digital elements and digital services necessary for the functioning of the goods bought. However, under the SGD, the only obligor of the consumer is the seller. In many situations, the seller is the least capable person to deliver updates among the several, often many market participants involved in business models based on goods with digital elements and their accompanying digital services. Therefore, the direct benefit for consumers may be rather limited. The consumers will hardly ever actually be in a position to enforce their right to updates against the seller. The position of the consumer has, nevertheless, improved to some extent since the SGD clarifies that, where necessary updates are not provided or promised digital services are not continuously upheld, then the consumer has the good old classical rights of a buyer to terminate the contract or to reduce the price and at least receive the money back.[29] Moreover, it is at least imaginable that the update obligations of sellers have some indirect effects by increasing the market pressure to ensure the necessary updates on producers, third-party service providers and other persons. It remains to be seen whether the update obligation has adverse effects on SMUs and competition in general.

The update obligation in the SGD, in particular, illustrates what the next step in the development of EU consumer law should be. EU consumer legislation should introduce a direct claim against producers and importers who put smart devices into circulation, in particular a right of consumers to receive the necessary updates. The classic counter-argument that it is not in the consumer's interest to have different remedies against different people[30] is a bogeyman. The goal must be a truly consumer-friendly legal situation in which the consumer can exercise all legal remedies against all persons that are significantly involved in the digital services promised together with the purchased goods. Such a right would somehow go beyond the classical doctrines of contract law, because, to

29 *Seritti*, EuCML 2021, 180, 181.

30 See only *Staudenmayer*, in Schulze / Staudenmayer, EU Digital Law (2020), Article 8 DCSD, No. 121 et seq., who justifies this solution even for the DCSD as an analogy with traditional sales law.

this day, there is often no contract concluded between the producer, who puts a smart device into circulation and the consumer who buys this device from a seller that is not the producer. However, the legislator is not bound to classical doctrines of contract law. Marketing goods with digital elements that need updates or the continuous provision of a digital service should be understood as an offer to the public. The task of consumer law is to ensure that consumers who accept this offer have the rights they can reasonably expect against all identifiable parties involved in the placing of the good on the market and selling it.

The Update Obligation – how to make it work in the relationship between seller, producer, digital content or service provider and consumer

*Christiane Wendehorst**

I. Introduction

From the point of view of consumers, the update obligation – together with the new concept of 'goods with digital elements' – is arguably the most important innovation resulting from Directives (EU) 2019/770 (Digital Content and Services Directive, DCD) and 2019/771 (Sale of Goods Directive, SGD).[1] It was only in exceptional constellations and under the law of some Member States that consumers may have had a right to receive software updates already on the basis of the previously applicable law (such as by way of a tacitly granted guarantee). In the vast majority of cases, a consumer did not have a right to software updates, but had to rely entirely on the producer's goodwill.[2] The initial DCD proposal from 2015[3] did not provide for an obligation to supply updates, and the first draft of the SGD[4] did not address digital elements at all, which was heavily

---

* Professor of Civil Law, University of Vienna.

1 Dirk Staudenmayer, in Reiner Schulze and Dirk Staudenmayer (eds), *EU Digtal Law* (Nomos 2020), Article 8 DCD, para 110.

2 See Sophia Fida, *Updates, Patches & Co – Zivilrechtliche Fragen zur Softwareaktualisierung* (Manz 2022) 13 ff with further references. See also Paul Schrader and Jonathan Engstler, 'Anspruch auf Bereitstellung von Software-Updates?' [2018] MMR, 356.

3 European Commission, 'Proposal for a Directive of the European Parliament and of the Council on certain aspects concerning contracts for the supply of digital content' COM (2015) 634 final.

4 European Commission, 'Proposal for a Directive of the European Parliament and of the Council on certain contract law aspects of online and other distance marketing of goods' COM (2015) 635 final. After severe criticism that the proposal's restriction to distance selling will lead to fragmentation and legal uncertainty, an amended proposal was put forward, European Commission, 'Amended Proposal for as Directive of the European Parliament and of the Council on certain aspects concerning contracts for the online and other distance sales of goods, amending Regulation (EC) No 2006/2004 of the European Parliament and of the Council

criticised, including by the author of this chapter.[5] The European legislator has reacted to the criticism and the final Directives reflect, among other changes, the author's 'five-factor model' of Internet of Things (IoT) products, which characterises IoT products as a combination of: (i) hardware, (ii) embedded software, (iii) ancillary software, (iv) updates for embedded and ancillary software and (v) ancillary digital services.[6] Regarding updates and ancillary digital services, the author had also argued in favour of an extended responsibility of the businesses involved. However, the suggestion to place the obligation to provide updates primarily on the manufacturer or the importer was not adopted by the Directives.[7]

The Directives provide rules on updates for two different scenarios that need to be delineated. In the first scenario, the trader needs to provide updates in order to maintain the conformity of the digital content or services or of the goods with digital elements with the contract. This may be the case either because updates have been promised under the contract

---

and Directive 2009/22/EC of the European Parliament and of the Council and repealing Directive 1999/44/EC of the European Parliament and of the Council' COM (2017) 637 final.

5 Christiane Wendehorst, 'Consumer Contracts and the Internet of Things' in Reiner Schulze and Dirk Staudenmayer (eds), *Digital Revolution: Challenges for Contract Law in Practice* (Hart/Nomos 2016) 189; Christiane Wendehorst, 'Sale of goods and supply of digital content – two worlds apart?' (Directorate-General for Internal Policies, Policy Department C, Citizen's Rights and Constitutional Affairs, 2016) <http://www.europarl.europa.eu/cmsdata/98774/pe%20556%20928%20EN_final.pdf> accessed 24.02.2022; Christiane Wendehorst, 'Hybride Produkte und hybrider Vertrieb' in Christiane Wendehorst and Brigitta Zöchling-Jud (eds), *Ein neues Vertragsrecht für den digitalen Binnenmarkt?* (Manz 2016).

6 Christiane Wendehorst, 'Verbraucherrelevante Problemstellungen zu Besitz- und Eigentumsverhältnissen beim Internet der Dinge' (Expert Opinion commissioned by the Sachverständigenrat für Verbraucherfragen, 2016); Christiane Wendehorst, 'Besitz und Eigentum im Internet der Dinge' in Hans-W. Micklitz et al (eds), *Verbraucherrecht 2.0 – Verbraucher in der digitalen Welt* (Nomos 2017).

7 Article 5 lit. d (Requirements for conformity of the goods) and Article 7a (Liability of the producer and the supplier of digital content) in Christiane Wendehorst, 'Sale of goods and supply of digital content – two worlds apart?' ' (Directorate-General for Internal Policies, Policy Department C, Citizen's Rights and Constitutional Affairs, 2016), <http://www.europarl.europa.eu/cmsdata/98774/pe%20556%20928%20EN_final.pdf> accessed 24.02.2022; see also the draft for the German Federal Government: § 477a and § 477b (Direct liability of the producer); the draft text for the EU institutions presented at the ELI Annual Conference on 4 September 2017: Art. 8a (Seller's guarantee for third party services) and Art. 9a (Producer's liability). With regard to the Austrian implementation, see also Christiane Wendehorst, 'Direkthaftung des Herstellers (Teil I)' [2020] VbR 94; Christiane Wendehorst, 'Direkthaftung des Herstellers (Teil II)' [2020] VbR 138.

(Art 7(d) DCD or Art 6(d) SGD) or because they are objectively necessary to maintain the conformity of the digital content or services or goods with digital elements (Art 8(2)-(3) DCD or Art 7(3)-(4) SGD). The relevant provisions of the DCD and SGD have been aligned to the maximum extent possible. The second scenario concerns updates and other modifications that are not required to maintain the conformity of the digital content or services with the contract, but which amount to a unilateral change of the performance owed under a long-term contractual relationship and may even be to the detriment of the consumer. This scenario is addressed by Art 19 DCD but no corresponding provision exists in the SGD. As the trader is not under an obligation to provide updates within the meaning of Art 19 DCD (quite on the contrary), such updates are not addressed by this Chapter (for details see the Chapters on Modifications of Digital Content/Services and Digital Elements in Smart Products).

II. Main elements of the update obligation

1. Single acts of supply and continuous supply over a period of time

a) General aspects of the distinction

A central distinction in the context of updates is that between single acts of supply (or a series of individual acts of supply) and continuous supply over a period of time. First of all, it needs to be stressed that in terms of the main obligations under the contract, the DCD covers both single acts of supply (e.g. software download, video download) and continuous supply over a period of time (e.g. software-as-a-service, social network, cloud storage). By contrast, the SGD only covers single acts of supply, i.e. the delivery of goods, but not goods-related services to be supplied over a period of time (e.g. not contracts on the rental of goods). While this striking divergence between DCD and SGD exists at the level of the main obligations under the contract, it no longer exists at the level of 'digital elements'. Under the SGD, goods supplied in a single act can have 'digital elements' that are continuously supplied over a period of time. Where, for example, the contract is about the sale of a smart refrigerator which, in order to maintain its functions, requires continuous supply of particular cloud services (e.g. a user account, platform shopping services and continuous data feeds), this is covered by the SGD. To a certain extent, the digital element turns traditional one-off obligations such as the delivery of goods into long-term legal relationships.

The update obligation needs to be analysed in relation to four different contractual constellations: (i) single act of supply (or series of individual acts of supply) of digital content or service, (ii) continuous supply of digital content or service over a period of time, (iii) delivery of goods with single act of supply of a digital element (e.g. embedded software), and (iv) delivery of goods with continuous supply of a digital element over a period of time (e.g. user account for the producer's cloud).

b) *Delimitation issues*

Recital 57 DCD (sentences 5–7) clarifies that the concept of continuous provision over a period of time is to be understood broadly and that the relevant period of time can also be relatively short, for example in the case of streaming a single video. Furthermore, sentence 7 of Recital 57 clarifies that cases where digital content or services are made available on a regular or recurring basis are also to be considered a continuous supply over a period of time. Since the Recital only refers to contracts with a fixed duration of supply and contracts with an indefinite period of supply, it is unclear whether the one-off supply of digital content combined with an obligation to provide regular updates qualifies as single act of supply or as continuous supply over a period of time. However, whether a contract falls in the former or latter category significantly affects the trader's obligations under the DCD (see II. 4.). Arguably, the decisive factor should be whether the updates are to be regarded as an essential part of the main obligation under the contract (then continuous provision over a period of time) or whether they are merely of accessory nature, i.e. the main digital content can still be used in a meaningful way even without the update.[8] For example, anti-malware protection software is useless without continuous updates, so a contract about anti-malware protection software should always be considered a case of continuous supply over a period of time.

While the 2015 DCD proposal only used the concept of 'digital content' and understood this to include also streaming subscriptions and contracts

8 Christiane Wendehorst, 'Aktualisierungen und andere digitale Dauerleistungen' in Johannes Stabentheiner, Christiane Wendehorst and Brigitta Zöchling-Jud (eds), *Das neue europäische Gewährleistungsrecht* (Manz 2019) 114.

with social networks,[9] the final text of the Directive distinguishes between 'digital content' on the one hand and 'digital services' on the other.[10] Article 2(2) DCD defines the latter as services that allow the consumer to create, process, store or access data in digital form; or services that enable the consumer to share or otherwise interact with data in digital form uploaded or created by the consumer or other users of the relevant service. The fact that it is hardly possible to draw a clear line between digital content and digital services (e.g. does streaming a single video qualify as digital content or service?) does not lead to legal uncertainty, as the distinction has virtually no consequences for the application of the DCD itself.[11] Quite generally, it can be said that digital services will typically be supplied over a continuous period of time. This includes, for example, software-as-a-service (SaaS) contracts or cloud storage contracts. Conversely, digital content is more likely to be supplied in a single act, such as downloading a particular copy of software or a video. However, there may also be constellations where digital content is supplied continuously over a period of time, for example if the trader undertakes to provide updates on a regular or recurring basis and these are to be regarded as an essential part of the main obligation under the contract (e.g. anti-malware protection software or the electronic maps in the case of a navigation service). The distinction between single act of supply and continuous supply over a period of time is thus not totally congruent with the distinction between digital content and digital services.[12]

9 European Commission, 'Proposal for a Directive of the European Parliament and of the Council on certain aspects concerning contracts for the supply of digital content' COM (2015) 634 final, and European Commission, 'Proposal for a

10 See the critical remarks of cMartin Schmidt-Kessel et al, 'Die Richtlinienvorschläge der Kommission zu Digitalen Inhalten und Online Handel (Teil II)' [2016] GPR 54, 55.

11 See, however, the parallel changes made to the Consumer Rights Directive made by Directive (EU) 2019/2161 of the European Parliament and of the Council of 27 November 2019 amending Council Directive 93/13/EEC and Directives 98/6/EC, 2005/29/EC and 2011/83/EU of the European Parliament and of the Council as regards the better enforcement and modernisation of Union consumer protection rules [2019] OJ L328/7. In the context of that Directive, the differentiation between digital content and digital services is clearly much more relevant.

12 Dirk Staudenmayer in Reiner Schulze and Dirk Staudenmayer (eds), *EU Digital Law* (Nomos 2020) Article 8 paras 136–138.

2. *What does the trader owe to the consumer?*

a) *Subjective and objective requirements*

The update-related provisions in the DCD and SGD are a core element of the new Directives. Updates may be owed for two reasons, either because they are a subjective requirement of conformity within the meaning of Art 7(d) DCD, Art 6(d) SGD or because they are part of the objective conformity requirements within the meaning of Art 8(2)-(4) DCD, Art 7(3)-(4) SGD. It is in particular the new concept of objective conformity requirements that constitutes a significant element of innovation for the consumer acquis.

Where updates are part of the subjective requirements, i.e. they are part of the contractual promise within the meaning of Art 7(d) DCD or Art 6(d) SGD, the extent and nature of the changes is determined by the parties. The parties may not only agree on updates that maintain initial level of quality of the digital service or content, but also on substantial improvements (e.g. upgrades that install new versions of an operating system). If this is the case, the update obligation also includes the obligation to provide upgrades, as substantial improvements are a subjective conformity requirement. By contrast, where updates are necessary only to maintain the conformity with objective requirements within the meaning of Art 8(2)-(3) DCD or Art 7(3)-(4) SGD, the update obligation is limited to what is necessary to keep (or re-establish) the initial level of quality (including compatibility, functionality, security etc.) of the digital content, service or element (Recital 30 SGD). Regardless of whether updates are a subjective or an objective requirement, their absence may trigger remedies for lack of conformity with the contract.

b) *Relationship with Art 19 DCD*

The provisions in Articles 7 and 8 DCD are not the only ones that deal with updates. Article 19 DCD provides a rule for unilateral modifications by the trader of digital content or a digital service supplied continuously over a period of time, which go beyond what is necessary to maintain the conformity of the services with the contract.[13] Whether a change

---

13 For a detailed analysis see Georg E. Kodek, 'Änderung digitaler Inhalte und digitaler Dienstleistungen (Art 19 DIRL)' in Johannes Stabentheiner, Christiane

constitutes an update owed by the trader pursuant to Articles 7 and 8 DCD or a modification which is only permissible under the restrictive conditions stated in Article 19, depends on whether the change is necessary for maintaining conformity with the contract. Assessing whether an update is "necessary" can be difficult task, particularly where updates are intended to maintain contractual conformity (for example, ensuring the agreed interoperability with (meanwhile modernised) other digital content) but, at same time also entail negative side effects for the consumer, such as requiring more storage space and computing power.

Since Article 19 DCD allows unilateral changes only under certain conditions, traders may argue that a particularly high level of functionality, compatibility, continuity and security is objectively required and therefore the provided update falls under Articles 7 and 8 DCD and does not need to meet the requirements of Article 19 DCD. The wording of Articles 7 and 8 DCD would suggest that the trader needs to limit updates to what is absolutely necessary in order to keep the digital content or digital services just in conformity with the contract. From a contract law perspective, however, the trader cannot be expected to keep digital content and digital services always as close as possible to the lowest end of conformity, as this would constantly expose the trader to a possible breach of contract. Furthermore, a trader cannot be expected to respond to all the different individual needs of consumers and, for example, refrain from updating a particular function in the interest of saving storage space for user groups that do not use that function anyway. In practice, this opens up a broad margin of discretion for the trader.

If an update (or update package) maintains the conformity of the digital content and digital services but also includes changes that go beyond what is necessary, one and the same update can fall under Articles 7 and 8 DCD as well as Article 19 DCD. In this case, the update package must meet the requirements of Article 19.

c) *Concrete actions owed by the trader*

Article 8(2) DCD and Article 7(3) SGD explicitly set out that the trader has to ensure that the consumer is informed about updates, including security updates, which are objectively required to maintain the conformity of

---

Wendehorst and Brigitta Zöchling-Jud (eds), *Das neue europäische Gewährleistungsrecht* (Manz 2019) 141.

the digital content or digital service. Unless specifically agreed otherwise, this should apply mutatis mutandis to updates that constitute a subjective conformity criterion within the meaning of Article 7(d) DCD and Article 6(d) SGD. While such information obligation sounds reasonable and harmless at first glance, it can pose a considerable challenge for traders in practice.[14] Informing consumers about updates presupposes that the seller can reliably contact the consumer, possibly even years after the contract was concluded. Not only does this require a considerable additional effort by traders, but it may also have negative effects on the protection of the consumer's personal data.

To comply with the information duty, it may be necessary for traders to store all available contact data of consumers as well as data on all their purchases for several years. Based on Article 6(1)(b) or (f) GDPR, the trader would either need to forward the data to the respective manufacturer/developer, or the trader itself would have to ensure that information about the availability of an update will in fact reach the consumer, even though the updates are usually provided by the manufacturer/developer and not the trader. At least technically, this could easily be achieved by online retailers (albeit at considerable additional cost for many businesses and at the price of additional processing of personal data). For brick-and-mortar stores, however, complying with this information duty could be a problem difficult to overcome in practice, as it would require traditional retailers to collect and store contact data of every consumer that buys a good with digital elements.

How all these new requirements relate to the GDPR's principles for the processing of personal data, in particular to the principle of data minimisation, is an open question. Article 3(8) DCD clarifies that the GDPR should prevail in case of conflict between the two instruments. This means an update management system used jointly by a trader and manufacturer/developer or other third parties must be in compliance with the GDPR, including the principle of data minimisation as well as the requirement of privacy by design and privacy by default (Article 25 GDPR). Arguably, the best solution both from the perspective of the consumer and the trader is if no personal contact data of the consumer (e.g. e-mail address, telephone number, residential address) is processed at all, but instead the information of an available update as well as the update itself is sent directly to the consumer's terminal device, as is currently common

14 See Zöchling-Jud, 'Das neue Europäische Gewährleistungsrecht für den Warenhandel' [2019] GPR 115, 123.

practice. This is also the only way to ensure that information and updates reach the person who actually uses the goods or digital content in the end because the individual who concluded the contract with the trader is not necessarily the person using the product.

To ensure compliance with the GDPR, the trader may rely on the manufacturer/developer, who can interact directly with the consumer via the digital content or services or a display on the goods or an online interface that comes with a digital element (such as a control app on the consumer's mobile), to fulfil the update obligations. Unlike the trader, the manufacturer/developer is in a position to ensure that the information about the availability of a new update appears on the display of, e.g., the connected household appliance, and that the consumer is given a reasonable opportunity to install the update. It would have been more appropriate if the respective legal requirements had been formulated as design requirements for the digital content or service or the goods with digital elements, instead of an obligation for the trader. It would also have been desirable if at least the Recitals had addressed issues of data protection and practical implementation in more detail. As the law stands now, there is a risk that retailers and manufacturers/developers may use the update requirement as a pretext for collecting consumer data on a large scale and opening up new communication channels for direct marketing. Even if data protection law sets certain limits, an obligation to contact the consumer regularly for updates seems almost like an invitation to utilise this data for marketing purposes. Moreover, the current legal framework disadvantages SMEs, which do not have the financial resources to build the infrastructure required for appropriate customer data and update management.[15]

d) *Admissibility of forced updates?*

Article 8(3) DCD, Article 7(4) SGD and Recital 30 SGD suggest that the European legislator in principle assumes that the consumer must actively trigger the installation of the update and can therefore decide whether and when to install an update. The question arises, however, whether this

15 Christiane Wendehorst, 'Aktualisierungen und andere digitale Dauerleistungen' in Johannes Stabentheiner, Christiane Wendehorst and Brigitta Zöchling-Jud (eds), *Das neue europäische Gewährleistungsrecht* (Manz 2019) 111, 123 ff; see also Sophia Fida, *Updates, Patches & Co – Zivilrechtliche Fragen zur Softwareaktualisierung* (Manz 2022) 54 ff.

already means that forced updates are not permissible under the Directives or whether businesses may be entitled or even obliged to design the update procedure in a way that updates are installed automatically.[16]

According to Recital 47 DCD and Recital 30 SGD, obligations under Union and national law to provide security updates remain unaffected. This concerns currently still voluntary security standards under the Cybersecurity Regulation in particular.[17] Also in the context of the Radio Equipment Directive[18], there has already been a discussion about introducing mandatory cybersecurity requirements through the principles of 'security by design and by default'.[19] However, it is unclear what exactly this means for forced updates under the law as it currently stands. Installing updates usually amounts to storing information on the consumer's terminal device, which means it has to meet the requirements of Article 5(3) of the E-Privacy Directive.[20] According to this provision, national law must

16 On the admissibility of forced updates, see LG Frankfurt a. M. 6.6.2013 – 2–24 O 246/12 (2013) CR 744 no. 59 according to which a consumer's blanket consent to the installation of future updates is an unfair contract term. See also Mirko A. Wieczorek, 'Softwarepflege bei Standard- und Individualsoftware' in Wolfgang Kilian and Benno Heussen (eds), *Computerrechts-Handbuch* (C.H. Beck 2018) para 18; Christiane Wendehorst, 'Aktualisierungen und andere digitale Dauerleistungen' in Johannes Stabentheiner, Christiane Wendehorst and Brigitta Zöchling-Jud (eds), *Das neue europäische Gewährleistungsrecht?* (Manz 2019) 111, 121Christiane Wendehorst, 'Hybride Produkte und hybrider Vertrieb' in Christiane Wendehorst and Brigitta Zöchling-Jud (eds), *Ein neues Vertragsrecht für den digitalen Binnenmarkt?* (Manz 2016) 45, 79; Christiane Wendehorst, 'Besitz und Eigentum im Internet der Dinge' in Hans-W. Micklitz et al (eds), *Verbraucherrecht 2.0 – Verbraucher in der digitalen Welt* (Nomos 2017) 379; Thomas Riehm, 'Updates, Patches & Co. – Schutz nachwirkender Qualitätserwartungen' in Martin Schmidt-Kessel and Malte Kramme, *Geschäftsmodelle in der digitalen Welt* (Jena 2017) 221.

17 Regulation (EU) 2019/881 of the European Parliament and of the Council of 17 April 2019 on ENISA (European Union Cyber Security Agency) and on cybersecurity certification of information and communication technology and repealing Regulation (EU) No 526/2013 (Cybersecurity Legislative Act), OJ 2019 L 151, 15.

18 Directive 2014/53/EU of the European Parliament and of the Council of 16 April 2014 on the harmonisation of the laws of the Member States relating to the making available on the market of radio equipment and repealing Directive 1999/5/EC, OJ 2014 L 153, 62.

19 Centre for Strategy & Evaluation Services, 'Impact Assessment on Increased Protection of Internet-Connected Radio Equipment and Wearable Radio Equipment, Final Report', European Commission, 2020, 24.

20 Directive 2002/58/EC of the European Parliament and of the Council of 12 July 2002 concerning the processing of personal data and the protection of privacy in the electronic communications sector OJ 2001 L 201, 37.

ensure that the storing of information in the terminal equipment of a user is only allowed on condition that the user has given consent after having been provided with clear and comprehensive information, in accordance with the GDPR. The only explicit exceptions are technical storage for the sole purpose of carrying out the transmission of a communication over an electronic communications network, or storage strictly necessary to enable the provider of an information society service to provide a service requested by the user. This already indicates that forced updates may be admissible only under very narrowly defined circumstances.

In principle, the consumer may well have a legitimate interest in not installing even those updates that are necessary to maintain the conformity of the digital content or goods with the contract.[21] This holds true in particular for updates that are not security-relevant but that rather concern the functionality of the digital content or service or element. Especially when consumers have integrated digital content or services or goods with digital elements into a complex digital environment – such as a comprehensive smart home solution – any change, no matter how minor, can result in high adaptation costs. On the other hand, given that the vast majority of consumers will not be fitting off-the-shelf products into complex digital environments, most consumers are likely to be more interested in having the products they purchase updated automatically. This may of course differ according to the type of digital content or service, or goods with digital elements, and the consumer must usually at least be able to decide at what point in time they want the update installed. For example, anyone who is forced to update their word processing programme while completing a paper to be submitted by midnight is likely to be only moderately pleased. If the timing cannot be influenced by the consumer, this circumstance would in itself constitute a lack of conformity – e.g., a word processing programme that occasionally sends the user into unforeseen 'forced coffee breaks' is hardly likely to be in conformity with Article 8(1)(a) and (b) DCD.

Apart from the timing issue, there are good arguments for allowing forced updates in order to protect consumers from the detrimental consequences their own inertia might have, considering the immense potential harm of uninstalled updates for consumers themselves and to third parties.

---

21 See Gerald Spindler, 'Verantwortlichkeit von IT-Herstellern, Nutzern und Intermediären' (Bundesamt für Sicherheit in der Informationstechnik, 2007) 129 <https://www.bsi.bund.de/SharedDocs/Downloads/DE/BSI/Publikationen/Studien/ITSicherheitUndRecht/Gutachten_pdf.pdf?__blob=publicationFile&v=2> accessed 24.02.2022.

There could even be an implied post-contractual duty to this end, since experience has shown that consumers with little digital affinity often postpone the installation of updates for a long time or do not carry it out at all.[22] In addition, the operation of insecure IoT devices is by no means just the consumer's 'private matter', but a gateway for so-called botnets, DDoS attacks and other illegal activities that can cause considerable damage worldwide.[23] The Directives do not have a blocking effect in this respect, although E-privacy law may be a hurdle to overcome.

3. *Liability of the trader in the context of updates*

a) *Liability for lack of conformity as a result of a failure to update*

Strictly speaking, all the trader owes to the consumer in the context of updates is to ensure that the consumer is informed of and supplied with updates, including security updates, that are necessary to keep the digital content or service or the goods with digital elements in conformity with the contract. Thus, the direct obligations of the trader are limited to post-contractual duties of information and duties of a more organisational nature. However, at least under the Directives, the trader is not directly liable to the consumer for the breach of these obligations. Rather, the trader is liable for a resulting lack of conformity, in very much the same way as the trader would be liable for any other lack of conformity with the contract.[24] It is irrelevant whether the lack of conformity actually already

---

22 Benajmin Raue, 'Haftung für unsichere Software' [2017] NJW 1841, 1842 f; cf also Gerald Spindler, 'Verantwortlichkeit von IT-Herstellern, Nutzern und Intermediären' (Bundesamt für Sicherheit in der Informationstechnik, 2007) 128 f <https://www.bsi.bund.de/SharedDocs/Downloads/DE/BSI/Publikationen/Studien/ITSicherheitUndRecht/Gutachten_pdf.pdf?__blob=publicationFile&v=2> accessed 24.02.2022.

23 *Cf* Benajmin Raue, 'Haftung für unsichere Software' [2017] NJW 1841 ff; Gerald Spindler, 'Verantwortlichkeit von IT-Herstellern, Nutzern und Intermediären' (Bundesamt für Sicherheit in der Informationstechnik, 2007) 38 ff with further references <https://www.bsi.bund.de/SharedDocs/Downloads/DE/BSI/Publikationen/Studien/ITSicherheitUndRecht/Gutachten_pdf.pdf?__blob=publicationFile&v=2> accessed 24.02.2022.

24 Wolfgang Faber, 'Bereitstellung und Mangelbegriff' in Johannes Stabentheiner, Christiane Wendehorst and Brigitta Zöchling-Jud (eds), *Das neue europäische Gewährleistungsrecht* (Manz 2019) 79; Brigitta Zöchling-Jud, 'Das neue Europäische Gewährleistungsrecht für den Warenhandel' [2019] GPR 115,123; Axel

existed at the time of supply or delivery or only arose later as a result of external developments. Things are different only if the failure to update pursuant to Article 8(3) DCD or Article 7(4) SGD has its cause in the sphere of the consumer.

With regard to the burden of proof, the question may arise whether Article 12(3) DCD and Article 11(3) SGD apply by analogy where a lack of conformity that is due to the absence of an update arises at a point in time after the one-off supply or delivery. According to these provisions, if a digital content or service or the digital element of goods is to be supplied continuously over a period of time, the trader/seller bears the burden of proof that the digital content or service or digital element had been in conformity with the contract until the lack of conformity became apparent. This reversal of the burden of proof does not apply directly where, e.g., a little more than one year after the one-off delivery of goods with digital elements, a lack of conformity that is due to the absence of an update becomes apparent. However, the situation is very similar to the situation where digital elements are to be provided continuously over a period of time. Therefore, it could be argued that the trader should bear the burden of proving that the need for an update did not arise earlier. In practice, this becomes relevant mainly if, exceptionally, the customer pays *pro ratio temporis* or where this factor is relevant for calculating a price reduction.

b) Liability for lack of conformity resulting from an update

It goes without saying that a lack of conformity that persists despite an unsuccessful attempt to remedy it by means of an update must give rise to liability in exactly the same way as if no update had been provided at all. What is less clear from the text of the Directives, however, is the question whether the trader becomes liable also where the digital content or services or the goods with digital elements were originally in conformity with the contract but then become defective as a result of an update. This situation is very common in practice, as many update packages are themselves defective and the update may, for example, result in the sudden loss of

---

Metzger, 'Verträge über digitale Inhalte und digitale Dienstleistungen: Neuer BGB-Vertragstypus oder punktuelle Reform?' [2019] JZ 577, 581; Dirk Staudenmayer in Reiner Schulze and Dirk Staudenmayer (eds), *EU Digital Law* (Nomos 2020) Article 8 para 115.

certain functionalities that had worked perfectly well previously.[25] Strictly speaking, the provisions on liability in Article 11 DCD and Article 10 SGD only refer to the time limits in Article 8(2)(b) DCD and Article 7(3) SGD, which in turn only mention updates to 'maintain' conformity with the contract. From Recitals 28 and 30 SGD it is clear, however, that the European legislator intended to establish liability also for a lack of conformity which is caused by an update and had not existed previously.[26] Treating the lack of conformity caused by defective updates in the same manner as the failure to provide an update seems fair and logical, but should have been stated more clearly also in the blackletter of the Directives.

Where lack of conformity is caused by a defective update, there are some uncertainties with regard to the burden of proof.[27] In particular, the question arises whether an update triggers a renewed one-year period with regard to the reversal of the burden of proof (see Article 12(2) DCD, Article 11(1) SGD). The fact that the reversal of the burden of proof must not be incompatible with the nature of the defect would then mean, inter alia, that it only applies to such defects as, according to their nature, might have been caused by the update. However, this interpretation also raises serious methodological concerns, especially under the SGD, where Article 11(1) clearly only refers to the delivery of the goods.

25 *Cf* Thomas Riehm and Metawi A. Abold, 'Mängelgewährleistungspflichten des Anbieters digitaler Inhalte' [2018] ZUM 82, 87; Thomas Riehm, 'Updates, Patches & Co. – Schutz nachwirkender Qualitätserwartungen' in Martin Schmidt-Kessel and Malte Kramme, *Geschäftsmodelle in der digitalen Welt* (Jena 2017) 220.

26 Recital 28 SGD states: 'Moreover, defective or incomplete updates should also be considered as a lack of conformity of the goods, given that that would mean that such updates are not performed in the manner stipulated in the sales contract.' Recital 30 SGD provides: 'If an update provided by the seller, or by a third party supplying the digital content or digital service under the sales contract, causes a lack of conformity of the good with digital elements, the seller should be liable for bringing the good into conformity again.'

27 Brigitta Zöchling-Jud, 'Beweislast und Verjährung im neuen europäischen Gewährleistungsrecht' in Johannes Stabentheiner, Christiane Wendehorst and Brigitta Zöchling-Jud (eds), *Das neue europäische Gewährleistungsrecht* (Manz 2019) 205; Brigitta Zöchling-Jud, 'Das neue Europäische Gewährleistungsrecht für den Warenhandel' [2019] GPR 115,125 f.

c) Liability for damages under national law?

The trader/seller who provides digital content or goods with digital elements on a one-off basis is liable under the Directives even if that trader has not breached any of their own duties of information or any of their own organisational duties at all. This applies in particular in those cases in which the manufacturer or other third party responsible for providing updates simply remained passive, and therefore there was nothing for the trader to inform the consumer about. In such cases, the trader becomes liable under the Directives even though that trader usually has no possibility whatsoever of influencing the manufacturer or other third party that would have been responsible for providing the update. Whether or not the seller may even face a claim for damages is left to the national law. Member States should be careful in this regard not to let the liability of sellers get out of hand.

4. Duration of the obligations and liability period

During the legislative procedure leading up to the two Directives, the duration of the period of time for which the trader must ensure that the consumer is informed of and supplied with updates was controversial right up to the end.[28] While most of the provisions on updates took their shape during the Austrian Council Presidency, a number of changes were made in this regard under the Romanian Presidency. The duration of the period is regulated in Article 8(2) DCD and Article 7(3) SGD. A difference is made between one-off supply and supply that is due continuously over a period of time.

a) Duration in the case of one-off supply

In the case of digital content or services or digital elements of goods that are to be provided in a single act of supply (such as software available for download onto the consumer's terminal device or the software embed-

---

28 Also the final provisions have been subject to criticism. See, for example, the remarks of Ivo Bach, 'Neue Richtlinie zum Verbrauchsgüterkauf und zu Verbraucherverträgen über digitale Inhalte [2019] NJW 1705, 1707, who argues that one could hardly have defined the moment of time more openly.'

ded in a smart refrigerator), updates are owed during the period that the consumer could reasonably expect according to the nature and purpose of the digital content, digital services or goods with digital elements, and according to the nature of the contract and all the circumstances of the individual case. Recital 31 SGD clarifies that the consumer may normally expect necessary updates at least during the warranty period.[29] However, the reasonable expectation of the consumer, especially in the case of high-priced items, may also extend considerably beyond the warranty period. In particular in the case of security gaps that make the use of the item by the consumer unsafe, the period during which updates can be reasonably expected is likely to correspond to the expected lifespan of the relevant item. This means, for example, that in the case of a connected elevator or heating system or other items typically designed to be used for a long time, provision of updates for periods of ten years or significantly longer may be required.[30] Conversely, reasonable consumer expectations may of course also be directed towards a shorter period than the regular warranty period, for example in the case of very short-lived goods.[31] In practice, the latter may not be particularly relevant at present, but in view of the observable tendency to equip even typical disposable items (such as product packaging for food or party gadgets) with digital elements and network connectivity, it is quite conceivable that updates may not even be expected for a period of two years from the initial supply. The same holds true for many apps that are provided, for instance, just for use during a particular event.

b) Duration in the case of continuous provision over a period of time

In the case of digital content or services or digital elements of goods to be provided continuously over a period of time, updates are owed during the period of time during which the relevant digital item itself is to be

29 Exentsivley on the reasonable expectations of the consumer see Dirk Staudenmayer in Reiner Schulze and Dirk Staudenmayer (eds), *EU Digital Law* (Nomos 2020) Article 8 para 139 ff.

30 Brigitta Zöchling-Jud, 'Das neue Europäische Gewährleistungsrecht für den Warenhandel' [2019] GPR 115,122; Sophia Fida, *Updates, Patches & Co – Zivilrechtliche Fragen zur Softwareaktualisierung* (Manz 2022) 59.

31 *Cf* Elize Rudloff, 'Der Vorschlag einer Warenhandels-Richtlinie der EU – Fortschritt auf dem Weg zu mehr Nachhaltigkeit?' VuR 2018, 323, 326 ff

provided.[32] For instance, where software is provided under an SaaS scheme and the contract is for one year, updates that are necessary for maintaining the software in conformity with the contract must equally be provided for one year. This rule may pose difficulties in cases of goods with long-term digital elements (e.g. a control app operated in the cloud of the manufacturer as SaaS), because the parties will normally not explicitly agree in such contracts on any specific duration. On the contrary, it is often made clear in the general terms and conditions that no representation or warranty of any kind with regard to a particular duration is being made. Arguably, one has to rely, in such cases on the objective requirement of a certain 'continuity' or 'durability' under Article 8(1)(b) DCD and Article 7(1)(b) SGD, which means that even in the case of continuous provision of digital elements over a period of time reasonable consumer expectations come into play, and any deviation from such objective requirements to the detriment of the consumer would require a qualified waiver. According to Article 10(2) SGD, goods with digital elements, which are provided for a over a period of time, the seller needs to ensure the conformity of the digital content or digital service for a period of at least two years from the time of delivery of the goods with digital elements.

5. *Remedies and their loss*

a) *Remedies for lack of conformity*

The consumer's remedies for lack of conformity which occurs or persists as a result of a failure to provide updates, or as a result of a defective update, coincide with the remedies generally available to the consumer in the case of a lack of conformity. Accordingly, the consumer is primarily entitled to having the relevant item brought into conformity according to Article 14(2) DCD and Article 13(2) SGD. This normally means that the required update is provided or the defective update is corrected. Alternatively, the delivery of a new item that has already been updated by the manufacturer may be requested or the trader may provide a more up-to-date version of

32 For more details see *Staudenmayer*, 'Kauf von Waren mit digitalen Elementen – Die Richtlinie zum Warenkauf' [2019] NJW 2889, 2891;Wolfgang Faber, 'Bereitstellung und Mangelbegriff' in Johannes Stabentheiner, Christiane Wendehorst and Brigitta Zöchling-Jud (eds), *Das neue europäische Gewährleistungsrecht* (Manz 2019) 71; Sophia Fida, *Updates, Patches & Co – Zivilrechtliche Fragen zur Softwareaktualisierung* (Manz 2022) 58.

the same digital content or the same digital services or digital element. In the case of goods with digital elements, where the consumer may normally choose between repair and replacement, this choice must arguably exist also where the lack of conformity only affects the digital element.

However, since the trader as the consumer's direct contracting partner often has no possibility whatsoever to influence the provision of updates, rendering the primary remedies of bringing into conformity (DCD) or repair or replacement (SGD) either impossible or at least unduly burdensome, price reduction or termination will very often be the appropriate remedy instead (Article 14(4) DCD, Article 13(4) SGD).[33] In this context, it is to be noted that the SGD grants the seller the right to refuse both repair and replacement where both are impossible or would cause disproportionate efforts (Article 13(3) SGD),[34] thus overruling the view taken by the ECJ in the *Weber* and *Putz* case.[35]

However, in many cases, the implementation of price reduction may not be quite simple in practice.[36] For example, where the price for a smart refrigerator was calculated as a lump sum, it is not readily clear what proportion of the price is attributable to the hardware and what proportion to the digital element in question. Comparing the value of the non-updated digital element, which makes the refrigerator being no longer in conformity with the contract, and the updated digital element may also be even more difficult than is the calculation of price reduction in general.

The remedy of termination can likewise give rise to uncertainties and practical difficulties.[37] Member States have considerable leeway with re-

33 Bernhard A. *Koch*, 'Das System der Rechtsbehelfe' in Johannes Stabentheiner, Christiane Wendehorst and Brigitta Zöchling-Jud (eds), *Das neue europäische Gewährleistungsrecht* (Manz 2019) 163.

34 See Johannes *Stabentheiner*, 'Hintergründe und Entstehung der beiden Richtlinien und die Bemühungen der österreichischen Ratspräsidentschaft um Konsistenz und Vereinfachung' in Johannes Stabentheiner, Christiane Wendehorst and Brigitta Zöchling-Jud (eds), *Das neue europäische Gewährleistungsrecht* (Manz 2019) 22; Bernhard A. *Koch*, 'Das System der Rechtsbehelfe' in Johannes Stabentheiner, Christiane Wendehorst and Brigitta Zöchling-Jud (eds), *Das neue europäische Gewährleistungsrecht* (Manz 2019) 188.

35 CJEU Joined Cases C-65/09 and C-87/09 *Weber/Wittmer and Putz/Medianess* [2011] ECLI:EU:C:2011:396; *cf* Brigitta *Zöchling-Jud*, 'Das neue Europäische Gewährleistungsrecht für den Warenhandel' [2019] GPR 115, 129..

36 *Cf* Thomas Riehm and Metawi A. *Abold*, 'Mängelgewährleistungspflichten des Anbieters digitaler Inhalte' [2018] ZUM 82, 87; also Matthias Wendland, 'Sonderprivatrecht für Digitale GüterInhalt' *(2019) 118* ZVglRWiss 191, 212 f.

37 *Cf* Thomas Riehm and Metawi A. Abold, 'Mängelgewährleistungspflichten des Anbieters digitaler Inhalte' [2018] ZUM 82, 87 who, in cases in which the con-

gard to the modalities of taking back goods and refunding the purchase price.[38] The SGD at least clarifies that returning the goods has to occur at the seller's expense (Article 16 para. 3 sentence 1 lit. a SGD), but it remains to be seen how the courts will deal with the issue. This includes the question to what extent the seller is obliged to remove the defective item upon termination of the contract and to what extent and under what conditions the consumer owes compensation for having used the item until termination of the contract.[39] This is, however, a general problem and not specifically related to updates.

b) Loss of remedies

While the Directives do not impose any obligations on the consumer and the consumer normally cannot be forced to install updates, the Directives do provide for unfavourable legal consequences for the consumer where the consumer fails to install an update. In this case, the consumer can no longer rely on a lack of conformity if that lack of conformity results solely from the absence of an update, and where the update was provided but failed to be installed by the consumer, providing this failure has its cause in the consumer's sphere (Article 8(3) DCD, Article 7(4) SGD). The Directives explicitly clarify that the consumer retains the remedies if the update was omitted only because the trader had not informed the consumer of the availability of the update and the consequences of not installing it, or because the installation instructions were defective. This raises questions in several respects.

Firstly, the question arises as to what is meant by information about the consequences of non-installation. It is unclear, for example, whether the consequences only have to be explained in legal terms, or also in technical terms, and whether blanket information can be provided when the contract is concluded or whether special and separate information has to be provided for every single update. Arguably, the legislator had not thought through all the practical implications of the trader's information

---

sumer was able to use the purchased software for several years, consider termination to be an unreasonable legal consequence for not providing a security update. So also Matthias Wendland, 'Sonderprivatrecht für Digitale GüterInhalt' *(2019) 118* ZVglRWiss 191, 212 f..

38 Recital 60 SGD.

39 See Brigitta *Zöchling-Jud*, 'Das neue Europäische Gewährleistungsrecht für den Warenhandel' [2019] GPR 115,129 f.

obligation in this respect either. Needless to say, blanket information provided at the point in time when the contract is concluded is hardly likely to attract the consumer's attention. If, on the other hand, information has to be provided specifically and separately for each individual update, this means a considerable burden for the trader that is hardly manageable, especially for small and medium-sized businesses. In practice, the manufacturer should provide the update over-the-air directly to the consumer's device (assuming that the device has a display or interacts with software on the consumer's computer or smartphone).

Secondly, the question arises as to how to deal with circumstances that make the installation of updates by the consumer appear unreasonable, but which are not explicitly addressed in the Directives. For example, where the manufacturer provides a mixed update package and combines essential security updates with functional enhancements or modifications to the design of the user interface, the question arises whether the consumer should lose their remedies with regard to the security gap if they refuse to install the update. While part of the problem may be resolved by Article 19 under the DCD,[40] a corresponding provision is missing in the SGD. Arguably, the consumer should retain their remedies in such cases where the consumer can demonstrate that they only refrained from installing the update because it was linked in an unjustified and unreasonable manner to other modifications.

Finally, it is surprising that the loss of remedies is regulated in Article 8 DCD and Article 7 SGD and thus may not even cover the case where updates have been contractually agreed upon within the meaning of Article 7 DCD or Article 6 SGD. However, this can hardly be correct. Subject to a decision by the CJEU, the provisions should therefore also apply where updates are part of the subjective requirements for conformity, but any agreement by the parties would, of course, take priority.[41]

---

40 See Georg E. *Kodek*, 'Änderung digitaler Inhalte und digitaler Dienstleistungen (Art 19 DIRL)' in Johannes Stabentheiner, Christiane Wendehorst and Brigitta Zöchling-Jud (eds), *Das neue europäische Gewährleistungsrecht* (Manz 2019) 142 ff.

41 But see Dirk *Staudenmayer* in Reiner Schulze and Dirk Staudenmayer (eds), *EU Digital Law* (Nomos 2020) Article 8 para 152, who argues the parties would need to agree on a clause corresponding to Art 8(3).

c) Qualified waiver

As far as the provisions on updates are part of the objective requirements for conformity, the trader can avoid liability by means of a qualified waiver under Article 8(5) DCD, Article 7(5) SGD. Thus, derogation from the objective requirements to the detriment of the consumer is possible (only) if the consumer was specifically informed that a particular characteristic was deviating from the objective requirements for conformity and the consumer expressly and separately accepted that deviation when concluding the contract by way of express and separate consent.[42] While the European legislator apparently trusts that qualified waivers will be the exception rather than the rule, this expectation may not come true with regard to the update obligation. Rather, it is to be expected that traders who can afford sound legal advice will routinely conclude a separate 'update agreement' with consumers in which the trader fully refers to the manufacturer for any obligations with regard to updates. It will be for the courts, and ultimately for the CJEU, to define the limits of routine waivers.[43]

III. Conceptualisation of triangular constellations

In practice, updates of digital content or services or of the digital elements of goods are only rarely provided by the trader with whom the consumer originally concluded the contract and who is the party liable under the Directives. If at all, this may be the case for online purchases of digital content or services, where there is typically a direct contract between the consumer and the producer, e.g. because the consumer directly made the contract on the producer's website (often facilitated by an app store). Beyond that, the vast majority of updates will be provided by the producer or a third party acting on behalf of the producer. This means that there is

42 For a detailed analysis see Wolfgang *Faber*, 'Bereitstellung und Mangelbegriff' in Johannes Stabentheiner, Christiane Wendehorst and Brigitta Zöchling-Jud (eds), *Das neue europäische Gewährleistungsrecht* (Manz 2019) 82 ff; Dirk *Staudenmayer* in Reiner Schulze and Dirk Staudenmayer (eds), *EU Digital Law* (Nomos 2020) Article 8 para 153 ff.

43 See also Brigitta *Zöchling-Jud*, 'Das neue Europäische Gewährleistungsrecht für den Warenhandel' [2019] GPR 115,120 ff.

at least a three-person constellation in which the consumer is confronted with several different traders acting in different roles.[44]

1. *Basic contractual models*

Generally speaking, when it comes to possible contractual arrangements, a distinction can be made between the package model, agency model and warranty model.[45] The difference will be illustrated with regard to the situation of goods with digital elements under the SGD, and the trader who is the consumer's contracting partner will be referred to as 'seller', but the same or very similar arrangements also arise under the DCD.

a) *Package model*

Where the contracting parties choose a package model, the seller makes a contractual promise in their own name to provide the digital elements as well as updates thereto. From a legal point of view, this amounts to an agreement on the provision of updates within the meaning of Article 6(1)(d) SGD. Insofar as the seller cannot factually provide these services themselves, the seller relies on the manufacturer or other third party as a vicarious agent, i.e. the situation is the same as if the manufacturer or other third party were the seller's subcontractor (and they may well be the

---

44 Axel *Metzger*, 'Verträge über digitale Inhalte und digitale Dienstleistungen: Neuer BGB-Vertragstypus oder punktuelle Reform?' [2019] JZ 577, 578; Beate Gsell, 'Der europäische Richtlinienvorschlag zu bestimmten vertragsrechtlichen Aspekten der Bereitstellung digitaler Inhalte' [2018] ZUM 75, 81; European Law Institute, Statement on the European Law Institute on the European Commission's Proposed Directive on the Supply of Digital Content to Consumers, COM (2015) 634 final [2016] 16 <https://www.europeanlawinstitute.eu/fileadmin/user_upload/p_eli/Publications/ELI_Statement_on_DCD.pdf> accessed 24.02.2022.

45 Christiane *Wendehorst*, 'Verbraucherrelevante Problemstellungen zu Besitz- und Eigentumsverhältnissen beim Internet der Dinge' (Expert Opinion commissioned by the Sachverständigenrat für Verbraucherfragen, 2016) <https://www.svr-verbraucherfragen.de/wp-content/uploads/Wendehorst-Gutachten.pdf> accessed 24.02.2022; Christiane Wendehorst, 'Hybride Produkte und hybrider Vertrieb' in Christiane Wendehorst and Brigitta Zöchling-Jud (eds), *Ein neues Vertragsrecht für den digitalen Binnenmarkt?* (Manz 2016) 60 f; Wendehorst, 'Besitz und Eigentum im Internet der Dinge' in Hans-W. Micklitz et al (eds), *Verbraucherrecht 2.0 – Verbraucher in der digitalen Welt* (Nomos 2017) 333 ff.

seller's subcontractor). If updates are not provided properly, the seller is directly liable, not only under the rules implementing the two Directives, but also for specific performance and/or damages under national law.[46] Whether or not the seller promises updates in their own name is a matter of interpreting the agreement. The mere mention of updates in the sales contract, which would be sufficient for Article 6(1)(d) SGD, does not necessarily lead to the qualification of the contract as relying on a package model. Rather, there must be clear indications that the seller itself indeed agreed to be legally bound and to be directly in charge of providing the updates.

b) Agency model

At the other end of the spectrum is the agency model, where the seller them itself selves has no contractual obligations of their own in relation to the digital element, but where the seller merely acts as an intermediary between the consumer and the manufacturer or other third party providing the digital elements and their updates. All the seller itself owes the consumer is delivery of the goods and appropriate instructions for the consumer how to conclude an end-user agreement (EUA) with the manufacturer or other third party, and possibly otherwise supporting the consumer in concluding that EUA. From a purely technical point of view, the conclusion of this EUA would take place online, for example when the consumer configures the digital element or puts the connected goods into service for the first time, accepting various terms and conditions by clicking buttons on a display.[47] Alternatively, the seller may conclude a

46 Christiane Wendehorst, 'Hybride Produkte und hybrider Vertrieb' in Christiane Wendehorst and Brigitta Zöchling-Jud (eds), *Ein neues Vertragsrecht für den digitalen Binnenmarkt?* (Manz 2016) 68 f; Wendehorst, 'Besitz und Eigentum im Internet der Dinge' in Hans-W. Micklitz et al (eds), *Verbraucherrecht 2.0 – Verbraucher in der digitalen Welt* (Nomos 2017) 371; Christiane Wendehorst, 'Aktualisierungen und andere digitale Dauerleistungen' in Johannes Stabentheiner, Christiane Wendehorst and Brigitta Zöchling-Jud (eds), *Das neue europäische Gewährleistungsrecht* (Manz 2019) 119; on this issue before the adoption of the Directives see Peter Bräutigam and Thomas *Klindt*, 'Industrie 4.0, das Internet der Dinge und das Recht' [2015] NJW 1137, 1138.

47 On the inclusion of end user agreements by so-called click wrap agreements Christiane Wendehorst, 'Hybride Produkte und hybrider Vertrieb' in Christiane Wendehorst and Brigitta Zöchling-Jud (eds), *Ein neues Vertragsrecht für den digitalen Binnenmarkt?* (Manz 2016) 50 f, 71; Wendehorst, 'Besitz und Eigentum im In-

separate update agreement in the manufacturer's or other third party's name, i.e. act as the manufacturer's or other third party's agent. Under the Directives, the agency model would mean qualified waiver pursuant to Article 7(5) SGD and full reference to the manufacturer or other third party for digital elements and their updates.

c) Warranty model

The warranty model lies somewhere between the package model and the agency model (but closer to the package model). If the parties opt for a warranty model, the seller does not undertake to provide updates in their own name. Therefore, the seller could not be sued under national law for the provision of updates, nor would normally not be liable for damages under national law if updates fail to be provided. However, the seller assumes a limited degree of responsibility and ultimately liability insofar as, where the manufacturer or other third party in charge fails to provide the updates, the seller is liable for the resulting lack of conformity as the seller would be liable for any other lack of conformity even if that lack of conformity had its cause exclusively in the manufacturer's sphere.

2. Solution adopted by DCD and SGD

The solution that the European legislator has now adopted as the default solution under Article 8(2) DCD and Article 7(2) SGD is probably best described as a 'qualified warranty model'. Recital 21 DCD and Recital 15 SGD state that the provision of digital elements is already part of the sales contract, which might be read as indicating a package model. However, the remedies available to the consumer under the Directives are characteristic of a warranty model, and even Article 5 DCD is silent on the provision of updates. According to Article 8(2) DCD and Article 7(3) SGD, the consumer's contracting partner only has to ensure that the consumer is

ternet der Dinge' in Hans-W. Micklitz et al (eds), *Verbraucherrecht 2.0 – Verbraucher in der digitalen Welt* (Nomos 2017) 342; Thomas Riehm, 'Updates, Patches & Co. – Schutz nachwirkender Qualitätserwartungen' in Martin Schmidt-Kessel and Malte Kramme, *Geschäftsmodelle in der digitalen Welt* (Jena 2017) 208 f; Thomas Fischl in Astrid Auer-Reinsdorff and Isabell Conrad (eds) *Handbuch IT-Recht*, 2016, § 17 para 86; Hubert Schmidt, 'Einbeziehung von AGB im Verbraucherverkehr' [2011] NJW 1633 ff.

informed about and receives available updates, including security updates. Where the seller can demonstrate that it is impossible for them to provide the update themselves, or that this would cause disproportionate effort, the seller must, at worst, only accept price reduction or termination of the contract. This warranty model is, however, qualified insofar as the seller is not only subject to the usual remedies for lack of conformity of the goods, but is at the same time subject to certain information and organisational obligations of their own.

As the Directives do not distinguish, as far as remedies are concerned, between lack of subjective and objective requirements, there is not much of a difference in practical terms between the package model and the warranty model. However, the difference may well become apparent where national law provides for a claim for damages. Since, under a package model, the seller is directly liable for providing the updates to the consumer, the seller is usually also directly liable for damages in contract where the updates fail to be provided (depending, of course, on the exact role of fault in the respective national legal system). Any failure on the part of the manufacturer is normally attributed to the seller under the rules on vicarious agency (depending, again, on national law). By contrast, under the warranty model, the manufacturer is usually not to be regarded as the seller's vicarious agent.[48]

48 For Germany, see BGH NJW 2020, 3313 para 18; NJW 2019, 292 para 97; NJW 2018, 291 para 24; NJW 2014, 2183 para 31; *Schaub* in Gsell et al (eds), BeckOGK BGB § 278 para 66.1; Stephan Lorenz in Georg Bamberger et al (eds), BeckOK, BGB § 278 para 27; Astrid Stadler in Rolf Stürner (eds), Jauernig BGB § 278 para 16. For a different view, see Stefan Grundmann in Jürgen Säcker et al (eds), MüKoBGB § 278 para 31; Malte Kramme in Hanns Prütting, Gerhard Wegen and Gerd Weinreich (eds), BGB § 278 para. 21; Ulrich G. Schroeter, 'Untersuchungspflicht und Vertretenmüssen des Händlers bei der Lieferung sachmangelhafter Ware' [2010] JZ 495; Frank Peters, 'Der Beginn der Verjährung bei Regressansprüchen' [2010] ZGS 24. For Austria, cf only the case law of the OGH RIS-Justiz RS0022662; cf also Brigitta Zöchling-Jud in Andreas Kletečka and Martin Schauer (eds), ABGB-ON [1.02] § 933a Rn. 4; Eva Ondreasova, *Die Gehilfenhaftung: eine rechtsvergleichende Untersuchung zum österreichischen Recht mit Vorschlägen zur Reform* (Manz 2013) 116; Erika M. Wagner in Michael Schwimann and Georg E. Kodek (eds), ABGB Praxiskommentar[4] § 1313a para 8a.

3. Parallel obligations under end-user agreements

If the default arrangement under the Directives is classified as a warranty model this also means that the consumer, if the relevant conditions are met – i.e. in particular if an exchange of corresponding declarations of intent can be established – may also have a parallel contractual remedies against the manufacturer or other third party under an EUA. Although the Recitals only mention the possibility of concluding end user license agreements,[49] there is no indication that the consumer should be deprived of the benefits the consumer may be afforded by direct contractual remedies against the manufacturer or a similar third party, in particular as these contractual remedies would be on top of the remedies the consumer already has against their contracting partner under the Directives. The consumer can then choose whether they will turn to the seller or to the manufacturer or other third party first.

IV. Critical evaluation

The update obligation may be the most important benefit that consumers derive from the DCD and SGD as compared with the situation under the previous law. It is thus to be considered a great legislative achievement. However, various problems have been identified regarding the update obligation's practical implementation. Once again the question has to be raised why the trader who is the consumer's contracting partner should be held liable at all for measures that are, at least normally, completely outside the trader's sphere of influence. The author of this Chapter had initially proposed to channel the responsibility for the provision of updates to the manufacturer or importer of a connected item,[50] including liability

49 See Recital 21 of Directive (EU) 2019/770, as well as Recital 15 of Directive (EU) 2019/771.

50 See Christiane Wendehorst, 'Sale of goods and supply of digital content – two worlds apart?' ' (Directorate-General for Internal Policies, Policy Department C, Citizen's Rights and Constitutional Affairs, 2016), <http://www.europarl.europa.eu/cmsdata/98774/pe%20556%20928%20EN_final.pdf> accessed 24.02.2022; in the 2017 draft for the German Federal Government: § 477a and § 477b; in the 4.9.2017 draft for the EU institutions presented at the ELI Annual Conference: Article 8a and Article 9a. With regard to the Austrian implementing act see also Christiane Wendehorst, 'Direkthaftung des Herstellers (Teil I)' [2020] VbR 94; Christiane Wendehorst, 'Direkthaftung des Herstellers (Teil II)' [2020] VbR 138.

for failure to provide updates or for the provision of defective updates, and to limit the trader's liability to the warranty period. Admittedly, the Directives provide that the trader may have recourse against other links in the supply chain, right up to the manufacturer. However, having only an action for recourse against the manufacturer or against the trader who imported the goods is certainly not the best solution: firstly, it causes unnecessary costs due to a potential multiplication of the number of legal disputes arising, and secondly, recourse as foreseen by the Directives is again very weak. Although Member States have leeway in this regard, and we are seeing some of them moving towards more robust recourse mechanisms,[51] protection of retailers in cross-border situations and/or where foreign law may be chosen remains to be limited.[52]

It would have been clearly preferable for the two Directives to provide for direct liability of the manufacturer or importer next to the liability of the retailer, with the latter's liability restricted to the warranty period. Direct action could be available to the consumer either right from the outset or in any case after the expiry of the regular warranty period (i.e. when the retailer would no longer be liable). On top of the question of direct action against the manufacturer or importer, the very similar question of liability of the platform operator arises, at least if the platform operator facilitates direct import from outside the EEA.[53]

The Directives left the question of direct action against the manufacturer, importer or other parties to the Member States.[54] However, it was not too hard to predict that, in an already difficult economic situation, Member State legislatures would not enthusiastically embark on new approaches, if only for reasons of domestic politics. Although liability of large platform operators would have been easier to communicate domestically, national solutions were mostly countered by wanting to wait for the

51 See for example Section 327u para 4 (German) BGB and Section 933b para 4 (Austrian) ABGB.

52 Gerald Spindler, 'Ausgewählte Rechtsfragen der Umsetzung der digitalen Inhalte-Richtlinie in das BGB' [2021] MMR 528, 533.

53 Christiane Wendehorst, 'Direkthaftung des Herstellers (Teil I)' [2020] VbR, 94, 96, 98; see also Christoph Busch, 'Effektiver Verbraucherschutz im Online-Handel: Verantwortung und Haftung von Internetplattformen' (Expert Opinion commissioned by Verbraucherzentrale Bundesverband e.v. 2019) 39 f; to some extent this is also indicated in Recital 18 DCD and Recital 23 SGD.

54 Recital 12 DCD; Recital 18 and Recital 63 SGD.

Digital Services Act.[55] Hopefully, the discussion will not be entirely over – there is a glimmer of hope that the issue of direct action will re-appear in the discussion we are going to see about adapting sales law better to sustainability goals.[56]

55 European Commission, 'Proposal for a Regulation of the European Parliament and of the Council on a Single Market For Digital Services (Digital Services Act) and amending Directive 2000/31/EC' COM (2020) 825 final

56 See European Commission, 'Sustainable consumption of goods – promoting repair and reuse' Ares(2022)175084 (Call for Evidence for an Impact Assessment).

The Update Obligation for Smart Products – Time Period for the Update Obligation and Failure to Install the Update

André Janssen[1]

I. General introduction

There is no question that smart products are on the rise and will continue to be so for a long time to come. The worldwide growth rates are rapid. The global market in this segment is growing by around 15–25 % annually.[2] While "only" around 14 billion smart products were in use in 2019, this figure is expected to reach 25 billion this year (2021) with a further upward trend.[3] Statistically, this means that every person on this planet owns about four smart products soon.

In Germany, too, smart products have become an integral part of many people's lives and their importance will continue to increase in the coming years. To name just one example, the number of households with smart home applications from the field of energy management alone will more than double to 10.7 million by 2024.[4] One might get the impression that almost all common technical products for consumers are now also available in a "smart version", as the emergence of smart tvs, smart cars, smart

1 Prof Dr. *André Janssen* is a Chair Professor of Civil Law and European Private Law at the Radboud University Nijmegen, The Netherlands. Postal address: Radboud University, Faculty of Law, Business & Law Research Centre, Montessorilaan 10, 6525 HR Nijmegen, The Netherlands. E-mail: andre.janssen@ru.nl. The article is based on a talk given by the author at the Münster Colloquia on EU Law and the Digital Economy on "Smart Products", which took place on 10 and 11 June 2021. The presentation style was largely retained.

2 Pieper, § 6.2. Vertragsschluss mit KI, Anfechtung und Schadensersatz, in: Kaulartz/Braegelmann (eds.), *Rechtshandbuch Artificial Intelligence und Machine Learning*, Munich 2010, 239, 240.

3 Pieper, § 6.2. Vertragsschluss mit KI, Anfechtung und Schadensersatz, in: Kaulartz/Braegelmann (eds.), *Rechtshandbuch Artificial Intelligence und Machine Learning*, Munich 2010, 239, 240.

4 Statista Recap: Die interessantesten Zahlen rund um Smart Home 2020, available at https://www.tink.de/blog/statista-recap-die-interessantesten-zahlen-rund-um-smart-home-2020/

locks, smart watches, smart meters, smartphones and smart refrigerators demonstrate.[5]

But what are smart products anyway? Various, slightly different definitions are discussed and handled, but they cannot and should not be discussed in detail here.[6] For the purposes of this article, we will assume that a smart product is a data processing object which has several interactive functions and which combines physical and software interfaces.[7] The Directive (EU) 2019/771 of 20 May 2019 on certain aspects concerning contracts for the sale of goods (hereinafter: the Sale of Goods Directive 2019/771) and the Directive (EU) 2019/770 of 20 May 2019 on certain aspects concerning contracts for the supply of digital content and digital services (hereinafter: the Digital Content Directive 2019/770) do not use the term "smart products", but use "*goods with digital elements*". Both directives define "goods with digital elements" as "*any tangible movable items that incorporate or are inter-connected with digital content or a digital service in such a way that the absence of that digital content or digital service would prevent the goods from performing their functions*".[8] The "goods with digital elements" are thereby uniformly subject in their entirety to the Sale of Good Directive 2019/771 and not to the Digital Content Directive 2019/770, irrespective of whether the digital content or the digital service of the good with digital elements is supplied by the seller or by a third party.[9] In the further course of this article, the terms "goods with digital elements" and "smart products" will be used largely synonymously, even though they might not be not completely identical.

This article will focus on the update obligation of the seller for smart products. As smart products are only subject to the Sale of Goods Directive 2019/771, there is a certain focus on the update obligations in this directive

5 Recitals 13, 14, 15 Sale of Goods Directive 2019/771 and recital 21 Digital Content Directive 2019/770 give some of the examples presented here.

6 See for the various possible definitions in more detail Gutiérrez, Garbajosa, Diaz, Yagüe, Providing a Consensus Definition for the Term "Smart Product", available at https://core.ac.uk/download/pdf/148668205.pdf; Raff, Wentzel, Obwegeser, Smart Products: Conceptual Review, Synthesis, and Research Directions, *Journal of Product Innovation Management* 2020, 379–404, also available at https://onlinelibrary.wiley.com/doi/full/10.1111/jpim.12544.

7 Clark, How smart connected products are transforming companies?, https://gotthisnow.com/how-smart-connected-products-are-transforming-companies.

8 See for the definition of "goods with digital elements" Art. 2(5)b Sale of Goods Directive 2019/771 and Art. 2(3) Digital Content Directive 2019/770.

9 See in this respect Art. 3(3) Sale of Goods Directive 2019/771 and Art. 3(4) Digital Content Directive 2019/770.

(more specifically, Art. 6(b) and Art. 7(3)-(5) of the Sale of Goods Directive 2019/771), although the Digital Content Directive 2019/770 also provides for a comparable update obligation for (pure) digital content and digital services.[10] In some places, however, reference is also made to the provisions of the Digital Content Directive 2019/770.

The discussion will mainly focus on two aspects of the update obligation under the Sale of Goods Directive 2019/771, namely (a) the time period for the update obligation and (b) the failure of consumers to install updates. However, some other issues related to the update obligation will also be addressed, without which the two main aspects cannot be fully understood. Unfortunately, it is not possible to go into the implementation in the individual countries here, as this would go beyond the scope of this contribution. Only in a few places is reference made to some specific implementation provisions in the German Civil Code (*Bürgerliches Gesetzbuch, BGB*).

II. Relevance of Update Obligation for Smart Products

Updates are of crucial importance for the functioning of smart products. Without updates, smart products very quickly become "dumb products" over time, become outdated, lose functionality or develop security gaps. Consumers therefore expect smart products to receive updates at regular intervals, especially if security of the smart product is at stake.[11] In Germany alone, it is assumed that there are around 29,000 security updates for smart products per year – with a strong upward trend.[12]

It is interesting to note that the first drafts of the two aforementioned directives almost completely disregarded the issue of updates, despite their already emerging importance. The initial proposal for a Digital Content Directive did not provide for an update obligation beyond those which

10 See Art. 7(d) Digital Content Directive 2019/770 and Art. 8(2), (3) Digital Content Directive 2019/770.

11 A free *upgrade*, on the other hand, cannot be expected (unless contractually agreed), although it can sometimes be difficult to distinguish between just a normal update.

12 Gesetzentwurf der Bundesregierung, Entwurf eines Gesetzes zur Regelung des Verkaufs von Sachen mit digitalen Elementen und anderer Aspekte des Kaufvertrags, Drucksache 19/27424,19 ff.

are contractually agreed.[13] Now, however, the update obligation of the seller, which was only introduced into the two directives at a late stage, has turned out to be a central element. It can even be said that it is probably the most innovative feature of the Sale of Goods Directive 2019/771, as it introduces a previously unknown new continuous obligation of the seller to update smart products into current law.[14] Also, for practical purposes, this can be seen as probably the most significant change brought by the Sale of Goods Directive 2019/771 compared to its predecessor, the Directive 1999/44/EC on certain aspects of the sale of consumer goods and associated guarantees. After the implementation of the Sale of Goods Directive 2019/771, the seller's obligations do not end with the delivery of the smart products, but a "latent continuing obligation" between the seller and the consumer is created by the new update obligation of the seller.[15]

III. The Subjective Conformity Requirement (Express Terms) and the Update Obligation

The contracting parties are free to regulate update obligations for smart products in more detail by contract themselves (*express terms* or *subjective conformity requirement*).[16] Art. 6(d) Sale of Goods Directive 2019/771 stipulates that "*(i)n order to conform with the sales contract, the goods shall (...), (...)*

---

13 Wendehorst, Aktualisierungen und andere digitale Dauerleistungen: Das neue Gewährleistungsrecht auf dem Prüfstand, in: Stabentheiner, Wendehorst, Zöchling-Jud (eds.), *Das neue Gewährleistungsrecht: Zu den Richtlinien (EU) 2019/771 über den Warenkauf sowie (EU) 2019/770 über digitale Inhalte und digitale Dienstleistungen*, Vienna 2019, 111, 112, Staudenmayer, in: Schulze, Staudenmayer (eds.), *EU Digital Law*, Baden-Baden 2020, 154.

14 As here, Kalamees, Goods with Digital Elements and the Seller's Updating Obligation, *Journal of Intellectual Property, Information Technology and Electronic Commerce Law* 2020, 131, 131 ("*groundbreaking*"); Wendehorst, Aktualisierungen und andere digitale Dauerleistungen: Das neue Gewährleistungsrecht auf dem Prüfstand, in: Stabentheiner, Wendehorst, Zöchling-Jud (eds.), *Das neue Gewährleistungsrecht: Zu den Richtlinien (EU) 2019/771 über den Warenkauf sowie (EU) 2019/770 über digitale Inhalte und digitale Dienstleistungen*, Vienna 2019, 111, 118.

15 Likewise Wendehorst, Aktualisierungen und andere digitale Dauerleistungen: Das neue Gewährleistungsrecht auf dem Prüfstand, in: Stabentheiner, Wendehorst, Zöchling-Jud (eds.), *Das neue Gewährleistungsrecht: Zu den Richtlinien (EU) 2019/771 über den Warenkauf sowie (EU) 2019/770 über digitale Inhalte und digitale Dienstleistungen*, Vienna 2019, 111, 111.

16 On the disputed question whether Art. 7(4) Sale of Goods Directive 2019/771 applies mutatis mutandis to Art. 6(d) Sale of Goods Directive 2019/771, see 5.3.

be supplied with updates as stipulated by the sales contract."[17] Not only regular updates can be contractually agreed, but also updates that ultimately represent *upgrades*.[18] As the question of updates is very important, one would now expect that at least the large sellers of smart products regularly regulate this topic in their standard contract terms. Surprisingly, a recent research of *Kalamees* shows that this is still uncommon until now – at least among large sellers such as Amazon or Mediamarkt in Germany.[19] However, with the implementation of the Sale of Goods Directive 2019/771, it is to be expected that at least the large sellers of smart products will adapt their standard contract terms and specify their update obligation in more detail.[20]

IV. Objective Conformity Requirement (Implied Terms) and the Update Obligation

Let us now turn to the objective conformity requirement (or *implied terms*) for updates under Art. 7(3) Sale of Goods Directive 2019/771, which sets out the minimum objective standard for updates (and the information about them). I first deal only with the beginning of the provision and the questions arising in this respect. If a good with digital elements is sold, "*the seller shall ensure that the consumer is informed of and supplied with updates, including security updates, that are necessary to keep those goods in conformity (...)*".[21]

---

17 See also recital 28 Sale of Goods Directive 2019/771. See also Art. 7(d) and recital 44 of the Digital Content Directive 2019/770 on this issue.

18 Staudenmayer, in: Schulze, Staudenmayer (eds.), *EU Digital Law*, Baden-Baden 2020, 130 (for the Digital Content Directive 2019/770).

19 Kalamees, Goods with Digital Elements and the Seller's Updating Obligation, *Journal of Intellectual Property, Information Technology and Electronic Commerce Law* 2020, 131, 133.

20 Likewise with this assessment Kalamees, Goods with Digital Elements and the Seller's Updating Obligation, *Journal of Intellectual Property, Information Technology and Electronic Commerce Law* 2020, 131, 134: "*It seems that the updating obligation and its regulation in contracts with consumers is still something rather new for the sellers. This situation will undoubtedly change after the provisions of the SGD have been transposed to the national laws of the Member States.*"

21 See for the parallel provision in Digital Content Directive 2019/770 Art. 8(2) Digital Content Directive 2019/770.

1. Content of the Update Obligation

The scope of the update obligation can be derived from the wording of the just mentioned provision. The seller is not obliged to provide all conceivable updates, but only those *which are necessary* to keep the goods with digital elements in conformity with the contract.[22] Although the European legislator mainly had security updates in mind, as can be seen from the wording itself, it goes without saying that other necessary updates are also covered by the update obligation stipulated here. Art. 7(3) Sale of Goods Directive 2019/771 also makes it clear that the seller is not obliged to provide any *upgrades*.[23] The view that the necessary updates may be provided by the seller only at a charge[24] is not convincing. It clearly contradicts the aim of both directives to raise the standard of consumer protection and is not supported by the text of the directives.[25]

The information obligation of the seller about the update is only described in a rather cryptic way. In order for him to fulfil the information obligation set out in Art. 7(3) Sale of Goods Directive 2019/771, it will however be sufficient to simply inform the consumer that an update is available. It is not required that the consumer receives any qualified technical information about the update itself. In practice, the information about the update will regularly coincide with the supply of the update itself. However, information about the updates (exclusively) at the time of the conclusion of the contract, but not at the time of the subsequent supply of

22 See also recital 30 of the Sale of Goods 2019/770.

23 Likewise Kalamees, Goods with Digital Elements and the Seller's Updating Obligation, *Journal of Intellectual Property, Information Technology and Electronic Commerce Law* 2020, 131, 134, Wendehorst, Aktualisierungen und andere digitale Dauerleistungen: Das neue Gewährleistungsrecht auf dem Prüfstand, in: Stabentheiner, Wendehorst, Zöchling-Jud (eds.), *Das neue Gewährleistungsrecht: Zu den Richtlinien (EU) 2019/771 über den Warenkauf sowie (EU) 2019/770 über digitale Inhalte und digitale Dienstleistungen*, Vienna 2019, 111, 122; Twigg-Flesner, Conformity of Goods and Digital Content/Digital Service, Working Paper 3/2020, 24, available at http://diposit.ub.edu/dspace/bitstream/2445/159600/4/WP_2020_3%20Christian%20Twigg_Flesner.pdf.

24 Peschel, Rockstroh, Sicherheitslücken als Mangel, *Neue Juristische Wochenschrift* 2020, 3345, 3348.

25 A seller's *right of modification* as in Art. 19 of the Digital Content Directive 2019/770 is missing in the Sale of Goods Directive 2019/771, which is regretted by some authors. See Lommatzsch, Prüfer, Zwei neue EU-Richtlinien zum Vertragsrecht – „Revolution" im Verbraucherrecht, *Gesellschafts- und Wirtschaftsrecht* 2020, 331, 333; Staudenmayer, Kauf von Waren mit digitalen Elementen – Die Richtlinie zum Warenkauf, *Neue Juristische Wochenschrift* 2019, 2889, 2891.

the updates, will have to be regarded as insufficient.[26] The function of the information obligation can only fully be fulfilled when the information is given with the supply of the update.

2. *Addressee of the Update Obligation*

The European legislator has decided to make only the seller of smart products the addressee of the update obligation. Other alternatives would have been conceivable, such as shifting the responsibility for updates to the producers of smart products or to another third parties who carry out the updates. The sole responsibility of the seller for the supply of updates is problematic for him, since he regularly has no control over the updates and possibly not even any information about upcoming updates, but he is fully liable for omitted or defective updates. The new update obligation for smart products will lead to a significant increase in liability for the seller, even though he has a right of redress, at least in purely legal terms.[27] In practice, however, this right of redress has often proved to be insufficient for the seller.

We will have to wait and see to what extent the extended catalogue of obligations for the seller will ultimately lead to higher prices for the consumer. It will also have to be seen whether the sellers will try to exclude the update obligation to a greater extent in accordance with Art. 7(5) Sale of Goods Directive 2019/771.[28] While some fear this,[29] others seem to be less afraid, as such an exclusion would have a negative impact on the competitiveness of the seller on the highly competitive market for smart products.[30]

---

26 Staudenmayer, in: Schulze, Staudenmayer (eds.), *EU Digital Law*, Baden-Baden 2020, 157 (for the Digital Content Directive 2019/770): *"(...) the trader has to inform the consumer about an update if, and when, this becomes available."*

27 See Art. 18 Sale of Goods Directive 2019/771.

28 Art. 8(5) Digital Content Directive 2019/770 provides for the same rule.

29 Wendehorst, Aktualisierungen und andere digitale Dauerleistungen: Das neue Gewährleistungsrecht auf dem Prüfstand, in: Stabentheiner, Wendehorst, Zöchling-Jud (eds.), *Das neue Gewährleistungsrecht: Zu den Richtlinien (EU) 2019/771 über den Warenkauf sowie (EU) 2019/770 über digitale Inhalte und digitale Dienstleistungen*, Vienna 2019, 111, 134.

30 Staudenmayer, in: Schulze, Staudenmayer (eds.), *EU Digital Law*, Baden-Baden 2020, 156 ff.; Staudenmayer, Kauf von Waren mit digitalen Elementen – Die Richtlinie zum Warenkauf, *Neue Juristische Wochenschrift* 2019, 2889, 2890.

But how can the seller actually comply with the update obligation under Art. 7(3) Sale of Goods Directive 2019/771? As already mentioned, the seller will regularly not be able to comply with the update obligation himself, as he often does not have the technical possibilities to provide the consumers with the updates or even the necessary information to inform them (e.g. in the case of an offline purchase of a smart product, where the smart product is paid for in cash). Ultimately, the seller's only option is to contractually ensure that the producer of the smart product or another third party inform the consumers and supply the updates.

Technically, the fulfilment of the update obligation could best be ensured by the producer or another third party in charge of the update sending the necessary information about the update and the link for the update itself directly to the smart product of the consumer.[31] The necessary information and the link to the update would then ideally appear on the display of the smart product – if this is already technically possible for the smart product in question. Of course, the legal responsibility for the updates would remain with the seller, even with the best design solutions. Nevertheless, one should not lose sight of the fact that the producers themselves and any third parties in charge of the updates have a vital self-interest in providing updates (and in a design solution). In the longer term, this is the best way for them to ensure sufficient consumer satisfaction and to help ensure that consumers continue to buy their products in the future.

3. *Time Period for the Update Obligation*

Let us now move to one of the central questions of this article, namely how long the seller of smart products is obliged to provide the buyer with updates. In order to answer this question, which was already hotly debated during the drafting phase of the Sale of Goods Directive 2019/771, we have

---

31 Wendehorst, Aktualisierungen und andere digitale Dauerleistungen: Das neue Gewährleistungsrecht auf dem Prüfstand, in: Stabentheiner, Wendehorst, Zöchling-Jud (eds.), *Das neue Gewährleistungsrecht: Zu den Richtlinien (EU) 2019/771 über den Warenkauf sowie (EU) 2019/770 über digitale Inhalte und digitale Dienstleistungen*, Vienna 2019, 111, 122; Twigg-Flesner, Conformity of Goods and Digital Content/Digital Service, Working Paper 3/2020, 24, available at http://diposit.ub.edu/dspace/bitstream/2445/159600/4/WP_2020_3%20Christian%20Twigg_Flesner.pdf; Staudenmayer, in: Schulze, Staudenmayer (eds.), *EU Digital Law*, Baden-Baden 2020, 157.

to distinguish between two different types of sales of smart products, as also provided for by Art. 7(3) Sale of Goods Directive 2019/771,[32] namely between (a) sales contracts that provide for a *single act of supply* of digital content or digital service (Art. 7(3)(a) Sale of Goods Directive 2019/771) and (b) sales contracts that provide for a *continuous supply* of digital content or digital services over a period of time (Art. 7(3)(b) Sale of Goods Directive 2019/771).[33]

a) *Sales Contracts that Provide for a Single Act of Supply of Digital Content or Digital Service*

If it is a so-called one-off contract, i.e. a sales contract that provides for a single act of supply of the digital content or digital service, the seller needs to ensure that the consumer is informed of and supplied with the relevant updates for a *reasonable period of time* under Art. 7(3)(a) Sale of Goods Directive 2019/771.[34] According to this provision, the type and purpose of the goods and the digital elements and the circumstances and nature of the contract are to be taken into account. The question is of course how long this reasonable period of time should be for one-off contracts. That this depends very much on the circumstances of the individual case is already clear from the list of relevant factors. Some assistance in answering this question is provided by recital 31 of the Sale of Goods Directive 2019/771. According to that recital a consumer would normally expect to receive updates for at least as long as the liability period for nonconformities lasts, which is according to Art. 10(1) Sale of Goods 2019/2019 also for goods with digital elements two years after delivery. In other cases, the reasonable period could be extended beyond that period, as might be the case particularly with regard to security updates. When the sales regards goods with digital elements the purpose of which is limited in time, the seller's obligation to provide updates would normally be limited to the liability period.

---

32 See for the parallel provision in Digital Content Directive 2019/770 Art. 8(2) Digital Content Directive 2019/770.

33 The delimitation between these two categories can sometimes be difficult. A more precise contractual specification may be advisable (Kumkar, Herausforderungen eines Gewährleistungsrechts im digitalen Zeitalter, *Zeitschrift für die gesamte Privatrechtswissenschaft* 2020, 306, 311).

34 See for the parallel provision in Digital Content Directive 2019/770 Art. 8(2)(b) Digital Content Directive 2019/770.

In the literature, three different opinions can be identified with regard to the length of the reasonable period of time. According to one opinion, the reasonable period of time can be shorter (for particularly short-lived goods with digital elements) or longer (for high-priced and long-lived goods with digital elements) than the two-year liability period under Art. 10(1) Sale of Goods Directive 2019/771.[35] According to another opinion, the reasonable period can be neither shorter nor longer than the liability period mentioned, i.e. the reasonable period of time for providing an update would always be two years.[36] However, most authors assume that the reasonable period of time for providing an update is at least two years, but that it can also be significantly longer depending on the circumstances.[37]

The latter opinion is preferable, as it is the only one that is compatible with the content of recital 31 of the Sale of Goods Directive 2019/771 and also takes sufficient account of the circumstances of the individual case. The first mentioned opinion does not sufficiently take into account that Art. 10(1) of the Sale of Goods Directive 2019/771 has set a minimum period not to be undercut also for the provision concerning updates. The second opinion mentioned here overlooks the fact that certain updates for high-priced and durable smart products are expected by the consumer for considerably longer than two years. One might think here of updates for a smart home security system or smart locks in general. If the legislator had really wanted a fixed period of two years for updates, it could have introduced it in Art. 7(3)(a) Sale of Goods Directive 2019/771. But that is precisely what he did not do, instead opting for a flexible reasonable period. Thus, according to the opinion preferred here, it must be assumed that the reasonable period for updates (one-off contracts) can be significantly

35 Wendehorst, Aktualisierungen und andere digitale Dauerleistungen: Das neue Gewährleistungsrecht auf dem Prüfstand, in: Stabentheiner, Wendehorst, Zöchling-Jud (eds.), *Das neue Gewährleistungsrecht: Zu den Richtlinien (EU) 2019/771 über den Warenkauf sowie (EU) 2019/770 über digitale Inhalte und digitale Dienstleistungen*, Vienna 2019, 111, 130.

36 Twigg-Flesner, Conformity of Goods and Digital Content/Digital Service, Working Paper 3/2020, 25, available at http://diposit.ub.edu/dspace/bitstream/2445/159600/4/WP_2020_3%20Christian%20Twigg_Flesner.pdf.

37 Kalamees, Goods with Digital Elements and the Seller's Updating Obligation, *Journal of Intellectual Property, Information Technology and Electronic Commerce Law* 2020, 131, 135; Kumkar, Herausforderungen eines Gewährleistungsrechts im digitalen Zeitalter, *Zeitschrift für die gesamte Privatrechtswissenschaft* 2020, 306, 316 ff.; Lommatzsch, Prüfer, Zwei neue EU-Richtlinien zum Vertragsrecht – „Revolution“ im Verbraucherrecht, *Gesellschafts- und Wirtschaftsrecht* 2020, 331, 332, 337.

longer than the liability period of two years. This must apply above all to security-relevant updates for high-priced and durable smart products. It can be assumed that in these cases the consumer expects updates even for the entire lifetime of the smart product.[38]

It is readily admitted that the reasonable period of time regulation for one-off products appears unsatisfactory from the point of view of the trade, as it leads to legal uncertainty with regard to the question of how long updates must be made available by the seller of smart products. He must ultimately make an assessment of the length of the reasonable period for updates, at least as long as there is no established case law for the product sold. Even if the decision made in the Sale of Goods Directive 2019/771 is unsatisfactory for the trade, it is nevertheless comprehensible in terms of content. The situations in the sale of smart products are too different for predefined time periods for updates to have made sense. The introduction of the flexible reasonable period of time is ultimately due to the nature of the matter.

This brings us to a subsequent problem, namely the question of how the reasonable time period for updates in Art. 7(3)(a) Sale of Goods Directive 2019/771 relates to the two-year liability period in Art. 10(1) Sale of Goods Directive 2019/771. No problem arises if the reasonable period for updates is not longer than the liability period, i.e. is also two years. The problems start, however, if the reasonable time period for updates of smart products should be longer than the liability period. Let us assume that the reasonable time period for updates for a specific smart product is five years, but the liability period is only two years and no more updates are provided after three years. Then, according to Art. 7(3) Sale of Goods Directive 2019/771, the seller would actually still be obliged to provide the consumer with the updates, but the buyer would no longer be able to legally enforce his right due to the expiry of the liability period of Art. 10(1) Sale of Goods Directive 2019/771. In order to prevent this situation, there are several possibilities for the national legislators who have to implement the Sale of Goods Directive 2019/771. The first possibility would be to let the liability period of Art. 10(1) Sale of Goods Directive 2019/771 start anew for each new update.[39] It would also be conceivable to make the length of

38 Staudenmayer, Kauf von Waren mit digitalen Elementen – Die Richtlinie zum Warenkauf, *Neue Juristische Wochenschrift* 2019, 2889, 2890 ff.; Stechern, Internet of things: Von Smartphones und Smart Homes, *IP-Rechtsberater* 2021, 76, 79.

39 So Kalamees, Goods with Digital Elements and the Seller's Updating Obligation, *Journal of Intellectual Property, Information Technology and Electronic Commerce Law* 2020, 131,138.

the liability period for updates dependent on the length of the reasonable period for the provision of updates, at least if the latter is longer than the two-year liability period. Another option would be to make the length of the liability period for updates dependent on the length of the reasonable period for the provision of updates, but then to extend the liability period by a certain period after the expiry of the reasonable period for updates.[40] Unfortunately, the advantages and disadvantages of the above models cannot be discussed in full here. However, all solutions have in common that they want to prevent the update obligation for smart products under Art. 7(3)(a) Sale of Goods Directive 2019/771 from running out. Due to the exception provided for in Art. 10(3) Sale of Goods Directive 2019/771, it is also possible for Member States to introduce or maintain a longer liability period despite the maximum harmonisation approach of the Directive.

b) Sales Contracts that Provide for Continuous Supply of Digital Content or Digital Service Over a Period of Time

The question of the time period for the update obligation is less problematic if it concerns a sales contract which provides for a continuous supply of the digital content or digital service over a period of time under Art. 7(3)(b) Sale of Goods 2019/770.[41] This is because in this case the length of the time period of the seller's obligation to provide updates is linked to the liability period applicable to sales contracts that provide continuous supply of digital content or digital service under Art. 10(2) s. 1 Sale of Goods Directive 2019/771. Both time periods, i.e. the time period for the update obligation of the seller and the liability period, are namely identical, i.e. two years beginning with the delivery of the smart product.[42] However, where the contract provides for a continuous supply for more than two years, the update obligation of the seller and the liability period for that digital content or that digital content are extended accordingly.[43] A clash between the time period for the update obligation and the limitation period as with one-off contracts is therefore not possible. Here too, as

40 The German legislator has chosen this solution in Section 475e(2) of the German Civil Code, according to which the liability period (more precisely limitation period) does not end until twelve months after the end of the update obligation.

41 See for the parallel provision in Digital Content Directive 2019/770 Art. 8(2)(a) Digital Content Directive 2019/770.

42 Art. 7(3)(b), Art. 10(2) s. 1 Sale of Goods Directive 2019/771.

43 Art. 7(3)(b), Art. 10(2) s. 2 Sale of Goods Directive 2019/771.

in the case of one-off contracts, it is possible for national legislators to introduce or maintain longer liability periods.[44]

V. *Consumer's Failure to Install Updates*

Art. 7(4) Sale of Goods Directive 2019/771 and also recital 30 of the Sale of Goods Directive 2019/771 make it clear that the consumer *is not obliged* to actually install updates made available to him. In principle, he is free to choose whether or not to install an update.[45] Thus, the consumer may have more or less understandable reasons for refraining (for the time being) from installing an update, for example if he is concerned about the functionality of the smart product after the update.[46] However, Art. 7(4) Sale of Goods Directive 2019/771 clarifies that the decision of the consumer *not* to install an update has a negative impact on his legal position. Because if the consumer fails to install within a reasonable time the update, the seller shall not be liable for any nonconformity resulting from the lack of the relevant update. This is therefore a classic German "*Obliegenheit*", i.e. the seller cannot sue for the installation of the updates or claim damages, but the buyer "only" worsens his own legal position.[47]

However, the loss of rights on the part of the consumer for the failure to install updates only occurs if (a) the seller informed the consumer about the availability of the update and the consequences of the failure of the

---

44 See Art. 10(3) Sale of Goods Directive 2019/771. This has happened, for example, in Germany. There, the new Section 475e(1) of the German Civil Code provides that in such cases claims based on a defect in the digital elements do not end before the expiry of twelve months after the end of the update obligation.

45 See for the parallel provision in the Digital Content Directive 2019/770 Art. 8(3) Digital Content Directive 2019/770.

46 On the question of whether there are circumstances that make the installation of updates indeed unreasonable for the consumer, see in more detail Wendehorst, Aktualisierungen und andere digitale Dauerleistungen: Das neue Gewährleistungsrecht auf dem Prüfstand, in: Stabentheiner, Wendehorst, Zöchling-Jud (eds.), *Das neue Gewährleistungsrecht: Zu den Richtlinien (EU) 2019/771 über den Warenkauf sowie (EU) 2019/770 über digitale Inhalte und digitale Dienstleistungen*, Vienna 2019, 111, 134.

47 Wendehorst, Aktualisierungen und andere digitale Dauerleistungen: Das neue Gewährleistungsrecht auf dem Prüfstand, in: Stabentheiner, Wendehorst, Zöchling-Jud (eds.), *Das neue Gewährleistungsrecht: Zu den Richtlinien (EU) 2019/771 über den Warenkauf sowie (EU) 2019/770 über digitale Inhalte und digitale Dienstleistungen*, Vienna 2019, 111, 132 ff.

consumer to install it;[48] and (b) the failure of the consumer to install or the incorrect installation by the consumer of the update was not due to shortcomings in the installation instructions provided to the consumer.[49] In particular, the first condition raises some questions, some of which already arose in a similar form under Art. 7(3) Sale of Goods Directive 2019/771.[50]

1. *Quality of Information*

Thus, a loss of rights on the part of the consumer for omitted updates requires, as said, according to Art. 7(4)(a) Sale of Goods Directive 2019/771, that the seller informed the consumer not only about the availability of the update, but also about the consequences of the failure of the consumer to install it. It is being discussed whether the seller must not only inform the consumer about the *legal consequences* of a failure to install the update, but whether he also needs to explain the main *technical features* of the update in a way that is understandable for a layperson.[51] But just as with Art. 7(3) Sale of Goods Directive 2019/771, one cannot demand explanations in technical terms or other qualified information from the seller. The wording of Art. 7(4)(a) Sale of Goods Directive 2019/771 is clear in this respect. Necessary, but also sufficient, is the notification that an update is available and what the legal consequences are of not installing the update.[52]

---

48 Art. 7(4)(a) Sale of Goods Directive 2019/771.

49 Art. 7(4)(b) Sale of Goods Directive 2019/771.

50 See also the comments under 4.1.

51 See on this discussion Wendehorst, Aktualisierungen und andere digitale Dauerleistungen: Das neue Gewährleistungsrecht auf dem Prüfstand, in: Stabentheiner, Wendehorst, Zöchling-Jud (eds.), *Das neue Gewährleistungsrecht: Zu den Richtlinien (EU) 2019/771 über den Warenkauf sowie (EU) 2019/770 über digitale Inhalte und digitale Dienstleistungen*, Vienna 2019, 111, 133 and Staudenmayer, in: Schulze, Staudenmayer (eds.), *EU Digital Law*, Baden-Baden 2020,161 ff. (for the Digital Content Directive 2019/770).

52 Likewise Staudenmayer, in: Schulze, Staudenmayer (eds.), *EU Digital Law*, Baden-Baden 2020, 162 (for the Digital Content Directive 2019/770): *"(...) Art. 8(3) does not contain any specific conditions. As a consequence, the information therefore should only relate to the simple availability of the update and is not required to include its technical details."*

2. *Time at Which the Information is Made Available*

A subsequent question concerns the point in time at which the consequences of the failure of the consumer to install must be pointed out. Since Art. 7(4)(a) Sale of Goods Directive 2019/771 is silent in this respect, two points in time can be considered, namely (only) the conclusion of the contract, or with the information to the consumer that a new update is available for installation. The better arguments are in favour of informing the consumer (again) with each new update about the legal consequences of a failure to install.[53] If an information at the time of conclusion of the contract were considered sufficient, it would be lost in the abundance of other pre-contractual and contractual information.[54] This would in turn lead to the fact that the actual (warning) function of the duty to inform could not be fulfilled.[55] It is true that this leads to a certain additional burden for the seller. However, this burden could be considerably reduced by the design solutions already discussed,[56] in which the information on a possible loss of rights due to failure to install an update appears directly on the display of the consumer's smart product.[57]

---

53 So also already represented on the interpretation of Art. 7(3) Sale of Goods Directive 2019/771. See on this point 4.1.

54 Likewise Wendehorst, Aktualisierungen und andere digitale Dauerleistungen: Das neue Gewährleistungsrecht auf dem Prüfstand, in: Stabentheiner, Wendehorst, Zöchling-Jud (eds.), *Das neue Gewährleistungsrecht: Zu den Richtlinien (EU) 2019/771 über den Warenkauf sowie (EU) 2019/770 über digitale Inhalte und digitale Dienstleistungen*, Vienna 2019, 111, 133.

55 Likewise Staudenmayer, in: Schulze, Staudenmayer (eds.), *EU Digital Law*, Baden-Baden 2020, 162 (for the Digital Content Directive 2019/770): "*If information is given in a summary manner at the time of conclusion of the contract or first supply, it cannot fulfil its purpose to allow the consumer to decide whether to install the update. Such an intention can only be fulfilled if the trader informs the consumer about an update if and when this becomes available.*"

56 See in more detail 4.2.

57 See also Wendehorst, Aktualisierungen und andere digitale Dauerleistungen: Das neue Gewährleistungsrecht auf dem Prüfstand, in: Stabentheiner, Wendehorst, Zöchling-Jud (eds.), *Das neue Gewährleistungsrecht: Zu den Richtlinien (EU) 2019/771 über den Warenkauf sowie (EU) 2019/770 über digitale Inhalte und digitale Dienstleistungen*, Vienna 2019, 111, 133 ff.

3. *The Consumer's Failure to Install Updates under Art. 7(4) Sale of Goods Directive 2019/771 and its Applicability to Agreed Updates*

An as yet unresolved question is the exact scope of application of Art. 7(4) Sale of Goods Directive 2019/771, because according to the wording of the law, this provision only applies if, *"the consumer fails to install within a reasonable time updates supplied in accordance with paragraph 3 (...)"*, i.e. only in the case of update obligations under Art. 7(3) Sale of Goods Directive 2019/771. The elephant in the room is whether Art. 7(4) Sale of Goods Directive 2019/771 is also applicable to update obligations stipulated by the sales contracts under Art. 6(d) Sale of Goods Directive 2019/771 – even though it is not explicitly mentioned by Art. 7(4) Sale of Goods Directive 2019/771. So can there also be a loss of rights for the consumer according to Art. 7(4) Sale of Goods Directive 2019/771 if it is a matter of a contractually agreed update obligation under Art. 6(d) Sale of Goods Directive 2019/771? According to one opinion, Art. 7(4) Sale of Goods cannot apply accordingly in these cases.[58] If the parties want to bring about a legal consequence comparable to Art. 7(4) Sale of Goods Directive 2019/771 it is argued that they must include a corresponding provision in the contract. However, the better arguments here speak for the other opinion, according to which Art. 7(4) Sale of Goods Directive 2019/771 is to be applied accordingly to contractually agreed update obligations pursuant to Art. 6(d) Sale of Goods Directive 2019/771.[59] Ultimately, there is no convincing reason for treating updates under Art. 6(d) Sale of Goods Directive 2019/771 and Art. 7(3) Sale of Goods Directive 2019/771 differently in this matter.

VI. *Conclusion*

The newly introduced update obligation for smart products will undoubtedly increase the level of consumer protection. In the long term, however, it will also probably concern many courts, since, as has been seen, numerous questions are unresolved yet. As an example, the determination of the

58 So Staudenmayer, in: Schulze, Staudenmayer (eds.), *EU Digital Law*, Baden-Baden 2020, 162 (for the Digital Content Directive 2019/770).

59 So Wendehorst, Aktualisierungen und andere digitale Dauerleistungen: Das neue Gewährleistungsrecht auf dem Prüfstand, in: Stabentheiner, Wendehorst, Zöchling-Jud (eds.), *Das neue Gewährleistungsrecht: Zu den Richtlinien (EU) 2019/771 über den Warenkauf sowie (EU) 2019/770 über digitale Inhalte und digitale Dienstleistungen*, Vienna 2019, 111, 134, who says the other view "*can hardly be correct.*"

reasonable time period for single act sales contracts for the supply of digital content or digital services under Art. 7(3)(a) Sale of Goods Directive 2019/771 can be mentioned here. For retailers, the update obligation for smart products leads to considerable additional burden and also to legal uncertainty. Ultimately, we will have to wait and see how retailers will adapt to the new situation. Above all, time will tell whether they will really make use of the possibility of an exclusion of the update obligation pursuant to Art. 7(5) Sale of Goods Directive 2019/771 on a large scale, as feared by some, or whether they will concentrate on regulating the update obligation in the general terms and conditions of business for sales to consumers in a meaningful way. It will also have to be seen whether sellers will ultimately pass on the costs of the update obligation imposed on them to consumers. In any case, sellers are advised to reach precise contractual agreements with producers regarding the update obligation. An essential component for coping with the new update obligation is the consistent use and further development of the design solution for smart products discussed here, in which the update appears as a download link together with all necessary information directly on the display of the consumer's smart product.

Modifications of digital content/services and digital elements in smart products

Modifications of digital content or services and of digital elements in smart products – Possible application problems*

Karin Sein[1]

I. Introduction

This paper aims at discussing the new rules of modifications foreseen in the Digital Content Directive[2] (DCD) as well as their potential application problems in practice. It also deals with the question of whether such a modification right would be necessary or desirable for smart goods, that is goods with digital elements regulated in the new Sale of Goods Directive (SGD).[3] To achieve these aims, the contribution starts with some general remarks on the trader's right to modifications and points out some application problems in the case of a triangular relationship between the consumer, the trader and the digital service provider (2.). Following that, it tries to define and delineate the concept of modification within the meaning of Article 19 DCD (3.); discusses the pre-conditions for modifying digital content or digital services and their legal consequences under the DCD (4.); and analyzes the specific case of interpersonal communications services as digital services and whether they underlie a specific modification regime (5.). Finally, it asks whether there is a need to provide for a right to modifications also in the case of goods with digital elements (6.). The contribution rounds up with some final conclusions (7.).

* The work leading to this publication has been supported by the Estonian Research Council's grant no PRG 124.

1 Prof. Dr. Karin Sein, Professor of Civil Law, University of Tartu.

2 Directive (EU) 2019/770 of the European Parliament and of the Council of 20 May 2019 on certain aspects concerning contracts for the supply of digital content and digital services [2019] OJ L136/1.

3 Directive (EU) 2019/771 of the European Parliament and of the Council of 20 May 2019 on certain aspects concerning contracts for the sale of goods, amending Regulation (EU) 2017/2394 and Directive 2009/22/EC, and repealing Directive 1999/44/EC [2019] OJ L136/28.

II. General remarks

Many digital services and smart products are constantly modified due to the ongoing technological developments in the digital environment. Traders offering such products often state in their terms and conditions that their services or products are subject to such modifications and refer to their changing product descriptions.[4] Sony, for example, has inserted the following clause in its End-User License Agreement:

> **Automatic Update Feature**
> From time to time, Sony may automatically update or otherwise modify the Software, including, but not limited to, for purposes of enhancement of security functions, error correction and improvement of functions, at such time as you interact with Sony's or third parties' servers, or otherwise. Such updates or modifications may delete or change the nature of features or other aspects of the Software, including, but not limited to, functions you may rely upon. You acknowledge and agree that such activities may occur at Sony's sole discretion and that Sony may condition continued use of the Software upon your complete installation or acceptance of such update or modifications. Any updates/modifications shall be deemed to be, and shall constitute part of, the Software for purposes of this EULA. By acceptance of this EULA, you consent to such update/modification.[5]

Indeed, it may be overly troublesome and impractical for a trader to keep up different versions of the same cloud computing service and it might be purely impossible to operate a multi-player online game with every participant using a different game version.[6] In order to prevent such problems and to allow certain flexibility, the digital content directive also has to deal with potential modifications to the contractual content for continu-

4 Georg E Kodek. 'Änderung von Leistungsmerkmalen und Vertragsbeendigung' in Christiane Wendehorst and Brigitta Zöchling-Jud (eds), *Ein neues Vertragsrecht für den digitalen Binnenmarkt?* (Manz 2016) 142.

5 Sony End User License Agreement for Certain Software <https://www.sonycreativesoftware.com/legal/eula> accessed 29 June 2021. By using Microsoft Office you consent that "Additionally, there may be times when we need to remove or change features or functionality of the Service or stop providing a Service or access to Third-Party Apps and Services altogether." Microsoft Services Agreement <https://www.microsoft.com/en/servicesagreement/> accessed 29 June 2021.

6 Recital 74 DCD refers to the necessity to adapt to the new technical environment or to an increased number of users as possible justifications for modifying digital content/services.

ous supply. Article 19(1) DCD regulates the possibilities of the trader to contractually agree on future modifications of the digital content or digital service and gives the trader the right to alter the supplied digital content or digital service, eg to adapt the service to changes in the digital environment such as new operating systems under certain conditions. The trader is explicitly allowed to modify features and functionalities of the digital content or digital service:[7] eg he may add a breakup-room functionality to an online-conferencing platform, a text-recognition feature to an e-mail service or just change the design or icon of an application. The trader may also change other features, eg connectivity or compatibility of the digital service but of course only if such a modification does not bring about lack of conformity: otherwise the consumer is entitled to use remedies.[8]

The trader's right to modifications under Article 19(1) DCD exists only in case of digital content or digital service supplied over a period of time, ie either continuously over a period of time (eg Facebook, Netflix or Dropbox) or in a series of individual acts of supply. It does not exist in case of one-off contracts (eg an e-book, wedding video or software bought on a CD or downloaded over the internet[9]). This restriction is necessary as modifications make sense only in case of a supply over a period of time during which the trader has an ongoing obligation to provide digital content or digital service and not in cases where he has already fulfilled his obligation to supply. Furthermore, it would clearly contradict reasonable consumer expectations and even the *pacta sunt servanda* principle[10] if the trader were allowed to modify the already downloaded e-books or music files.

The problem, however, emerges in the case of multi-party relationships, that is where the trader and the digital service provider are different persons. It may well be that the trader concludes a one-off contract with the consumer, but it would still be in the legitimate interest of the actual digital service provider to apply modifications. Let us take an example where the consumer buys a CD with Microsoft Office or Windows 10 from the local electronics shop and installs it on his PC. The consumer has concluded a sales contract, ie a one-off contract with the trader, ie the local shop. This means that the trader has no right to modifications under

---

7 Recital 75 DCD.

8 Recital 77 DCD.

9 So also Kristina Ehle and Stephan Kreß, 'Neues IT-Vertragsrecht für digitale Inhalte und Dienste gegenüber Verbrauchern' (2019) 11 CR 730.

10 In this sense Christina Möllnitz, 'Änderungsbefugnis des Unternehmers bei digitalen Produkten. Auslegung und Folgen des § 327f BGB-RefE' (2021) MMR 116.

Article 19(1) DCD simply because the trader does not have an obligation to supply over a period of time. As the consumer has no contract with Microsoft (other than the EULA concluded at the time of installation), Microsoft has no right to modifications either as in this constellation Microsoft is not a trader within the meaning of the digital content directive. Therefore, the only option for the trader (the local electronics store) not to be liable for modifications made by Microsoft later is to use the possibility in Article 8(5) DCD and obtain an express and separate consent from the consumer when concluding the contract.[11] As the rule on modifications in Article 19(1) DCD is exhaustive it is also not within the competence of the Member States to provide for an additional modification right in the national law for one-off contracts. The same situation can also arise in the case of smart goods, for instance when buying a smart watch using a connected digital service.[12]

One could ask whether Microsoft could have a modification right agreed on in the EULA: it can be argued that depending upon its wording, such an EULA could be seen as an additional contract for the supply of digital content between Microsoft and the consumer.[13] This would, however, not solve the problem at least for offline sales of digital content as the EULA would constitute a shrink-wrap license and it is highly questionable whether it can validly be incorporated in the consumer contract.[14] The situation would be more easily solved in the case of online sale of software as it would be possible to refer to the respective EULA on the seller's webpage.[15]

---

11 Similarly but in the end critically Ivo Bach, 'Neue Richtlinien zum Verbrauchsgüterkauf und zu Verbraucherverträgen über digitale Inhalte' (2019) NJW 1707: no right of modification in case of one-off contracts.

12 See below in Ch 6.

13 Christiane Wendehorst, 'Aktualisierungen und Andere digitale Dauerleistungen' in Johannes Stabentheiner, Christiane Wendehorst and Brigitta Zöchling-Jud (eds), *Das neue europäische Gewährleistungsrecht: zu den Richtlinien (EU) 2019/771 über den Warenkauf sowie (EU) 2019/770 über digitale Inhalte und digitale Dienstleistungen* (Manz 2019), 121–122.

14 Astrid Auer-Reinsdorff and Isabell Conrad, *Handbuch IT- und Datenschutzrecht* (3rd edn CH Beck 2019) § 17, paras 104–107.

15 Eg stating in the product description that in order to use it, one must accept the Microsoft's Terms of Use available at <www.microsoft.com/useterms> accessed 29 June 2021.

III. What is a modification within the meaning of Article 19 DCD?

Before moving on to analyze the necessary conditions for the trader's right to modify, it is important to distinguish between modifications and updates necessary for maintaining the digital content or service in conformity with the contract. Article 19 DCD regulates only these modifications which are not required to keep the digital content or digital service in conformity with the objective and subjective conformity requirements.[16] Consequently, modifications under Article 19 DCD are neither updates agreed in the contract nor updates required to maintain conformity under Article 8(2) DCD[17], nor deviations from the conformity requirements agreed under Article 8(5) DCD.[18] As Wendland puts it, they are cases of "permitted non-conformity".[19] Most importantly, it is necessary and often complicated to distinguish whether an update is a modification within the meaning of Article 19 DCD or an update necessary for keeping up with the conformity requirements which the trader is obliged to provide under Article 8(2) DCD. Let us take the example of a legal tech application for contract drafting and a change in the national unfair terms legislation which calls for a change of the legal tech service as well. In my view, such a change in the contract-generating software is not a modification within the meaning of Article 19 DCD but rather a conformity requirement within the meaning of Article 8 DCD because such a modification is necessary to maintain the conformity of the legal tech application. In other words, updates are the obligation, modifications the right of the trader. The consumer may exercise remedies for lack of conformity if updates are not provided; in the case of modifications, the consumer either must accept them or is entitled to terminate the contract, provided that the modification has a detrimental impact on him. It is only the detrimental impact that matters: the directive does not operate with the concept of the

---

16 „beyond what is necessary to maintain the digital content or digital service in conformity in accordance with Articles 7 and 8", see Article 19(1) DCD. It is also necessary to stress that the directive uses the notion of „modification" as a general one in Recital 75 which also includes updates.

17 Eg security updates.

18 Recitals 74–75 DCD.

19 Matthias Wendland in Reiner Schulze and Dirk Staudenmayer, *EU Digital Law* (Nomos, Hart, CH Beck 2020) Art 19 DCD para 8.

extent of the modification and does not *per se* forbid even very far-reaching changes in the digital content.[20]

In contrast to updates, modifications do not need installation by the consumer and may be done automatically by the trader. Updates, on the other hand, need to be installed by the consumer, according to Article 8(3) DCD.[21] Recital 47 DCD also stresses that "the consumer should remain free to choose whether to install the updates provided" – hence, the directive does not foresee an obligation to install updates.[22] It should, however, be legitimate to obtain general consent from the consumer for automatic updates in the contract, including in its standard terms and conditions. By using such consent, the trader can avoid the problem that might otherwise arise if he wants to include eg a security update and a modification in the same patch, as modifications may be done automatically but updates may not. Nevertheless, in my view, such general consent of the consumer must

20 Möllnitz (n 10) 118. She argues that the purpose of the norm still requires that the core of the digital content or service remain unchanged: the trader has no justified interest to be allowed to supply a totally different product than originally agreed.

21 See also Ehle and Kreß (n 9) 728. They refer to the current practice of automatic updates, especially for operating systems and consider such practice to be allowed under the directive if such updates are necessary for maintaining conformity requirements and the trader complies with the notification obligation under Article 8(2) DCD. This argumentation oversees that Article 8(3) DCD clearly leaves the choice of installing updates to the consumer. Wendehorst, however, rightly points out that there are situations where the wider interest of avoiding systemic risks would justify automatic updates. Wendehorst (n 13) 125–126. Indeed, Recital 47 DCD clarifies that the updating rules of the directives should not affect obligations to provide security updates laid down in Union or national law. Such Union or national law might provide the obligation – and the right – of the digital service provider to enact updates against the consumer's will. For instance, § 10 of the Estonian Cybersecurity Act obliges the digital service provider to ascertain the risks posed to the security of their system and take organisational and technical measures appropriate for risk management. Such technical measures could include mandatory security updates. Wiesemann, Mattheis and Wende also argue for the service provider's right to automatic security updates at least for IT-security reasons. Hans Peter Wiesemann, Clemens Mattheis and Susanne Wende, 'Software-Updates bei vernetzten Geräten' (2020) MMR 139–142.

22 Dirk Staudenmayer, 'Auf dem Weg zum digitalen Privatrecht – Verträge über digitale Inhalte' (2019) NJW 2501. Where the consumer decides not to install the updates, the consumer should, however, not expect the digital content or digital service to remain in conformity. See Recital 47 DCD.

be coupled with the possibility to withdraw it later:[23] this is necessary for keeping the control over installation of updates with the consumer.[24]

Another interesting question is whether a modification within the meaning of Article 19 DCD also includes a change of terms of use of the digital service. Notably, Article 19(1) DCD allows "modification of digital content or digital service"[25] and not modification of contract terms. Digital service, in turn, means: (a) a service that allows the consumer to create, process, store or access data in digital form; or (b) a service that allows the sharing of or any other interaction with data in digital form uploaded or created by the consumer or other users of that service.[26] Clearly, not all cases where the trader modifies its terms and conditions can be qualified as modifications within Article 19 DCD: for instance, jurisdiction or applicable law clauses most certainly do not need changes in the digital content or digital service and hence cannot be qualified as modifications under Article 19 DCD. Similarly, changing the payment conditions or rate of late payment interest is not a modification of the digital service as these clauses regulate the obligations of the consumer rather than the obligation of the trader to provide a digital service according to the contract. The obligations of the consumer are mostly outside the scope of the digital content directive anyway[27] and contract terms allowing their unilateral

---

23 Eg Apple iOS and iPadOS Software License Agreement 1(c): "By using the Apple Software, you agree that Apple may download and install automatic Apple Software Updates onto your Device and your peripheral devices. You can turn off automatic updates altogether at any time by changing the Automatic Updates settings found within Settings." <https://www.apple.com/legal/sla/docs/iOS13_iPadOS13.pdf> accessed 29 June 2021.

24 By contrast, Google Play Terms of Service do not always allow consumers such a choice as required by Article 8(3) and Recital 47 DCD. Section 2(4) of the Terms stipulate: „By agreeing to these Terms and using Google Play, you agree to receive such Updates automatically. You may be able to manage Updates to certain Content via Settings in Google Play." Google Play Terms of Service <https://play.google.com/intl/en-us_us/about/play-terms/index.html> accessed 29 June 2021.

25 Moreover, Article 19(1) DCD does not allow modifying consumer's digital environment outside the supplied digital content or digital service. See Möllnitz (n 10) 120.

26 Article 2 DCD.

27 On the obligations of the consumer in case of data-paid contracts, see Axel Metzger, 'Data as Counter-Performance: What Rights and Duties do Parties Have?' (2017) 8(1) JIPITEC para 2ff.

modification are to be assessed according to the Unfair Terms Directive (UCTD).[28]

In other cases, distinguishing between a modification of the digital service and a modification of the contract terms is complicated, as eg modifying the functionality of the digital service also means modification of the contract, ie the conformity criteria.[29] The delineation becomes complicated also in cases such as AirBnB changing its cancellation policy due to the COVID-19 pandemic: are these changes also modifications under Article 19 DCD? AirBnB is clearly a digital service falling under the scope of the DCD: it is a service that allows consumers to process or access data in digital form. If a natural person rents out his flat via AirBnB only twice a year, he is still a consumer within the meaning of Article 2(6) DCD. But is the change of cancellation policy (ie a change of the rental contract already concluded between the host and the tenant) also a modification of a feature of the digital service of AirBnB?[30] Is it a unilateral change of conformity criteria (characteristics) of the digital intermediary service to the detriment of the hosting consumer as he is now subject to worse cancellation terms? Or is this situation completely outside the scope of the DCD?

If this case does not fall within the scope of the DCD, then the respective standard term of AirBnB falls within the scope of the Unfair Terms Directive. According to the Unfair Terms Directive, unilateral change of contract terms or characteristics of the service is allowed only if there is a valid reason specified in the contract.[31] Admittedly, point 2(b) of the Annex of the UCTD makes an exception for terms under which a supplier reserves the right to alter unilaterally the conditions of a contract of indeterminate duration, provided that he is required to inform the consumer with reasonable notice and that the consumer is free to dissolve the contract.[32] However, as AirBnB changed rental contracts already concluded

---

28 Council Directive 93/13/EEC of 5 April 1993 on unfair terms in consumer contracts [1993] OJ L95/29.

29 The Unfair Terms Directive also distinguishes between „change of contract terms“ in point 1(j) and „change of characteristic of the service“ in point 1(k) of the Annex whereby the German literature considers the latter *lex specialis*. *Münchener Kommentar zum Bürgerlichen Gesetzbuch* (8th edn 2019) BGB § 308 no 4 para 2.

30 Recital 75 states that „the trader should be allowed under certain conditions to modify features of the digital content or digital service“.

31 Annex of the UCTD, points 1(j) and (k).

32 See also Case C-92/11 *RWE Vetrieb v Verbraucherzentrale Nordrhein-Westfalen* [2013] paras 49ff.

between the host and the tenant, this would have required a valid reason in the contract; otherwise the unilateral change of cancellation policy is illegal and hence the hosting consumer could claim damages from AirBnB.

Consequently, if the situation falls within the scope of the DCD, then it is clearly a detrimental modification and the consumer could only terminate the contract with AirBnB under Article 19(2) DCD[33] but not claim damages or prevent the change of cancellation policy – nor can the consumer protection authorities interfere with an injunction. However, if it falls within the scope of UCTD, then – depending on the national law and the wording of the standard terms – the behavior of AirBnB could be either totally legal (hence, no extraordinary termination right for the consumer) or, on the contrary, be based on an unfair contract term and hence entitle the consumer to damages or restitution. In my view, it would be problematic to consider cancellation policy as part of the objective conformity criteria of a digital rental intermediary service; therefore, I would tend to leave it outside the scope of the DCD and within the scope of the UCTD but drawing the line is surely complicated.

IV. Conditions for using the right to modifications

1. Modifications not detrimental to the consumer

In order to make use of the right to modify, the trader has to meet the following conditions: (i) the right to modify must be stipulated in the contract, including a valid reason for the modification, (ii) the modification may not cause additional costs to the consumer[34], and (iii) the consumer must be informed of the modification in advance in a clear and comprehensible manner.

First, it must be stressed that the trader's modification right must be contractually agreed: the directive does not foresee a statutory modification

33 It is clearly not a case for Article 19(1) DCD as the modification does cause costs for the consumer.

34 Otherwise the trader could unilaterally raise the price just by adding a new functionality to eg Spotify or MS Office 365. It is another question, though, whether the trader can raise the price for reasons other than modifications: this is not regulated by the directive and is subject to national law, including the rules on unfair terms. Cf also G. E. Kodek who brings out that the free-of-cost requirement was also found in Art. 85 of the Common European Sales Law but absent in Art. II-9:401 (1) of the Draft of Common Frame of Reference. Kodek (n 4) 166.

right.[35] The valid reasons foreseen in the contract must be clear and specific and not merely in generic terms.[36] Such valid reasons as required by the directive could encompass cases where the modification is necessary to adapt the digital content or digital service to a new technical environment or to an increased number of users or for other important operational reasons.[37] Consequently, the consumer needs to be informed about the trader's modification right and the valid reasons for it at the stage of conclusion of the contract, ie in the contract terms.[38] The valid reasons must be specified in the contract; it is not enough to merely stipulate that the trader has a modification right in case of a valid reason.[39] However, specific features or extent of the modifications do not need to be stipulated in the contract: it should be enough to describe the categories and reasons for modifications in order to inform the consumer about the possible future modification possibilities. Further, it is not necessary that a particular modification should be reasonably expected by the consumer at the time of conclusion of the contract.[40]

---

35 Kodek suggests deriving a statutory modification right from the doctrine of change in circumstances – however, only for extreme cases. Kodek (n 4) 146.

36 Karin Sein and Gerald Spindler, 'The new Directive on Contracts for the Supply of Digital Content and Digital Services – Conformity Criteria, Remedies and Modifications – Part 2' (2019) 15(4) ERCL 388–389. Differently Wendland who sees the requirements of Article 19(1) DCD met already if the nature (and not the wording) of the contract provides a sufficient reason for modifications. In his opinion most, if not all, contracts concerning the supply of digital content or digital services meet that requirement. Wendland (n 19) Art 19 DCD para 12.

37 Recital 75 DCD.

38 As Article 19(1) DCD lays down mandatory transparency requirements for the agreement on trader's modification right, there is no need nor possibility to assess their transparency under the Unfair Terms Directive. Möllnitz (n 10) 118. In this sense also Kodek who considers the DCD *lex specialis* to the UCTD. Kodek (n 4) 146. Differently Wendland (n 19) Art 19 DCD para 7: Article 19 serves as the legal standard ('Leitbild') towards which general terms and conditions are to be reviewed in application of Article 3 of the Unfair Terms Directive.

39 In this sense also Möllnitz (n 10) 119.

40 Such a requirement was suggested by the European Parliament. See Report of the European Parliament on the proposal for a directive of the European Parliament and of the Council on certain aspects concerning contracts for the supply of digital content (COM(2015)0634 – C8-0394/2015 – 2015/0287(COD)) amendment 114 <https://www.europarl.europa.eu/doceo/document/A-8-2017-0375_EN.html> accessed 30 June 2021. The changes in the digital environment and hence the necessity for modifications are, however, often not predictable at the time of conclusion of the contract. Thomas Riehm, 'Updates, Patches & Co. – Schutz

A modification must not result in additional costs for the consumer.[41] This also includes indirect costs.[42] Raising the price of the digital service for reasons other than the particular modification does not fall under Article 19 DCD either as such a change does not constitute a "modification of the digital content or digital service" but concerns only the payment obligation of the consumer. Hence, it is outside the scope of the directive and subject to the applicable national law, including the rules on unfair terms.[43] The directive also allows the parties to conclude a new contract, eg on the new version of the software[44] and agree upon a higher price for that. Therefore, an option suggested in the literature is to keep the contract periods relatively short and in case of modifications offer consumers a new version of the digital content for an increased price.[45]

The specific information concerning each modification must be given "in a clear and comprehensible manner" before or at the time of its factual application and not already at the conclusion of the contract.[46] In case the modification is not detrimental to the consumer, notification does not need to be made on a durable medium.[47] While the original proposal of the directive obliged the trader to use a durable medium[48] for all notifications[49], during further legislative process it was rightly found that such a requirement would end up in constant e-mailing and therefore turn out to be too burdensome for traders as well as for consumers. Consequently, the consumer may be notified of a modification eg via a pop-up window.

---

nachwirkender Qualitätserwartungen' in Martin Schmidt-Kessel and Malte Kramme (eds), *Geschäaftsmodelle in der digitalen Welt* (JWV 2017) 202.

41 Article 19(1)b DCD.

42 Möllnitz (n 10) 119.

43 See Annex 1 point 1(l) of the Unfair Terms Directive which blacklists contract terms that allow a supplier of services to increase their price without in both cases giving the consumer the corresponding right to cancel the contract if the final price is too high in relation to the price agreed when the contract was concluded.

44 Recital 75 DCD.

45 Ehle and Kreß (n 9) 730. This of course puts the consumer in a take-it-or-leave-it situation, see Wendland (n 19) Art 19 DCD para 13.

46 Ehle and Kreß (n 9) 729.

47 Article 19(1)c, Recital 76 DCD.

48 Durable medium means any instrument which enables the consumer or the trader to store information addressed personally to that person in a way that is accessible for future reference, for a period of time adequate for the purposes of the information and which allows the unchanged reproduction of the information stored, see Article 2(13) DCD. On the notion of durable medium see Case C-49/11 *Content Services v Bundesarbeitskammer* [2012].

49 Article 15(1)b of the Commission's proposal of DCD.

Whether or not a modification is detrimental to the consumer must be decided objectively and not from the perspective of each individual consumer.[50] If a modification only results in minor negative consequences and all the conditions described above are met, the trader has effectively changed the contract and the conformity criteria of the digital content or digital service.[51] Hence, the consumer has no right to terminate the contract: thus, the consumer must accept and bear such modifications without any possibility to use remedies.

2. *Modifications detrimental to the consumer*

As detrimental modifications entitle the consumer to termination under Article 19(2) DCD, it is first necessary to determine under which circumstances a modification can be considered as having more than a merely minor negative impact on the consumer.[52] In this context, Recital 75 DCD refers to „the nature and purpose of the digital content or digital service and to the quality, functionality, compatibility and other main features which are normal for digital content or digital services of the same type“ and foresees an objective perspective test. Surely, there is a detrimental modification if a major functionality change of software leads to a considerably increased use of memory space of the consumer's end device which affects the use of other digital content.[53] Furthermore, negative impact may result from increased use of the consumer's personal data[54] or

---

50 Recital 75 provides: the extent to which modifications negatively impact the use of or access to the digital content or digital service by the consumer should be objectively ascertained having regard to the nature and purpose of the digital content or digital service and to the quality, functionality, compatibility and other main features which are normal for digital content or digital services of the same type.

51 Möllnitz (n 10) 119.

52 See Article 19(2) DCD. It was not clear in the original proposal whether the right to termination also existed in case of modifications advantageous to the consumer, cf Gerald Spindler, 'Contracts for the Supply of Digital Content – Scope of Application and Basic approach. Proposal of the Commission for a Directive on contracts for the supply of digital content' (2016) ERCL 12(3) 214.

53 Ehle and Kreß (n 9) 730. Similarly Wendland: negative impact if additional hardware requirements have to be met. Wendland (n 19) Art 19 DCD para 17.

54 Wendland (n 19) Art 19 DCD para 17; Kodek considers such cases as causing additional „costs“ to the consumer. Kodek (n 4) 147. From the data protection side, it must be noted that it is not always necessary to obtain consumer's (data subject's) consent for such increased data use: in certain cases the legitimation

even change of login possibilities in a way that only a specific highly secure authentication method is accepted without any clear security justification. On the other hand, just changing the design or color scheme of the digital service does not constitute a more than a minor negative impact even if it may be considered troublesome and subjectively unwanted by a particular consumer.

If a modification negatively impacts the consumer's access to or use of the digital content or digital service in more than a minor manner, several important legal aspects must be considered. First, in such cases, notification has to follow on a durable medium and it has to provide information on the features and time of the modification and of the right to terminate the contract, or, alternatively of the possibility to maintain the digital content or digital service without the modification.[55] The specific information concerning each modification must be given reasonably in advance before its factual application: this allows the consumer to decide whether to use his right to termination or not.[56]

Second, as already indicated, in case of detrimental modifications, Article 19(2) DCD entitles the consumer to terminate the contract within 30 days after the receipt of the information or after the content or service has been modified. The consumer may terminate the contract free of any charge[57] and termination has the same consequences as termination due to lack of conformity, including the right to retrieve user-generated content.[58] True, termination is not really of interest to consumers in case of data-paid contracts such as those with Facebook as these service providers allow instant termination anyway. But terminating the contract may be an adequate option eg in the case of paid services such as the paid yearly subscriptions of Spotify or Netflix where modifications are clearly of major importance.

The trader may also offer the consumer the continuation of the supply of digital content or digital service without any modification at no additional cost and in conformity with the contract in which case the con-

---

may be based on Article 6(1)b GDPR, ie when increased processing of personal data is necessary for the (now modified) performance of the contract.

55 Article 19(1)d DCD.

56 Ehle and Kreß (n 9) 729.

57 Consequently, any sort of cancellation or processing fee required from the consumer is unlawful under the directive.

58 Article 15ff DCD. Möllnitz considers partial termination also possible, see Möllnitz (n 10) 121.

sumer will not be entitled to terminate the contract.[59] Again, if the digital content or digital service that the trader enabled the consumer to maintain is no longer in conformity with the contract, the consumer is entitled to rely on the remedies for a lack of conformity.[60] It must be stressed, though, that the consumer has no right to demand the continuation of the old version; he can continue using it only if the trader offers it. Otherwise, he can just terminate the contract.[61]

If a modification results in a lack of conformity, then the consumer can exercise remedies, eg demand that the service be brought into conformity.[62] The consumer has a similar right in situations where the lack of conformity was not caused by the modification but nevertheless arises after the digital content or digital service was modified by the trader.

V. *Modifications in the case of interpersonal communications services*

A specific issue arises with respect to modifications of publicly available interpersonal communications services. Namely, whereas electronic communications services, including number-dependent interpersonal communications services (such as SkypeOut) are outside the scope of the DCD

59 Article 19(4) DCD.

60 Recital 77 DCD.

61 Sein and Spindler (n 36) 389. Critical in this respect Hugh Beale, 'Digital Content Directive and rules for contracts on continuous supply' (2021) 12(2) JIPITEC 102; Beate Gsell, 'Der europäische Richtlinienvorschlag zu bestimmten vertragsrechtlichen Aspekten der Bereitstellung digitaler Inhalte' (2018) 62(2) ZUM 80. The European Law Institute suggested that Member States should be able to provide for a consumer's right to roll-back under national law. European Law Institute, 'Statement on the European Commission's proposed directive on the supply of digital content to consumers' (ELI 2016) 23.

62 This is clarified in Recital 77 DCD which states: „if the digital content or digital service that the trader enabled the consumer to maintain is no longer in conformity with the subjective and the objective requirements for conformity, the consumer should be able to rely on the remedies for a lack of conformity as provided for under this Directive. Where the requirements for such a modification as laid down in this Directive are not satisfied and the modification results in a lack of conformity, the consumer's right to bring the digital content or digital service into conformity, have the price reduced or the contract terminated, as provided for under this Directive, should remain unaffected."

and instead subject to the Electronic Communications Code (EECC)[63], the Digital Content Directive is applicable to number-independent interpersonal communications services such as FB Messenger, Zoom, MS Teams or Whatsapp.[64] At the same time, these number-independent interpersonal communications services form a subtype of electronic communication services and are partly subject to the EECC.[65] To put it simply: Skype is subject to the DCD and partially also to the EECC, SkypeOut only to the EECC. Interestingly, they are subject to somewhat different modifications regimes.

Number-independent interpersonal communications services falling within the scope of the DCD benefit from a more generous modifications regime: their providers are entitled to modify their services under the conditions of Article 19(1) DCD and consumers may terminate their contracts only if such modifications have a considerable negative impact on them.[66] By contrast, other public electronic communications services, including number-dependent interpersonal communications service providers face the possible termination in all cases where they change their contractual conditions, unless these changes are duly notified[67], are either exclusively to the benefit of the end-user, or of a purely administrative nature and have no negative effect on the end-user, or are directly imposed by Union or national law.[68] To use a simple example: Skype users have to tolerate modifications slightly detrimental to them while SkypeOut users do not.

---

63 Directive (EU) 2018/1972 of the European Parliament and of the Council of 11 December 2018 establishing the European Electronic Communications Code (Recast) [2018] OJ L321/36.

64 Article 3(5)b DCD. They are often also referred to as OTT-s. On the notion and different subtypes of OTTs, see Marcin Rojszczak, 'OTT regulation framework in the context of CJEU Skype case and European Electronic Communications Code' (2020) 38 Computer Law and Security Review 3–4. He points out that there is no universally accepted definition of an OTT.

65 See more on the issue Karin Sein, 'Interplay of Digital Content Directive, European Electronic Communications Code and Audiovisual Media Directive in Communications Sector' (2021) 12(2) JIPITEC 169ff.

66 Article 19(2) DCD.

67 The trader must notify the end-users at least one month in advance in a clear and comprehensible manner on a durable medium, see Article 105(4) EECC. The right to terminate the contract must be exercised within one month after notification.

68 This is considerably different from the principle found in Article 19(2) DCD, which entitles the consumer to terminate only if the modification negatively impacts the consumer's access to or use of the digital content or digital service, unless such negative impact is only minor.

The question of the applicable modifications regime becomes important also in the case of bundle contracts. For example, if we have a telecom bundle involving internet access, digital TV and a mobile phone subscription, the digital TV part falls within the scope of the DCD[69] while the other parts are subject to the EECC. As the DCD's modifications regime is somewhat more favorable to the trader than the one in the EECC, there may be an overlap or conflict between them. In order to ensure consistency with the sector-specific provisions of the EECC, Article 3(6) DCD declares Article 19 DCD, ie the rules on modifications of digital content or digital services, not applicable if a bundle contract includes elements of an internet access or a number-based interpersonal communications service. Instead, the relevant provisions of the EECC apply to all elements of the bundle.[70] Thus, if a digital service such as digital TV forms part of a telecom bundle, the consumer benefits from the easier termination possibility in case of modifications in the contract. As in practice consumers often use digital TV in a bundle with other electronic communications services, changes in the digital TV program package must usually be assessed under Article 105(4) EECC, ie be notified at least 1 month ahead, on a durable medium and the consumer may terminate the digital TV package even in case of minor negative effects.[71]

VI. Modifications in the case of goods with digital elements

Trader's right to modifications could also play a role in the case of smart goods as many smart goods are interconnected with digital services, eg a receiver which is connected to Spotify to play music, a smart TV having YouTube and Netflix applications, or a smart car with embedded software and different digital accessory services. There are also products where hardware and software are totally intertwined: the new Microsoft Surface

69 Recital 31 DCD.

70 Recital 33 DCD.

71 See also an earlier decision of the German Federal Supreme Court of 15 November 2007 no III ZR 247/06. The Court declared a standard term in the paid-TV package contract unfair even if the standard term allowed to change the package only for the benefit of the consumer but contained no valid reason for the change of quantity or composition of the channel package. The Court ruled that such a clause does not enable the consumer to predict at the conclusion of the contract which changes may occur without his consent and especially what changes are considered to be „for the benefit of the consumer“. In particular, it is not enough that the changes in programs are favorable to the majority of the clients.

Earbuds allow the user to control music and calls, catch up on emails in the Outlook mobile app for iOS and even dictate in Word, Outlook, and PowerPoint.[72]

The new Sale of Goods Directive adopted together with the Digital Content Directive does not include a provision comparable to Article 19 DCD regarding modifications.[73] Consequently, if a fitness tracker app is sold together with a fitness tracker device, which falls under the Sale of Goods Directive, the seller is obliged to deliver updates under Article 7(3) SGD but is not entitled to make modifications to the app. One might ask whether it would be possible and even advisable to foresee such a right also for goods with digital elements in the national law. It is indeed within the competence of Member States to foresee a comparable rule on modifications because this question is outside of the scope of the new Sale of Goods Directive. Under Article 10(1) SGD conformity of the good must be assessed at the moment of delivery: after that point in time the directive only regulates the seller's obligation to deliver updates to the digital elements[74] but not his right to enact modifications. However, Member States should not lower the consumer protection standard of the Unfair Terms Directive as point 1(k) of its Annex qualifies terms enabling the seller to alter unilaterally any characteristics of the product without a valid reason as being unfair.

But should one advise for such a national modifications rule? First, one should most certainly not provide for such a right for hardware as the seller has no legitimate interest in it. In case of sales contracts, consumers should be protected against non-voluntary although non-detrimental modifications. Otherwise, it may lead to situations where a car brought to annual maintenance is repainted in a different color and the seller could argue that such a modification was not detrimental to the consumer. Secondly, one must keep in mind that such national rules would create fragmentation of consumer protection rules in the European Union.

More importantly, the modification rules of the DCD, especially their legal consequences would not be fit for tangible goods, including goods with digital elements. Under Article 19(1) DCD, the modification right

72 Microsoft Surface Earbuds <https://www.microsoft.com/en-us/p/surface-earbuds/8r9cpq146064?activetab=pivot%3aoverviewtab> accessed 30 June 2021.

73 Metzger considers this as diminishing the consumer protection level in the SGD compared to that of the DCD. Axel Metzger, 'Verträge über digitale Inhalte und digitale Dienstleistungen: Neuer BGB-Vertragstypus oder punktuelle Reform?' (2019) 12 JZ 578.

74 See Article 7(3) SGD.

is explicitly foreseen only for contracts of continuous supply and not for one-off contracts. Sales contracts, however, are typical one-off contracts and therefore the rules of Article 19(2) DCD, which entitle the consumer to termination of the contract in case of detrimental modifications, are not suitable for them. Whereas termination with *ex nunc* effect makes sense in case of long-term contracts, it could be simply too burdensome for the seller to risk with termination of the sales contract and the following restitution in case of a detrimental modification of embedded software. Additionally, it would create difficult legal questions as to eg the compensation of use of the good. True, one could imagine such a right for a continuous digital service such as a digital navigation system offered together with a car on a subscription basis.

Moreover, there is no practical need for introducing such a modification rule into national law. Whereas the trader might have a valid interest in modifying the operating system of a smart phone to adjust it with the changed digital environment[75], he may also agree upon such a right in the sales contract. True, this can only be done in accordance with the unfair terms rules as point 1(k) of the Annex of UCTD blacklists contract terms which enable the seller to alter unilaterally without a valid reason any characteristics of the product or service to be provided. Therefore, such modifications, eg changes in the design of the icons on the smart phone's display, are only allowed if there is a valid reason stipulated in the contract which is sufficiently clear and transparent.[76] Even then, modifications of the operating system that significantly reduce the memory space of the phone promised in the sales contract should qualify as lack of conformity of the phone:[77] such modifications are only allowed in an express and separate agreement under Article 7(5) SGD. Otherwise traders could effectively force consumers to change phones or other electronic devices just by making space-consuming modifications to the operating system resulting in a situation where consumers are not able to use apps or other content on their devices. The same is true in cases where software modifications lead to battery degradation and slower charging of an electric car.[78]

75 Updates necessary to maintain conformity are required anyway under Article 7(3) SGD.

76 Of course, as Annex of the UCTD is only of indicative nature, the exact requirements stem from the applicable national law.

77 Sein and Spindler (n 36) 370–371.

78 See Sarah D Young, 'Tesla ordered to pay fine in Norway for throttling battery charging speeds. Customers have reported battery degradation following a software Update' *Consumer Affairs* (24.05.2021) <https://www.consumeraffairs.com/ne

The problem here is of course the time for assessing the lack of conformity of the smart good: according to Article 10(1) SGD, the liability of the seller presupposes that the lack of conformity existed at the time of delivery of the good, but at the time of delivery the good was in order: the modification leading to non-conformity was made only afterwards.[79] The problem is not solved by Recital 39 SDG either which states that goods with digital elements should be deemed to have been delivered to the consumer when both the physical component of the goods has been delivered and the single act of supply of the digital content or digital service has been performed or the continuous supply of the digital content or digital service over a period of time has begun. In the case of a smart phone or a smart car, this point in time usually more or less coincides with the delivery of the tangible good itself and hence does not help to establish non-conformity in cases where the digital elements are modified later and cause a lack of conformity of the smart good. Nevertheless, Recital 30 SGD clearly states that if an update causes a lack of conformity of the good with digital elements, the seller should be liable for bringing the good into conformity again: this implies that in the case of update-induced defects, it is not required that the lack of conformity exist at the time of delivery.[80] The other way to help consumers would be treating the operating system as a continuous supply of the digital content or digital service over a period of time, as then the seller would be liable for its conformity for either 2 years or even longer, depending upon the contract and the applicable national law.[81]

In many cases, however, the question about modifications of goods with digital elements does not even arise as the digital elements are not part of the sales contract. Namely, the new consumer contract law directives allow an express agreement that digital content or digital service is not

---

ws/tesla-ordered-to-pay-fine-in-norway-for-throttling-battery-charging-speeds-052421.html> accessed 30 June 2021.

79 In this sense also Peter Rott, 'The Digitalisation of Cars and the New Digital Consumer Contract Law' (2021) 12(2) JIPITEC 164. The problem was also pointed out by Jasper Vereecken and Jarich Werbrouck, 'Goods with Embedded Software: Consumer Protection 2.0 in Times of Digital Content?' (2019) 30(1) Indiana International and Comparative Law Review 64.

80 Wendehorst (n 13) 127–128. This is also in line with the second sentence of Article 10(1) SGD, which makes a „without prejudice"reference to the updating obligation in Article 7(3) SGD for goods with digital elements.

81 See Article 10(2) and (3) SGD. Smart TV software is indeed considered continuous supply of digital content or digital service by Vereecken and Werbrouck (n 79) 76.

part of the sales contract but rather constitutes a separate contract on supply of digital content or digital services subject to the DCD, provided that the application requirements of the latter are met.[82] The recitals of the directives name as an example the sale of a smart phone where its operating system is later obtained from a third party under a separate contract.[83] If this is the case and the operating system is not part of the sales contract of the smart phone, the digital service provider has a right to modify the operating system under Article 19 DCD.[84] Of course, this presupposes that the supply of the operating system can be qualified as a supply over a period of time and not merely a one-off contract, it must be without additional costs for the consumer and modifications must be agreed upon in the contract and duly notified. The problem, however, starts if the modifications to the operating system prove to be objectively detrimental to the consumer: termination of the operating system contract alone under Article 19(2) DCD offers little consolation as this does not enable the consumer to claim back his money from the seller. In order to help consumers in such cases, the detrimentally modified operating system should be considered not only a slightly detrimental modification but a lack of conformity of the phone entitling the consumer to use remedies. Otherwise it would be possible to shift virtually all security obligations to the digital service provider and relieve the seller of most of its liability.

VII. Conclusions

Article 19(1) of the newly adopted DCD offers traders a possibility to contractually agree on future modifications of the digital content or digital service, eg to adapt the service to changes in the digital environment under certain conditions. Most importantly, the right to enact modifications

---

82 On that, see Karin Sein and Gerald Spindler, 'The new Directive on Contracts for the Supply of Digital Content and Digital Services – Scope of Application and Trader's Obligation to Supply – Part 1' (2019) 15(3) ERCL 269–276.

83 Recital 22 DCD, Recital 16 SGD.

84 This of course presupposes that the DCD is applicable to the digital service contract. This is, for example, not the case if the operating system is a free and open-source software, as Article 3(4)f DCD excludes such software from the scope of the DCD provided that the consumer does not pay a price and the personal data provided by the consumer are exclusively processed by the trader for the purpose of improving the security, compatibility or interoperability of that specific software. In these cases, the digital service provider cannot agree upon the right to modifications under the DCD – but may do so under the UCTD.

must be expressed in a clear and transparent manner indicating a valid reason in the contract. In case of non-detrimental modifications, notifying the consumer does not need to follow on a durable medium, which is required only in case of detrimental modifications. The latter entitles the consumer to termination of the contract unless the trader offers a free-of-cost continuation of the old version of the digital content or service. Non-detrimental modifications, on the contrary, must be tolerated by the consumer without any possibility to resort to remedies.

Although often delivered in the same patch, on the legal level one must distinguish between a modification and an update: modifications are a right, updates an obligation of the trader. Modifications may be enacted automatically whereas updates need installation by the consumer. Further, modifications of digital content or digital service must also be distinguished from modifications of the contract, such as changes in payment terms: the latter are outside the scope of the DCD and subject to the rules of the Unfair Contract Terms Directive.

A specific regime applies to publicly available number-independent interpersonal communications services, such as SkypeOut, falling outside the scope of the DCD and within the scope of the EECC: their providers do not have the right to modifications under Article 19 DCD and face possible contract termination in all cases where they change their contractual conditions, unless these changes are duly notified, are either exclusively to the benefit of the end-user, or of a purely administrative nature and have no negative effect on the end-user, or are directly imposed by law.

Trader's right to modifications may also play a role in the case of smart goods, ie goods with digital elements: the trader might have a valid interest eg in modifying the operating system of a smart phone to adjust it with the changed digital environment. The new Sale of Goods Directive, however, does not foresee a seller's right to modifications comparable to the one in Article 19 DCD. Still, the seller may agree upon such a right in the sales contract but must respect the unfair terms rules as point 1(k) of the Annex of UCTD blacklists contract terms which enable the seller to alter unilaterally without a valid reason any characteristics of the product or service to be provided. One must also keep in mind that modifications leading to a lack of conformity of the smart good (eg modifications of the operating system that significantly reduce the memory space of the phone promised in the sales contract or software modifications leading to battery degradation and slower charging of an electric car) are only allowed in an express and separate agreement under Article 7(5) SGD. The problem of Article 10(1) SGD requiring the existence of the lack of conformity of the smart good at the time of delivery can be overcome by the interpretation offered in Recital 30 SGD.

Modifications of digital content/services and digital elements in smart products – how to design the contracts

Isabell Conrad & Dr. Alin Seegel[1]

I. Introduction

Considering the fast-evolving character of digital content and digital services – in particular streaming services and online games – such products can or rather *will* be subject to significant modifications during their lifespan. However, not all modifications are welcome within the respective user groups. Therefore, providers (traders) typically reserve the right to modify a digital product[2] by virtue of the applicable terms of service. In B2B and B2C terms and conditions, variations of direct and indirect modification rights exist, e.g.:

- unilateral right of the trader to change the contractual terms after conclusion of the contract;
- click-wrap contracts (in particular license terms such as EULA) to be accepted by consumers after they have purchased e.g. an IT device;
- short contract terms (period of subscription) requiring renewals (with new terms)[3];
- trader reserves the right to change, restrict or discontinue digital products which the trader provided free of charge but to offer them unmodified by charging fees for future use;
- reservation of the right to improve enhance the services and/or modify them for IT security and/or legal and regulatory requirements reasons;
- right to modify the digital products only in good faith if trader has no other reasonable options and consumer has no disadvantages;
- reservation of the right to either add or reduce or change features / functionalities;

1 The authors thank *Raphaela Rab* for her support in preparing this article.

2 Section 327 par. 1 German Civil Code (BGB) coming into effect on January 1, 2022 (see below footnote 18) jointly defines digital content and digital services as "digital products". In this article the term "digital product" is used in this sense.

3 See recital 75 of Directive (EU) 2019/77.

- right to suspend the service, e.g. modification of "maintenance windows";
- dynamic linking of documents, e.g. description of the digital product and reservation to modify these linked documents "from time to time";
- dynamic links to list of sub-providers and right of provider to modify this list;
- incorporation of terms and conditions (e.g. End User License Agreements EULA) of sub-providers (e.g. End User License Agreements EULA) and modification of the sub-providers' terms and conditions by the sub-providers.

German law provides rather restrictive rules for modification rights in standard terms. This refers in particular to section 308 no. 4[4] and no. 5[5], section 308 no. 8[6], section 309 no. 2[7] and section 346 BGB[8] (German Civil Code). These provisions are not limited to digital products. Modification rights in standard business terms have repeatedly been subject of court decisions in Germany: The German Federal Court of Justice[9] (BGH) ruled in 2005 that the standard business terms of a web shop granting the trader a right to replace unavailable goods with goods of equal value are ineffective even if the customer has the right to withdraw from the contract within 14 days of receipt of the goods.[10] In contrast to that, in a very controversial

4 Reservation of the right to modify: „*the agreement of a right of the user to modify the performance promised or deviate from it, unless the agreement of the modification or deviation can reasonably be expected of the other party to the contract when the interests of the user are taken into account*".

5 Provision regarding the validity of fictitious declarations. The provision is relevant for the user's acceptance of a change of the contract terms.

6 Reservation of non-availability of performance / service is only valid if the user of the clause informs the other party without undue delay, of the unavailability, and reimburses the other party without undue delay.

7 Right to refuse performance and other parties' right to retention.

8 Effects of revocation: restitution or return and – in case of violation of this obligation – the trader may demand damages; in lieu of restitution or return, compensation for value; if compensation for value does not apply, remaining enrichment must be returned.

9 German Federal Court of justice (BGH), highest German court in civil cases, decision of 21.09.2005 – VIII ZR 284/04.

10 English translation of the warranty clause in this specific case: ""*3. Warranty* [...]. *If a certain article is not available, we will send you an article of the same quality and price (replacement article) in individual cases. If you are not satisfied, you can return this article within 14 days. If replacement articles are not available, we are entitled to free ourselves from the contractual obligation to deliver; we also undertake to inform*

decision of 2013 the Higher Regional Court of Cologne (OLG Köln)[11] ruled in the specific case of a mileage program that a rather extensive modification clause was deemed valid.[12] In a recent decision of April 2021, the BGH[13] forced the banking sector to change their long standing practice with regard to modifications of their business terms. According to the bank's standard terms, changes to the terms were offered to customers in textual format at least two months before the proposed date of their entry into force. The customer's consent was deemed to be given if the customer did not indicate their rejection before the proposed time for the changes to take effect. The bank specifically notified about this effect in its offer and the customer had the option of termination. According to the BGH, such clauses which imply the customer's acceptance of changes of the bank's T&Cs are ineffective.

The DCD regulates the right of the trader to modify digital content or digital services and sets out additional requirements for the right of the trader to modify such content and services (Art. 19 DCD). In general, contracts and contractual obligations are binding for the contracting parties. However, in cases of digital content or digital services, supplied or made accessible over a period of time, there can be a need for modifications of the contractual content.[14] Such modifications may be necessary and are often advantageous for the consumer.[15] However, according to Recital 75 of the DCD there may be instances where such modifications negatively impact the use of or access to the digital content or digital service in more

---

you immediately about the non-availability and to reimburse any consideration received without delay."

11 OLG Köln, decision of 08.01.2013 – I-15 U 45/12.

12 Translation of the relevant clauses: "*xy reserves the right to use selected co-publishers of the program in certain countries (..) Via xy it is also possible to collect or redeem miles with various xy partner companies (...).*
A few conditions apply to the acquisition of miles, the redemption of miles and the general implementation of xy, which we have summarized for you here. Special regulations can also result from other program documents (...) as well as from the xy communication media (e.g. newsletter, bonus catalog, account statement). xy reserves the right to make changes or additions to the conditions of participation, the bonuses, the bonus scale or other processes described in the program documents for xy at any time, as far as this appears necessary and the participant is not disadvantaged in good faith. Changes or additions to these conditions of participation will be announced in writing. They are considered approved if a participant continues to use his xy customer number or if he does not object in writing within one month of the announcement ..."

13 BGH, decision of 27.4.2021 – XI ZR 26/20.

14 Recital 74, 75 of Directive (EU) 2019/770.

15 Recital 74 of Directive (EU) 2019/770.

than only a minor manner. For a fair balance of interests between the trader and consumer, Art. 19 DCD determines necessary requirements for such unilateral modifications.

As the Directive requires full harmonization[16], the German legislator has decided to adapt the existing provisions of the German Civil Code[17] and to insert new provisions. Art. 19 DCD therefore has been transposed into German law in the form of section 327r BGB.[18] Section 327r BGB will be applicable from January 2022. If a unilateral right of modification concerning digital content or digital services is to be agreed in the contract, the requirements of Art. 19 DCD/section 327r BGB must be observed and implemented when drafting the contract. This article deals with the drafting of contracts, considering the newly standardized right of modification in Art. 19 DCD/section 327r BGB.

II. Requirements of the right of modification according to Art. 19 DCD

1. General remarks

Relevant for the discussion about modification rights are not only direct modifications of digital products by the trader but also if the trader e.g. wants to exclude damage and warranty claims in the event of a modification.[19]

Modifications within Art. 19 DCD must be differentiated from updates that are required to maintain the conformity of the digital content or digital service. The trader's duty to provide updates for maintaining the digital product's conformity results from Art. 6, 7 (d), 8 (2) DCD. Accordingly, it is required that the trader provides updates as stipulated in the contract (see Art. 7 (d) DCD) as well as updates that are necessary to maintain certain objective qualitities in the sense of Art. 8 (1) DCD. Only updates that

16 See Art. 4 DCD, recitals 6 et seq.

17 "Bürgerliches Gesetzbuch", short "BGB".

18 On 25 June 2021 the German Bundestag passed the law transposing Directive (EU) 2019/770 on certain aspects concerning contracts for the supply of digital content and digital services: https://www.bmjv.de/SharedDocs/Gesetzgebungsverfahren/Dokumente/Bgbl_Digitale_Inhalte.pdf?__blob=publicationFile&v=2

19 MüKoBGB/*Wurmnest*, 8. ed. 2019, BGB section 308 Nr. 4 Rn. 5.

exceed these duties qualify as modifications within the meaning of Art. 19 DCD.[20][21]

2. Requirements of the right of modification according to Art. 19 DCD

Art. 19 DCD establishes requirements that must be met in case digital content and digital service is modified beyond what is necessary to maintain the digital content or digital service in conformity. The requirements apply to any change of the contractual service covered by the provision, i.e. irrespective of whether it is advantageous or disadvantageous for the consumer.[22]

According to Art. 19 DCD modifications are only allowed if all of the following requirements are met:

(1) contractual agreement on a right of modification and the contract provides a valid reason for the modification;
(2) the modification is made without additional cost to the consumer;
(3) the consumer is informed in a clear and comprehensible manner of the modification;
(4) where the modification negatively impacts the consumer's access to or use of the digital content or digital service, the consumer is informed reasonably in advance on a durable medium (e.g. e-mail) of the features and time of the modification and of the right to terminate the contract, or (if applicable) of the possibility to maintain the digital content or digital service without the modification.

The option to terminate the contract and the corresponding information requirement do not apply in case the modification's negative impact for the consumer is only minor.

---

20 If an update simultaneously serves to maintain conformity and goes beyond this, differentiation must be made with regard to the individual elements of the update and the appropriate provision must be applied in each case; see recital 74, 75 and BT-Drucksache 19/27653 p. 77.

21 Both Art. 7 (d) DCD and Art. 19 DCD concern the contractual agreement of modifications. However, they differ about the intention of the parties. In the case of Art 7. (d) DCD, an agreement of updates leads to a quality agreement, the trader therefore has a duty to provide the agreed updates. Such an agreement will therefore regularly serve the interest of the customer. In contrast, an agreement under Art. 19 DCD grants the trader a right to make updates to the product in his own interest.

22 BT-Drucksache 19/27653 p. 77.; *Möllnitz*, MMR 2021, 116 (117).

In summary, Art. 19 DCD requires a sufficient contractual agreement, the existence of a valid reason for the modification, the absence of additional cost for the consumer, and adequate notice to the consumer.

3. Contracts affected by Art. 19 DCD

Only contracts in a consumer-trader relationship are covered by the DCD. Contracts that concern the objects mentioned in Art. 3(5) DCD are excluded from the scope of the Directive from the outset. The same applies to gratuitous contracts. Whereby the consumer's obligation to provide personal data beyond what is strictly necessary for the fulfilment of the contract is sufficient for the application, a monetary payment is not required.

Art. 19 DCD itself restricts the applicability to contracts under which the digital content or digital services are made available to the consumer for a period of time, i.e. only continuing obligations.

III. Transposition of Art. 19 DCD into German law: section 327r BGB

In the German civil code, a right to change performance has not been explicitly included so far. With the implementation of the DCD, section 327r BGB will be inserted into the BGB with effect from January 2022 as a counterpart to Art. 19 DCD. The following table compares the structure of Art. 19 DCD and section 327r BGB and shows some differences:

Art. 19 (1)(a)-(c) DCD „*(a) the contract allows, and provides a valid reason for, such a modification;*" Recital 75: "*In addition to modifications aimed at maintaining conformity, the trader should be allowed under certain conditions to modify features of the digital content or digital service, provided that the contract gives a valid reason for such a modification. Such valid reasons could encompass cases where the modification is necessary to adapt the digital content or digital service to a new technical environment or to an increased number of users or for other important operational reasons.* [...]"	Sec. 327r (1) nos. 1–3 BGB „*(1) Bei einer dauerhaften Bereitstellung darf der Unternehmer Änderungen des digitalen Produkts, die über das zur Aufrechterhaltung der Vertragsmäßigkeit nach § 327e Absatz 2 und 3 und § 327f erforderliche Maß hinausgehen, nur vornehmen, wenn* 1. *der Vertrag diese Möglichkeit vorsieht und einen triftigen Grund dafür enthält*"
Art. 19 (1)(d)	Sec. 327r (2) „[1]*Eine Änderung des digitalen Produkts, welche die Zugriffsmöglichkeit des Verbrauchers auf das digitale Produkt oder welche die Nutzbarkeit des digitalen Produkts für den Verbraucher beeinträchtigt, darf der Unternehmer nur vorneh-*

	men, wenn er den Verbraucher darüber hinaus innerhalb einer angemessenen Frist vor dem Zeitpunkt der Änderung mittels eines dauerhaften Datenträgers informiert. ²Die Information muss Angaben enthalten über: 1. *Merkmale und Zeitpunkt der Änderung sowie* 2. *die Rechte des Verbrauchers nach den Absätzen 3 und 4.* *³Satz 1 gilt nicht, wenn die Beeinträchtigung der Zugriffsmöglichkeit oder der Nutzbarkeit nur* ***unerheblich*** *ist."*
Art. 19 (2) "*The consumer shall be entitled to terminate the contract if the modification negatively impacts the consumer's access to or use of the digital content or digital service, unless such negative impact is only* ***minor***. [German version of the DCD: "***geringfügig***"].	Sec. 327r (3) "*¹Beeinträchtigt eine Änderung des digitalen Produkts die Zugriffsmöglichkeit oder die Nutzbarkeit im Sinne des Absatzes 2 Satz 1, so kann der Verbraucher den Vertrag innerhalb von 30 Tagen unentgeltlich beenden. ²Die Frist beginnt mit dem Zugang der Information nach Absatz 2 zu laufen. ³Erfolgt die Änderung nach dem Zugang der Information, so tritt an die Stelle des Zeitpunkts des Zugangs der Information der Zeitpunkt der Änderung."*
Art. 19 (4)	Sec. 327r (4)
Art. 19 (5)	Sec. 327r (5)
Art. 15 – 18	Secs. 327o – 327p
Art. 22	Sec. 327s

Under German law modification rights are considered to be a "foreign object" and are therefore supposed to be interpreted very strictly.[23] This interpretation shall apply to section 327r BGB as well.[24] As part of section 327 et seq. BGB, section 327r BGB is a provision of the general law of obligations, which applies irrespective of the specific type of contract. As does the Directive, sections 327 et seq. BGB only apply in a consumer-trader relationship.

1. *Applicability of section 327r BGB to the respective modification*

Section 327r BGB applies only to cases where digital products shall be modified beyond what is necessary to maintain conformity in accordance with section 327e and 327f BGB (Art. 7, 8 DCD). If the modification is required for maintaining conformity, the modification procedure does not need to comply with the strict requirements of section 327r BGB. There-

23 Begr. RegE, BT-Drs. 19/27653, 89; *Möllnitz*, MMR 2021, 116 (116).
24 Begr. RegE, BT-Drs. 19/27653, 89; *Möllnitz*, MMR 2021, 116 (116.

fore, it is very likely and foreseeable that traders will try to introduce modifications under section 327e, 327f BGB (and not under section 327r BGB).

Furthermore, section 327r BGB shall not apply to situations where the parties conclude a new contract for the supply of digital products.[25] As a result and as stated above[26], short contract terms (period of subscription) requiring renewals with new terms will very likely remain a solution for the trader to deal with modifications.

2. *Requirements regarding the modification clause*

The basic prerequisite for a right of modification is that it needs a prior valid agreement in the in the contract. The right does not arise automatically from the law[27] but requires an explicit and specific agreement between the contracting parties.[28] It is necessary that the right to modify is limited by the existence of a valid reason, i.e. that the trader is only granted such a right in the event that a valid reason exists.

Furthermore, Art. 19 DCD states that the contract shall provide valid reasons for the modification.[29] Recital (74) of the Directive states, "… other modifications, which would deviate from the objective requirements for conformity and which are foreseeable at the time of conclusion of the contract, would have to be expressly agreed to by the consumer when concluding the contract." That means that the contract must provide a comprehensible specification of the valid reasons. A clause stating that the valid reason is a condition for the modification is not sufficient.[30]

According to section 327r (1) no. 1 BGB the contract must provide and specify exhaustively the valid reason which shall allow the modification.[31] The abstract reference to a lawful modification in the event of a valid reason is thus insufficient. Rather, a concretisation of this indeterminate

---

25 Recital 75 of Directive (EU) 2019/770; *Möllnitz*, MMR 2021, 116 (118).

26 See I., third bullet point.

27 *Möllnitz*, MMR 2021, 116 (116).

28 Begr. RegE, BT-Drs. 19/27653, 77; *Staudenmayer*, NJW 2019, 2497 (2501); *Spindler*, MMR 2021, 528 (531); *Spindler/Sein*, MMR 2019, 488 (493); *Pech*, GRUR-Prax 2021, 547 (548); *Bach*, NJW 2019, 1705 (177).

29 *Möllnitz*, MMR 2021, 116 (118/119); *Spindler/Sein*, MMR 2019, 488 (493).

30 In so far the draft version of section 327r no. 1 BGB-E (BT-Drucksache 19/27653) differed from Art. 19 DCD (*Möllnitz*, MMR 2021, 116, 118 f.) but was finally adopted to the wording of the DCD.

31 Spindler, MMR 2021, 528 (531); Möllnitz, MMR 2021, 116 (118/119); Spindler/Sein, MMR 2019, 488 (493).

legal term is necessary for the consumer's understanding. Recital (75) DCD provides a list with valid reasons. These reasons could be involved in the trader's modification clause, provided they fit to the trader's respective situation. The agreement shall exhaustively cover all reasons, which could lead to a modification in the sense of section 327r BGB in the specific case.

For the trader to be entitled to change the service in the specific case, a valid reason must actually exist. In this context, one might refer to recital (75) of the Directive, according to which a valid reason exists if "the modification is necessary to adapt the digital content or digital services to a new technical environment or to an increased number of users or for other important operational reasons".

The modification must be made without any additional cost to the consumer, section 327r (1) no. 2 BGB. This concerns only costs that are caused by the modification and covers direct as well as indirect[32] additional costs.

3. *Requirements and consequences of the consumer information*

The consumer shall receive a clear and comprehensible information prior to the modification, section 327r (1) no. 3 BGB. Section 327r (2) BGB requires the information to be provided in a reasonable time before the modification. In the case of section 327r (1) no. 3 BGB this must happen at the latest when the modification is made.[33] In case the information does not correspond with the actual modification, the trader is not entitled to modify.[34]

Where the planned modification to the service has more than a minor negative impact on the use of or access to the digital content or digital services of the consumer, the additional requirements of section 327r (2) BGB must be observed. The German translation of a "minor" negative impact within the meaning of Art. 19 (1)(d), section 327r (2) BGB has been adapted to the terminology of the German Civil Code; the term "insignificant" impact is therefore used.

According to Recital (75), whether there is a minor negative impact is to be ascertained by means of objective criteria. The relevant criteria are the nature and purpose of the digital content and services as well as the

32 For example: if the modification causes the necessity of further modifications at/in the consumer's digital settings/environment.

33 *Möllnitz*, MMR 2021, 116 (119).

34 *Spindler*, MMR 2021, 528 (531).

quality, functionality, compatibility and other essential characteristics as they are usual for comparable services of the same kind. The graphical modification of the user interface without impact on functionality is probably insignificant.[35]

The information to the consumer about the modification must be provided in a clear and comprehensible manner. The notification of the change must additionally contain information about the features and the time of the modification. Further, the consumers must be informed about their rights under section 327r (3), (4) BGB. According to section 327r (2) BGB this information must be provided within a reasonable time in advance and on a durable medium. Art. 2 no. (13) DCD defines the term “durable medium”. Section 126b (1) sentence 2 BGB contains a provision corresponding to the definition in Art. 2 No. 13 DCD. In this respect, information in text form is required. Such durable media are in particular paper, DVDs, CDs, USB sticks, memory cards and hard drives as well as e-mails. Publishing the information on the website is not sufficient.[36] A durable medium should enable the consumer to store the information for as long as is necessary to protect the interests of the consumer arising from the consumer's relationship with the trader.[37]

4. *Right of the consumer to terminate the contract, section 327r (3), (4) BGB*

If the modification does not only have a minor impact, the consumer has an extraordinary right to terminate the contract according to section 327r (3), (4) BGB. The consumer can terminate the contract for digital products free of charge within 30 days after receipt of the above-mentioned information by the trader or after the modification in the service, whichever is later. However, a right to terminate the contract is not given despite more than a minor negative impact if the trader has made it possible for the consumer to retain the original content or service unchanged without additional costs. Still, the contractual conformity of the performance must be ensured. In this case, there is no need for the consumer to have a right to terminate the contract.

The consequence of the right to terminate the contract is that the provisions of section 327o BGB and section 327p BGB apply via section

35 Begr. RegE, BT-Drs. 19/27653, 79.

36 EuGH, MMR 2012, 730 – Content Services Ltd/Bundesarbeitskammer.

37 Recital 76 of Directive (EU) 2019/770.

327r (5) BGB. According to these, the consumer must exercise the right of termination by making a statement to the trader. This statement must clearly express the intention to terminate the contract.

The following obligations of the trader result from section 327o BGB. The trader shall in principle reimburse all payments made under the contract. However, there is a restriction in section 327o (3) BGB, that a refund is only to be made on a pro rata basis for the period in which the digital content or digital services had not been in conformity and for such payments that were made in advance for the remaining contractual period. The refund must be made within 14 days of receipt of the notice of termination at the latest. It shall be made using the means of payment that the consumer used. Another means of payment can only be used if the consumer agrees, and no additional charges are incurred by him.

In return, the trader can prevent further use of the content or services by the consumer (section 327p BGB). At the same time, the consumer is obliged to refrain from further use and disclosure to third parties. Insofar as the consumer has provided or created content when using the digital content or digital services, he can demand these within section 327p (3) BGB. If digital content was also provided by the trader on a physical data carrier, the trader may demand that the consumer return it within 14 days of the termination notice (section 327o (5) BGB).

5. *Contract design in terms and conditions*

In B2C business traders ordinarily use standardised clauses regulating the modification right in the form of general terms and conditions. Under German law, standard clauses are governed by specific rules (section 305 et seq. BGB). In particular, section 308 no. 4 BGB remains unaffected[38] by section 327r BGB and must be taken into account. In principle, section 808 no. 4 BGB prevents a unilateral right to modify the contractually agreed performance obligations of the trader or deviate from them, unless the agreement of the modification or deviation can reasonably be expected of the consumer to the contract when the interests of the trader are taken into account.

On EU level Annex No. 1 lit. j) and k) of Directive 93/13/EEC regulate that contractual provisions are unfair which permit a unilateral alter of terms of the contract or unilateral alter of characteristics of the product or

38 *Spindler*, MMR 2021, 528 (531).

services to be provided by the trader without a valid reason which – in case of Annex No. 1 lit. j) – the trader has to specify in the contract. Art. 19 DCD and section 327r BGB do not prescribe examples for valid reasons or reason what can be reasonably expected by the consumer. But Art. 19 DCD and section 327r BGB provide a more detailed and balanced regime for taking into account the interests of both parties and give them appropriate rights. Both rules are in line with and specifications of Annex No. 1 lit. j) and k) of Directive 93/13/EEC resp. section 308 no. 4 BGB.

According to Art. 22 (1) DCD the above-mentioned provisions are of a mandatory nature. In the case of the modification right, an exclusion or variation to the detriment of the consumer is only permitted after the consumer has become aware of the specific change through the trader, see section 327s (2) BGB. A deviation from the regulation that is disadvantageous to the consumer would not be valid. In contrast, a consumer-friendly deviation is possible and contractual provisions that increase the protection in favour of the consumer can be valid.

However, for the time being it is advisable for traders not to deviate from section 327r BGB and wait for the courts to create a higher level of certainty on possible consumer-friendly deviations.[39] As a result, the trader's right of modification should correspond with the explicit requirements of section 327r BGB. Contract clauses which correspond with the essential principles of statutory provisions – such as section 327r BGB – can still be ineffective if they are not clear and comprehensible, section 307 (1) sentence 2 BGB. Copying the wording of the statutory provision within the contract does not necessarily qualify for a clear and comprehensible contract term.[40]

---

39 German Federal Court of justice (BGH), decision of May 13, 2014 – XI ZR 405/12. A user of a standard clause has used a clause that under former German jurisdiction was regarded ineffective because of section 307 BGB. However, the relevant jurisdiction of the highest court changed and the user of the clause was confident that now the clause will be effective. The BGH ruled against this confidence of the user.

40 Under German law in B2C standard terms for digital products the notification about the consumer's cancellation right (Widerrufsbelehrung) is subject to extensive jurisdiction. Among others it was discussed whether the official „BGB-Informationspflichtenverordnung" (BGB-InfoV) which provided a template for a cancellation notification was sufficiently transparent and whether standard clauses copying the BGB-InfoV template could violated the transparency requirement of section 307 (1) section 2 BGB and be regarded ineffective. See e.g. BGH, decision of August 15, 2012 – VIII ZR 378/11.

In the context of section 307 (1) sentence 2 BGB, the provision concerned must be sufficiently defined which requires a detailed description of the individual rights and obligations resulting from the right of modification. Recently it can be observed in the B2C market that traders inform consumers about their B2C business terms in a non-legal and very consumer friendly language. For example, Google informs customers about "How our business works" which includes explainations about how Google makes money with customers' data[41] which can be relevant for contracts where the consumers does not pay money but has an obligation to provide data beyond what is strictly necessary for the fulfilment of the contract. Furthermore, Google informs consumers about their modifications of the terms of use coming into effect on January 5, 2022.[42] Google informed about "what you can expect from Google and what Google can expect from you when you continue to use the service". The customer can active links to a preview of the new terms of use and a summary of the most important changes.

Broad and generic clauses which need to be interpreted by the consumer are not recommended. This applies in particular for the valid reasons to be given by the trader in the contract. In particular, an exhaustive enumeration of specified valid reasons is required. This is the only way for the consumer to know without any special effort when the trader has a right of modification and when he does not, and which rights and obligations result for him from this.

IV. Examination of contract clauses regarding the new legal provisions

If one examines currently used provisions in terms and conditions that provide a right of modification for the trader, it is noticeable that these provisions on a regular basis do not comply with the new requirements of section 327r BGB. Some examples are shown below:

41 https://about.google/intl/de_DE/how-our-business-works/ (link activated on October 5, 2021).

42 https://policies.google.com/terms?hl=de (link activated on November 20, 2021).

No	Clauses in terms and conditions	Right of modification according to Art. 19 DCD and section 327r BGB		
		Art. 19 (1) DCD / section 327r (1) BGB: "contract provides that the digital content or digital service is to be supplied or made accessible […] over a period of time"	Art. 19 (1)(a) DCD / section 327r (1) No. 1 BGB: "contract allows, and provides a valid reason for, such a modification"	Art 19 (1)(b) DCD/ section 327r (1) No. 2 BGB: "modification is made without additional cost to the consumer"
1	**Amazon Prime Video** **"d. Modification of Service.** Amazon reserves the right to *modify, suspend, or discontinue the Service, or any part of the Service, at any time and without notice* (except as required by applicable law), and Amazon will not be liable to you should it exercise such rights, even if your ability to use Digital Content is impacted by the change." https://www.primevideo.com/help?nodeId=202095490&language=de_DE&view-type=content-only (07.05.2021)	✓ Contract concerning provision of videofiles via streaming for a monthly monetary payment	× "Amazon reserves the right to modify (…)" Contract allows modification only in general, but does not contain a restriction by the requirement of a valid reason (in the contract and in case of a specific modification)	× No exclusion of additional costs
2	**Microsoft** "c. We are continually working to improve the services and, to that extent, we reserve the right at any time to change the services, delete features or discontinue access to third party apps and services. This applies especially if our contracts with third parties no longer allow us to provide their material, if it is no longer practical for us to do so, if technology evolves or if customer feedback indicates that a change is necessary. We will notify you in advance if a change to the services will result in you no longer having access to your content. For paid services, we will also notify you in advance of other significant changes to the services. […]. If we terminate a chargeable service, we will refund to you on a pro rata basis the amount of any payments you have made in respect of the unpaid por-	✓ Contract concerning provision of different digital contents or services like communication or cloud services and applications for a monetary payment or a payment with personal data	× "(…) we reserve the right at any time to change the services, delete features or discontinue access to third party apps and services. This applies in especially if our contracts with third parties no longer allow us to provide their material, if it is no longer practical for us to do so, if technology evolves or if customer feedback indicates that a change is necessary."	× No exclusion of additional costs

	tion of the relevant Service at the time of termination." https://www.microsoft.com/de-de/servicesagreement/ (translated) (07.05.2021)		Contract allows modification any time; reasons for change only examples ("especially") but no requirement	
3	**Apple iCloud**	✓	✗	✗
	"YOU EXPRESSLY UNDERSTAND AND AGREE THAT APPLE […] SHALL NOT BE LIABLE TO YOU FOR ANY […] DAMAGES, INCLUDING, BUT NOT LIMITED TO, DAMAGES FOR LOSS OF PROFITS, GOODWILL, USE, DATA, COST OF PROCUREMENT OF SUBSTITUTE GOODS OR SERVICES, OR OTHER INTANGIBLE LOSSES […], RESULTING FROM: (I) THE USE OR INABILITY TO USE THE SERVICE (II) ANY CHANGES MADE TO THE SERVICE OR ANY TEMPORARY OR PERMANENT CESSATION OF THE SERVICE OR ANY PART THEREOF; […]" https://www.apple.com/uk/legal/internet-services/icloud/en/terms.html (07.05.2021)	Contract concerning provision of cloud-services via access to storage capabilities for a monthly monetary payment or a payment with personal data	Clause leads to indirect right to modify services (as liability for damages resulting from changes to the service is excluded) No explicit right of modification in case of a valid reason for the modification	No exclusion of additional costs

No	Clauses in terms and conditions	Right of modification according to Art. 19 DCD and section 327r BGB-E		
		Art. 19 (1)(c) DCD/ section 327r (1) No. 3 BGB: "consumer is informed in a clear and comprehensible manner of the modification"	Art. 19 (1)(d) DCD/ section 327r (2) BGB: additional rights in the case of negative impacts on the access or use	General requirements of section 307 et seq.. BGB
1		✗	✗	✗
		"(…) without notice (except as required by applicable law)"	No differentiation between "positive" and "negative" modifications for the consumer No right of termination for the consumer	"(…) without notice (except as required by applicable law)" No certainty due to blanket reference to applica-

				ble law, section 307 (1) BGB Conflict with section 308 no. 4 BGB, as no valid reason is required for modification
2	**Amazon Prime Video** **“d. Modification of Service.** Amazon reserves the right to *modify, suspend, or discontinue the Service, or any part of the Service, at any time and without notice* (except as required by applicable law), and Amazon will not be liable to you should it exercise such rights, even if your ability to use Digital Content is impacted by the change.” https://www.primevideo.com/help?nodeId=202095490&language=de_DE&view-type=content-only (07.05.2021)	× “We will notify you in advance if a change to the Services will result in you no longer having access to your content. For paid services, we will also notify you in advance of other significant changes to the Services.” Notification is only provided in cases of loss of access or significant changes of paid services; no notification in other cases	× “We will notify you in advance if a change to the Services will result in you no longer having access to your content. For paid services, we will also notify you in advance of other significant changes to the Services […]. If we terminate a chargeable Service, we will refund to you on a pro rata basis the amount of any payments you have made in respect of the unpaid portion of the relevant Service at the time of termination.” No special requirements for the notification No right of termination for the consumer; refund of payment only if trader terminates the service	×
3	**Apple iCloud** “YOU EXPRESSLY UNDERSTAND AND AGREE THAT APPLE […] SHALL NOT BE LIABLE TO YOU FOR ANY […] DAMAGES, INCLUDING, BUT NOT LIMITED TO, DAMAGES FOR LOSS OF PROFITS, GOODWILL,	× Notification is not provided	× Notification or right of termination depending on impact on access to services is not provided	× section 309 nos. 7, 8 BGB must be observed

	USE, DATA, COST OF PROCUREMENT OF SUBSTITUTE GOODS OR SERVICES, OR OTHER INTANGIBLE LOSSES […], RESULTING FROM: (I) THE USE OR INABILITY TO USE THE SERVICE (II) ANY CHANGES MADE TO THE SERVICE OR ANY TEMPORARY OR PERMANENT CESSATION OF THE SERVICE OR ANY PART THEREOF; […]" https://www.apple.com/uk/legal/internet-services/icloud/en/terms.html (07.05.2021)		

V. Clause proposal considering the new legal regulations

A sample wording for a right of modification in legal language (not in everyday consumer language which should be improved in the following example) could look like this:

Section X Right of modification by the trader

(1) The trader is entitled to modify the contractually agreed service[43]*or a part of the service beyond what is necessary to maintain the contractually agreed service in conformity according to section xx of this agreement at any time, provided the contractually agreed service is supplied or made accessible to the consumer over a period of time and there is valid reason to do so.*[44] *This applies to both modifications in favour of the consumer and to modifications to the detriment of the consumer.*[45]

(2) A valid reason within the meaning of this provision is given if the modification is necessary in order to adapt the contractually agreed service to

43 The term "contractually agreed service" shall be defined in the agreement under der section "Definitions". The contractually agreed service contains the provision of digital content or digital service, which is supplied or made accessible to the consumer by the trader.

44 See Art. 19 (1)(d) DCD, section 327r (1) no. 1 BGB.

45 Clarification for reasons of certainty, see section 307 (1) BGB.

a new technical environment or to an increased number of users, or if it is necessary for other important operational reasons.[46]

(3) The modification shall be made without any additional cost to the consumer[47]

(4) In the case that the modification has only a minor negative impact on the access to or use of the contractually agreed service, the customer shall be informed of this in text form at the latest when the modification is made.[48]

(5) In the cases that the modification has a more than a minor negative impact on the use of the contractually agreed service, the consumer shall be informed of the modification in text form within a reasonable period before the modification is made.[49] *This notification shall contain information on the features and the time of the modification, as well as the right of the consumer to terminate the contract.*[50]

(6) In case of a more than minor negative impact, the consumer shall be entitled to terminate the contract free of charge within 30 days of receipt of the notification as regulated above in paragraph 5 or after the digital content or digital services have been modified, depending on whichever is later.[51]

(7) The consumer is not entitled to terminate if the trader has enabled the consumer to keep the contractually agreed service unchanged without additional costs, and the conformity of the contractually agreed service is preserved.[52]

(8) Any declaration of termination by the consumer in accordance with paragraph 6 above, shall be made in text form or written form.[53] *In the*

---

46 Clarification for reasons of certainty, see section 307 (1) BGB; see Recital 75 for the exemplary enumeration. Please note, that the clause has to cover all reasons due to them trader should be entitled to modify the contractually agreed service in the specific case.

47 See Art. 19 (1)(b), section 327 (1) no. 2 BGB.

48 See Art. 19 (2) DCD, section 327r (2) BGB and Art 19 (1)(c) DCD, section 327r (1) No. 3 BGB; although no spe-cific form is specified for this case, regarding the provability text form might be better suited than no form.

49 See Art. 19 (1)(d) DCD, section 327r (2) BGB; text form within the meaning of section 126b BGB corresponds to the definition of the durable medium in Art. 2 (13) DCD.

50 Clarification for reasons of certainty, see section 307 (1) BGB.

51

52 See Art. 19 (4) DCD, section 327r (4) BGB.

53 See Art. 19 (3), 15 DCD, sections 327r (5), 327o (1) BGB.

case of a termination, the trader shall reimburse, at no additional cost to the consumer, all sums paid under the contract within 14 days of receipt of the termination declaration, using the same means of payment that the consumer has used for their payments. Provided that no additional charges are incurred by the consumer and the consumer has agreed to this, the refund may also be made by other means.[54] *The trader shall reimburse the consumer for the proportionate part of the price paid corresponding to the period of time during which the service was not in conformity. Furthermore, refunds shall be made for payments the consumer made in advance for any period of the contract that would have remained if the contract had not been terminated.*[55]

In return, the trader is entitled to prevent any further use.[56] *At the same time, the cosumer is obliged to refrain from using the contractually agreed service and from making them available to third parties.*[57]
The consumer may demand the return of content provided or created by the consumer during the use of the contractually agreed service – insofar as it is not personal data – within a proper period of time from the trader in a commonly used and machine-readable format.[58]
The trader is entitled to demand the return of the physical data carrier on which the contractually agreed service / digital content was provided from the consumer within 14 days of knowledge of the consumer's termination declaration. In this case, the consumer shall be obliged to return it immediately at the expense of the trader.[59]

VI. Contract design regarding the right of modification in B2B relationship

Traders in B2B context are more flexible to create on standard terms. Both the DCD and section 327r BGB apply only to contracts in the business-consumer relationship.[60] According to section 310 (1) sentence 1 BGB

54 Art. 19 (3), 16 (1), 18 DCD, section 327r (5), 327o (2), (3), (4), 327n (4) BGB.
55 Art. 19 (3), 16 (1) DCD, section 327r (5), 327o (2), (3) BGB.
56 Art. 19 (3), 16 (5) DCD, section 327r (5), 327p (1) BGB.
57 Art. 19 (3), 17 (1) DCD, section 327r (5), 327p (1) BGB.
58 Art. 19 (3), 16 (4) DCD, section 327r (5), 327p (3) BGB; only required if provision or creation is possible at all within the scope of the concrete digital content or digital services.
59 Art. 19 (3), 16 (4) DCD, section 327r (5), 327p (3) BGB; only required if digital content was made available on data carriers.
60 Art. 3 (1) DCD, section 327 (1) BGB.

for B2B business terms section 308 no. 4 BGB does not apply directly. However, the principles of section 308 BGB are indirectly relevant for the assessment whether a B2B clause is ineffective in accordance with section 307 (1) BGB.

Within a supply chain the recourse-provisions of Art. 20 DCD and section 327t BGB must be observed. Moreover, the (last) trader in the supply chain is in a "sandwich position". If the trader does not technically modify the digital product but receives modified products by the suppliers, the B2C trader should agree with its suppliers clauses corresponding with section 327r BGB. It would even be necessary that the suppliers' information obligations go beyond what is required under section 327r BGB regarding when and how the trader is to be informed. In particular, the trader will probably need even more details about the specific modification and consequences for consumers than the consumer will receive from the trader. Otherwise, the trader risks that the trader cannot inform the consumer as required by section 327r BGB. It is likely that section 327r BGB exceeds its relevance for consumer law and will, in practice, be very important in B2B context, too. Regarding section 327r BGB the relevance of passing on the legal requirements within the supply chain is obvious.

Another effect of the DCD could be that in future, B2B end customers want to be treated equally as consumers with regard to modification rights but also with regard to update obligations of the trader. A trader concluding contracts with consumers and B2B end customers probably will not have good arguments why B2B end customers a discriminated although they probably have to pay a much higher price and the relevance of modifications and negative impact for them could be much higher.

VII. Conclusion

The advantages of a modification right are that traders are more flexible in their product design and can regularly offer only one version of their digital product to all customers. For the consumer, however, such changes can also be advantageous, as they improve the products. Art. 19 DCD and its transposition into section 327r BGB create a balance of interests as the modification right must have narrow limits and the consumer's right to terminate the contract is stipulated under certain conditions. It is to be expected that the courts will have to deal with the question of when a "minor" or "insignificant" impact within the meaning of Art. 19 (2) DCD, section 327r (2) BGB is given and which specific deviations from the provisions in favour of the consumer are permissible within the Art. 22 (2) DCD, section 327s (2) BGB.

One will see how the new right of modification proves itself in practice and case law. The DCD will not only affect B2C standard business terms, but also back-to-back agreements with suppliers / sub providers (B2B). Example: the trader can only inform the consumer about details of a modification with negative impact if the software supplier has informed the trader correspondingly and in timely manner. Furthermore, it is very likely that consumer rights will influence the expectations and requirements of B2B customers who probably in the future will not accept a weaker position in their contracts.

By rule of thumb the following recommendations apply for the design of a valid modification clause:

- The clauses should clearly differentiate between modifications necessary to keep the digital content / service in conformity and modifications beyond that.
- The reasons for modifications beyond keeping conformity should (a) be in line with recital 75 DCD, (b) be comprehensibly specified, including specification of "*other important operational reasons*"[61], (c) provide specification of positive and negative impacts for the consumer, (d) taking into account legitimate reasons of the consumer, including e.g. the consumer's reliance on market standards, (e) be exhaustive[62].
- In general, it is not necessarily helpful to repeat the wording of the DCD / German Act in the clauses. However, deviations of the DCD's wording could be risky too: E.g. the meaning of „*the negative impact is only minor*" is not identical with terms such as „*the consumer is entitled to terminate if the negative impact is substantial*" and a trader using the latter term would violate Art. 19 DCD and section 327r BGB.
- No specific form (e.g. textual form) for the consumer's declaration of termination is required in the DCD. However, a clause that states the consumer's declaration shall be in written form (section 126 BGB) will very likely be considered ineffective.[63]

61 Recital 75 DCD.

62 A non-exhaustive exemplary list of reasons („*valid reasons such as…*") should be avoided.

63 *Spindler*, MMR 2016 (223).

Non-contractual liability for smart products

Software as a Product

Gerhard Wagner[1]

I. Introduction: Why the Question is Important

1. The Impact of Digitization

The digital transformation of industry and society is well under way. Again, technological advances change the world around us in general, and the commodities that we buy und use in particular. The industrial revolutions of the past brought the steam engine and electricity, the current industrial revolution is powered by software. The very term "software" has developed in opposition to "hardware", i.e. corporeal artefacts. Software itself is non-corporeal, but a major part of its function is to operate hardware in space and time. The capacity of software to operate hardware gadgets is not entirely new. It is familiar since the invention of the computer, i.e. digital machines whose sole purpose it is to run software. What is new to the digital transformation that is under way now is the spread of software from computers into products of any kind, from machinery stacked in factories, to ships, trains, airplanes and cars, to household appliances of any kind, from refrigerators to lawn mowers. As these products tend to be connected to each other and to cloud-based servers, they establish what has come to be called the "Internet of Things" (IoT).

Digitization in general, and the Internet of Things in particular, pose serious challenges to existing liability regimes. The shift from user control to manufacturer control necessitates that liability rules zoom in on manufacturers and abandon their focus on users, such as owners, keepers, and operators of machinery or other products.[2] This shift in focus from users to

---

1 Chair for Private Law, Business Law, and Law and Economics at the Humboldt University in Berlin.

2 Gerhard Wagner, 'Robot Liability' in Sebastian Lohsse, Reiner Schulze, Dirk Staudenmayer (eds), *Liability for Artificial Intelligence and the Internet of Things* (Nomos 2019) 27, 37–39; Gerhard Wagner, 'Produkthaftung für autonome Systeme' (2017) 217 Archiv für die civilistische Praxis 707, 709 seq, 761 et seq; Gerhard Wagner, 'Verantwortlichkeit im Zeichen digitaler Techniken' (2020) Zeitschrift für Versicherungsrecht 717, 724; Herbert Zech, 'Entscheidungen digitaler autonomer

manufacturers places one area of law into the limelight that is particularly designed to govern the liability of manufacturers, namely products liability.

2. *Products Liability*

Within the European Union, products liability is one of the few areas of non-contractual liability governed by Union law. Council Directive 85/374/EEC on the approximation of the laws, regulations and administrative provisions of the Member States concerning liability for defective products, the so-called Product Liability Directive (PLD),[3] defines a uniform framework for the liability of manufacturers vis-á-vis victims, i.e. product users as well as bystanders. Among the class of liable parties the Directive includes original equipment manufacturers, i.e. the producers that put the product into the stream of commerce, as well as component manufacturers, alongside importers and, under certain conditions, merchants (Art. 4 PDL).

Responsibility under the Directive does not require the establishment of fault on the part of the producer or another liable entity. Rather, the framers of the Directive assumed that liability for defective products was a form of strict liability. In the time since 1985, legal scholarship has come to realize that the concept of product defect incorporates much of the analysis that also determines the concept of negligence. This is particularly true for the most important categories of product defect, namely design defects, and failure to warn.

Given the dominance of the Product Liability Directive in European Union law, the question arises whether software qualifies as a "product" for purposes of the Directive. Unfortunately, the answer is far from clear.

3. *National Law*

If software did not qualify as a product and thus fell outside the scope of the Product Liability Directive, this would not be the end of the world for the law of tort or delict. Products liability is not an exception to a general

Systeme: Empfehlen sich Regelungen zu Verantwortung und Haftung?' (Verhandlungen des Deutschen Juristentags 2020), at A 88 seq.

3 OJ L 210/29.

principle of no-liability but rather a special segment of tort law that exclusively deals with the liability of product manufacturers. Pursuant to the jurisprudence of the ECJ, the Directive is conclusive with regard to the liability of product manufacturers in the sense that national law must not derogate from its provisions.[4] However, outside the scope of the Directive, national tort law applies. If software did not qualify as a product within the meaning of Art. 2 PLD, software "manufacturers" would not be exempt from liability, but rather would be subject to the liability regimes of national tort law.

The tort law regimes of the Member States of the European Union are quite diverse, but they rest on common principles.[5] The bedrock principle of the common European law of tort is the principle of fault, i.e. the responsibility of private parties for negligent behavior or violation of a duty of care. Another common element in European tort law is the countervailing principle of strict liability which serves as a supplement to the fault principle. The scope of application of strict liability varies greatly among the legal systems of the Member States. The common denominator is that strict liability applies to certain categories of machinery and installations, and potentially even to any "thing" under anyone's "guard".[6] The most common head of strict liability in Europe involves motor traffic, i.e. the operation of a motor car on a public road.[7]

4 Case C-52/00 *Commission v France* [2002] ECR I-3827, para 24; Case C-154/00 *Commission v Greece* [2002] ECR I-3879, para 20; Whittaker, 'Form and Sustance in the Harmonisation of Product Liability in Europe. Judgement of the European Court of Justice of 10 January 2006' (2007) Zeitschrift für Europäisches Privatrecht 858 (note); Case C-621/15 *Sanofi Pasteur* [2017] EU:C:2017:484, para 20.

5 Christian von Bar, *The Common European Law of Torts*, vol. 2 (Oxford UP 2000) para 224 et seq; Gerhard Wagner, 'Comparative Tort Law' in Mathias Reimann, Reinhard Zimmermann (eds), The Oxford Handbook of Comparative Law (2nd edn, Oxford UP 2019) 994, 1013 et seq; Cees van Dam, *European Tort Law* (2nd edn, Oxford UP 2013) 230 et seq.

6 Gerhard Wagner, 'Custodian's Liability' in Jürgen Basedow, Klaus J. Hopt, Reinhard Zimmermann (eds), *The Max Planck Encyclopedia of European Private Law*, vol. 1 (Oxford UP 2012) 441–442; Gerhard Wagner, 'Strict Liability' in Jürgen Basedow, Klaus J. Hopt, Reinhard Zimmermann (eds), *The Max Planck Encyclopedia of European Private Law*, vol. 2 (Oxford UP 2012) 1607–1609; Francois Terré, Philippe Simler, Yves Lequette, Francois Chénedé, *Droit civil. Les obligations* (12th edn, Dallos 2018) para 1011.

7 Cees van Dam, *European Tort Law* (2nd ed., Oxford UP 2013) 408–420.

II. A Primer on the Scope of the Product Liability Directive

The scope of products liability law is defined in an almost tautological way: it applies to products, and not to non-products. But what are products? Without much ado, legal systems that operate a distinct branch of tort law dealing with liability for harm caused by product defects generally assume that products are things, i.e. corporeal assets. If one looks closer, however, the boundaries become blurred. The difficulties arise precisely in those areas where intellectual property, or rather: information, comes into play. The old-school version of the problem arose when information was "stored" in books, journals, or newspapers, and the information turned out to be inaccurate.[8] A book undoubtedly qualifies as chattel and thus as a product, but the information contained in the book is not physical but intellectual. Thus, it is far from clear whether product liability law applies to inaccurate reports in books, journals, and newspapers, and, if so, who qualifies as the manufacturer of such information. Here, the choice is between the author and the publisher.

The processes of technological innovation summarized under the term digitization are driven by computer programs. Without software, the digital hardware would be literally useless. For a long time, software was stored on physical assets, such as floppy disks, hard disks, CDs, DVDs, USB-Sticks and the like. As long as this was the case, courts and commentators could use an intellectual detour and focus on the corporeal storage device, which clearly qualified as a product. The obvious questions of whether the computer code stored on the device shared the same classification and whether a storage device was rendered defective for purposes of products liability law if the information stored on that device was inaccurate were never asked.

Under Union law these same questions arise under the special regime of the Product Liability Directive. The Directive itself provides a definition of "product" in Art. 2. In relevant part, Art. 2 PLD provides that "product" means "all movables", regardless of whether incorporated into another movable or immovable, including electricity. Now the problem lying at the core of this article has become clear: Does software qualify as a "movable" within the meaning of Art. 2 PLD?

---

8 Cf. Gerhard Wagner in *Münchener Kommentar zum Bürgerlichen Gesetzbuch: BGB* (8th edn, CH Beck 2020) § 2 ProdHaftG para 16 et seq; Simon Whittaker, *Liability for Products* (Oxford UP 2005) 477 seq; as to U.S. law David G. Owen, *Products Liability Law* (3rd edn, West Academic 2015) 1040 et seq.

Before delving into the interpretation of Art. 2 of the Directive, it is advisable to broaden the horizon. The Product Liability Directive is not the only legal instrument that grapples with the problem of classification of software. In today's economy, software is an important subject matter of commercial transactions. Therefore, one would expect that the question as to whether software qualifies as a product arises in other contexts as well. As we shall see, this is exactly the case.

III. Software under Union Law

Products liability law is not the only branch of the legal system where the classification of software as a product surfaces. As a survey of current Union law reveals, the classification of software is problematic across the full range of legal sources, from the EU treaties down to the customs regulation, VAT, product safety, contract law, and commercial law.

1. Fundamental Freedoms

In its chapter on the internal market, the TFEU enshrines the fundamental economic freedoms, particularly the free movement of goods (Art. 28 et seq TFEU), and the freedom to provide services (Art. 56 et seq. TFEU). As different regimes of protection apply to goods and services, respectively, it is important to distinguish between the two categories. When applying the treaty provisions on the customs union, the ECJ clearly distinguishes between goods and services. The scope of the EC treaties' provisions on the free movement of goods was held to be confined to "tangible property", to the exclusion of "incorporeal property such as processes, services or know-how".[9] This jurisprudence is reflected in the Union Customs Regulation which applies to "goods brought into or taken out of the customs territory of the Union".[10] The Customs Regulation explicitly distinguishes between goods on the one hand, and "goods and services" on the other, for the pur-

9 Case 1/77 *Bosch v Hauptzollamt Hildesheim* [1977] ECR 1473, para 4.

10 Union Customs Code Regulation (EU) 952/2013 of 9 October 2013, OJ L 269/1, Art. 1 (1).

pose of determining the customs value of the merchandise.[11] In this context, the CJEU has classified software as a service, and not as a good.[12]

In the context of Art. 34 TFEU, i.e. the prohibition of quantitative restrictions on imports and other measures having the same effect, the Court is more lenient. In particular, the Court classifies electricity as a "good" within the meaning of the provisions protecting the freedom of movement.[13] However, the inclusion of electricity into the scope of protection of freedom of movement of goods does not mean that any asset, whether corporeal or not, qualifies as a good and comes within the protective perimeter of the guarantee of free movement of goods. Thus, the Court rejected the idea of classifying a television signal as a "good" for the purpose of the fundamental freedoms and squarely classified it as a service.[14]

Thus, the Court refused to accept fishing rights as "goods" within the meaning of the EU treaties, Art. 23 EC at the time. To come under the umbrella of the freedom of movement of goods it was held not to be enough, that the object in question could be valued in money and was capable of forming the subject of commercial transactions.[15] The main reason for withholding the status of goods was the lack of an identifiable object of the transaction. It was said the grant of fishing rights and the issue of fishing permits were activities, not goods. Thus, the Court concluded that the grant of fishing rights qualified as a service.[16]

2. VAT

The value added tax regime of the European Union is contained in Directive 2006/112/EC which,[17] in relevant part, clearly distinguishes between goods and services. While both categories are subject to VAT, exemptions and rates of taxation may differ. The CJEU ruled that the supply of electronic books must be classified as a service, and not as the supply of a

---

11 Ibid, Art. 71 (1) (b).

12 Case C-509/19 *BMW v Hauptzollamt München* [2020] EU:C:2020:694, para 18.

13 Case C-393/92 *Almelo v Energiebedrijf Ijsselmij* [1994] ECR I-1508, para 28; cf. also Case 6/64 *Costa v Enel* [1964] ECR 585, 587, 597 et seq.

14 Case 155/73 *Sacchi* [1974] ECR 409, para 6.

15 Case C-97/98 *Jägerskiöld v Gustafsson* [1999] ECR I-7319, para 33.

16 Ibid, para 30 et seq, 36.

17 Council Directive 2006/112/EC of 28 November 2006 on the common system of value added tax, [2006] OJ L347/1.

good. This conclusion was based on the argument that electronic books are non-corporeal and thus do not qualify as "tangible property".[18]

3. Product Safety

Product safety law is the public law equivalent of products liability law. The current Product Safety Directive 2001/95/EC[19] does not address the issue whether software qualifies as a product. The Commission proposal for a Regulation on general product safety of 2021,[20] which is designed to replace the Product Safety Directive, explicitly sets the aim of clarifying that product safety law also applies to software.[21] However, the definition of "product" in Art. 3(1) of the Commission proposal remains silent in this regard.[22] At least, the proposed regulation would create a right to software updates, which implies that software embedded in a tangible product must be regarded as being part of such product and thus as being subject to product safety regulation.[23]

Within current EU law, the Machinery Directive clarifies that the safety requirements for control systems do not apply to the hardware, but also to the software.[24] Similar obligations are imposed by the Radio Equipment Directive.[25] These acts recognize that software exists and poses risks but do not move beyond embedded software. In doing so, they classify software that operates hardware as part of this hardware, but not as a product in its own right.

---

18 Case C-479/13 *French Republic v Kingdom of Belgium* [2015] EU:C:2015:141, para 35.

19 Directive 2001/95/EC of the European Parliament and the Council of 3 December 2001 on general product safety [2002] OJ L11/4.

20 Commission (EC) 'Proposal for a Regulation of the European Parliament and the Council on general product safety' COM (2021) 346 final, 30 June 2021.

21 Ibid, 14.

22 Ibid, Art. 3 para 1.

23 Ibid, Art. 35 para 2.

24 Directive 2006/42/EC of the European Parliament and the Council of 17 May 2006 on machinery, [2006] OJ L157/24, Annex I Section 1.2.1.

25 Directive 2014/53/EU of the European Parliament and of the Council of 16 April 2014 on the harmonisation of the laws of the Member States relating to the making available on the market of radio equipment [2014] OJ L153/62, Art. 3(3)(i).

Regulation (EU) 2017/745 on medical devices[26] goes one important step further and addresses the issue of software head-on. Art. 2(4) of the Regulation defines the term "active device" as a device that depends on a source of energy for its operation, and adds the clarification that "software shall also be deemed an active device". This definition is remarkable as it does not cover the case of software being embedded in a hardware device. Rather Art. 2(4) says that software as such, even without hardware, shall be classified as a device, thus unlocking the application of the Medical Devices Regulation. In the Brain Products case the CJEU affirmed that, even under the Medical Devices Directive 1993, as amended in 2007, software is a medical device "in its own right" when designed for use in medical services.[27]

4. *Contract and Commercial Law*

Union legislation in the area of contract and commercial law did not address particular types of contracts and refrained from regulating contracts with a view to particular items which are the subject matter that the parties are contracting about. This has changed with the Digital Content Directive of 2019.[28] Art. 2(3) of the Directive defines the concept of "goods with digital elements" as "any tangible movable items that incorporate or are interconnected with, digital content or a digital service in such a way that the absence of that digital content or digital service would prevent the goods from performing their functions". Likewise, the sister Directive on the sale of goods incorporates special provisions on tangible movable items that incorporate or are inter-connected with digital content".[29] Again, the focus remains on the hardware, while the software is not addressed directly but only as a feature of the tangible product.

There is also jurisprudence dealing with software products under the Commercial Sales Agent Directive of 1986. Art. 1(2) of the Directive defines the concept of a "commercial agent" in terms of a self-employed person who serves as an intermediary with authority to negotiate the sale or

26 Regulation (EU) 2017/745 of the European Parliament and the Council of 5 April 2017 on medical devices, [2017] OJ L117/1.

27 Case C-219/11 *Brain Products v BioSemi et al.* [2012] EU:C:2012:742, para 16.

28 Directive (EU) 2019/770 of the European Parliament and the Council of 20 May 2019 on certain aspects concerning contracts for the supply of digital content and digital services, [2019] OJ L136/1.

29 Ibid, Art. 2(5).

purchase of "goods" on behalf of another. In the Software Incubator case, the issue arose whether software that was not to be delivered via a physical storage device but which was to be downloaded from the cloud qualified as "goods" within the meaning of Art. 1(2) of the Directive. The Advocate General answered in the affirmative, based on the argument that "... an interpretation of 'goods' in Article 1(2) of Directive 86/653 as limited to tangible items would allow a principal to circumvent the mandatory provisions of Directive 86/653 [...] simply by arranging for the supply of goods by intangible means. This would undermine the objectives pursued by that directive to provide protection for commercial agents and to promote the security of commercial transactions".[30] The CJEU went along and held that the concept of "goods" under the Commercial Sales Agents Directive was not limited to tangible items but rather included software.[31] The Court was of the view that the term "goods" was neutral as to the tangible or intangible nature of the asset. All that counted was that the item in question had commercial value, which computer software surely had.[32] Moreover, the Court stressed that, from a commercial point of view, the modes and mediums through which computer programs are distributed, be that via a CD, a DVD or a download from the internet, were equivalent so that the application of the Directive could not be dependent on which particular technology was used.[33]

In its opinion in the Software Incubator case, the CJEU relied heavily on its earlier decision in UsedSoft.[34] That case did not involve the question of whether computer programs qualify as "goods" or "products" but concerned the concept of exhaustion under copyright law.[35] But regardless, the UsedSoft Court clearly expressed its unwillingness to treat computer programs differently, depending on whether they were distributed with the help of tangible storage devices, such as CDs or DVDs, or by way of a download from the internet.[36] In doing so, the justices referred to Directive 2009/24/EC[37] and concluded that it made "abundantly clear the

30 Case C-410/19 *The Software Incubator Ltd v Computer Associates (UK) Ltd* EU:C:2020:1061, Opinion of Advocate General Tanchev, para 75.

31 Ibid, para 34 et seq.

32 Ibid, para 35.

33 Ibid, para 38.

34 Ibid, para 38, 41, 42.

35 Case C-128/11 *UsedSoft GmbH v Oracle International* [2012] EU:C:2012:407.

36 Ibid, para 43, 47, 61.

37 Directive 2009/24/EC of the European Parliament and the Council of 23 April 2009, on the legal protection of computer programs [2009] OJ L111/16.

intention of the European Union legislature to assimilate, […] tangible and intangible copies of computer programs".[38] In addition, they pointed to the commercial equivalence of sale on a corporeal storage device and sale via download from the internet.[39]

This position, that the classification of software must not depend on the particular channel and medium through which it is distributed, is not limited to copyright law but lends itself to generalization across different areas of the law. The CJEU seems to share this view, as evidenced by its reliance on UsedSoft when deciding Software Incubator, a case that arose under the Commercial Sales Agent Directive.

5. Conclusions and Observations

As this short survey of Union law reveals, there is no uniform solution to the categorization of software. In some contexts, it is classified as a good, in others it is categorized as a service. With a view to the distinction between the "sale of goods" and contracts for the "provision of services" under the European rules on jurisdiction in civil and commercial matters, the CJEU explicitly rejected the proposition that the concept of services must have a uniform meaning across Union law. The Court acknowledged that it had interpreted the freedom to provide services under what is now Art. 56 TFEU (Art. 50 EC) broadly, but indicated that this approach was motivated by the desire to avoid excluding certain economic activities from the protections of the Treaties.[40] The Court went on to conclude that in the context of the Brussels I Regulation, there was no need to interpret the second indent of the former Art. 5 (1) (b) Regulation 44/2001[41] (now Art. 7 (1) (b) Brussels I Regulation Recast)[42] broadly, so as to ensure that certain types of contracts would not fall outside the scope of jurisdiction over contract-based claims. The crucial point was that Art. 5 (1) (a) and (c) (now Art. 7 (1) (a) and (c) Brussels I Regulation Recast) offered a default mechanism

38 Case C-128/11 *UsedSoft GmbH v Oracle International* [2012] EU:C:2012:407, para 58.

39 Ibid, para 61.

40 Case C-533/07 *Falco Privatstiftung v Weller-Lindhorst* [2009] ECR I-3369, para 35.

41 Regulation (EC) 44/2001 of 22 December 2000 on jurisdiction and the recognition and enforcement of judgments in civil and commercial matters, OJ L12/1.

42 Regulation (EU) 1215/2012 of 12 December 2012 on jurisdiction and the recognition and enforcement of judgments in civil and commercial matters, OJ L351/1.

for all contracts that qualified neither as sales nor as services contracts.[43] For the same reason, the proposition that the concept of "services" under the VAT regime should be identical to the one under the Union law on jurisdiction in civil and commercial matters was rejected.[44] This confirms that the distinction between goods and services, together with the interpretation of the very concepts of "goods" and "services" remains highly context-specific.

In conclusion, at a conceptual level, nothing stands in the way of including intangible, non-corporeal assets into the category of "goods". On the other hand, there is no compelling terminological reason to expand the concept of "goods" to nontangible assets. Given that the terminological analysis remains inconclusive, everything depends on context and purpose. Given that the legislative goals and normative functions underlying legal areas such as the fundamental freedoms, customs, tax law as well as contract, commercial and copyright law, differ widely, a uniform classification is not even desirable. The controlling element must always be the purpose and function of the respective legal instrument or other source.

It is important to note that the terminological question remains truly open. It is not clear *a priori* that the concept of "goods" must be limited to tangible items. This paves the way towards a dynamic approach that allows the development of traditional concepts in light of changing circumstances in technology, the economy, and society. In doing so, the CJEU seems to follow a special version of the principle of equal treatment: Software cannot be categorized differently, i.e. as a good or as a service, depending on the medium and mode of distribution, be that via a tangible storage device or intangible download from the internet. By implication, the characterization of software as a "good" cannot be based on the nature of the storage device as a tangible unit. In other words, software stored on a DVD cannot be characterized as a "good" simply because the DVD undoubtedly qualifies as one. If that is so, then it is also unacceptable to categorize software as a service, only because it is downloaded from the internet and thus lacks a tangible storage device. At its root, the CJEU, in its UsedSoft decision, postulated the principle of technological neutrality:

43 Case C-533/07 *Falco Privatstiftung v Weller-Lindhorst* [2009] ECR I-3369, para 36 et seq; cf. also Matthias Lehmann in Andrew Dickinson & Eva Lein (eds), *The Brussels I Regulation Recast* (Oxford UP 2015) para 4.45.

44 Ibid, para 38.

Software must be categorized on its own terms, regardless of the technology used for storage and transmission.

IV. Interpretation of the Products Liability Directive

1. Methods of Interpretation

Pursuant to standing jurisprudence of the CJEU, the interpretation of EU law must not stop with an analysis of the terminology that was used but go further. The context of the respective provision is equally relevant to its interpretation, as is its legislative history and its purpose.[45] As the Court has confirmed in a recent decision, these elements also govern the interpretation of Art. 2 PLD.[46]

2. Art. 2 of the Directive

In the 1985 version of the Product Liability Directive, Art. 2 contained a definition of "product" that provided exceptions for primary, i.e. unprocessed, agricultural products and game. These exemptions that excluded meat and other foodstuffs from the scope of the Directive were abolished in 1999, as a response to the BSE (mad cow) crisis. Directive 99/34/EC[47] deleted the exemptions and streamlined the language. In its current version, Art. 2 PLD reads:

"For the purpose of this Directive, 'product' means all movables even if incorporated into another movable or into an immovable. 'Product' includes electricity."

---

45 Case C-621/18 *Wightman v Secretary of State for Exiting the European Union* [2018] EU:C:2018:999, para 47; Case C-548/18 *BGL BNP Paribas SA v TeamBank AG Nürnberg* [2019] EU:C:2019:848, para 25; Case C-410/19 *The Software Incubator Ltd v Computer Associates (UK) Ltd* [2021] EU:C:2021:742, para 31.

46 Case C-65/20 *VI v. Krone-Verlag* [2021] EU:C:2021:471, para 25.

47 Directive 1999/34/EC of the European Parliament and the Council of 10 May 1999 amending Council Directive 85/374/EEC on the approximation of the laws, regulations and administrative provisions of the Member States concerning liability for defective products [1999] OJ L141/20.

3. *Movables*

Art. 2 of the Directive defines its scope with a view to the concept of a "movable". The crucial question thus becomes whether software does qualify as such. Upon first blush, this may be possible as software certainly is not immovable but may be moved around, but such reasoning leads astray. The distinction between movables and immovables does not exhaust the world of legal subjects.[48] The real question is not whether software is movable or immovable but whether the concept of a movable (and likewise an immovable) is limited to corporeal assets. The answer seems to be "no", as the common law distinguishes between corporeal movables and incorporeal movables.[49] Bonds are a pertinent example of a movable that is not corporeal. In French legal discourse, it is accepted that the provisions of the code civil transposing the Product Liability Directive also apply to intangible assets or "meubles incorporels".[50]

On the other hand, the German version of the Product Liability Directive refers to a "movable thing" (bewegliche Sache) and thus limits the scope of the concept to corporeal assets. Analysis of the terminology used in Art. 2 of the Directive thus supplies no definite answer. Given the confusion surrounding the concept of a "movable", or rather the distinction between movables and immovables in the European legal systems, it is not surprising that the framers of the Product Liability Directive proved to be unable to resolve the ambiguities surrounding the concept of a "movable". It is simply unclear whether it is restricted to corporeal assets or also includes non-corporeal ones.

4. *Electricity*

The notion that the concept of a "movable" is confined to corporeal assets is supported by the fact that Art. 2 Product Liability Directive explicitly refers to electricity. In doing so, it may be argued, the framers of the Direc-

48 Christian von Bar, *Gemeineuropäisches Sachenrecht*, vol. 1 (CH Beck 2015) paras 218–219.

49 Legal Definition of 'Movable', *Merriam Webster Dictionary* <https://www.merriam-webster.com/dictionary/movable#legalDictionary> accessed 15 November 2021; cf. also Christian von Bar, *Gemeineuropäisches Sachenrecht*, vol. 1 (CH Beck 2015) paras 220 et seq.

50 Francois Terré, Philippe Simler, Yves Lequette, Francois Chénedé, *Droit civil. Les obligations* (12th edn, Dallos 2018) para 1221.

tive implicitly indicated that Art. 2 was limited to corporeal assets. If it were otherwise, there would have been no need to specifically mention electricity. Exactly this was the view of Hans-Claudius Taschner, the EU Commission staff member who drafted the Product Liability Directive in the early 1980s.[51] He thought that Art. 2 was limited to corporeal assets, that the inclusion of electricity was an exception, and that exceptions were to be interpreted narrowly. But, again, even the view of the godfather of the Directive was clouded by contradictions. While Taschner vigorously argued for a narrow interpretation of the "electricity-exception" he was of the view that computer programs qualified as movables within the meaning of Art. 2 PLD, without explaining why this should be so.[52]

Against this background it would be wrong to draw a reverse conclusion from the fact that Art. 2 PLD explicitly mentions electricity. The inclusion of electricity into the scope of the Product Liability Directive did not implicate the decision to exclude all other non-tangible items. The truth of the matter seems to be that the framers focused on the non-tangible item that was most salient at the time when the Directive was drafted and negotiated. In the early eighties of the last century, the computer industry was still in its infancy, at least if compared to its current state. More importantly, computers were almost exclusively used by businesses and hardly at all by consumers. As a consequence, software as such never reached consumer markets. Given the focus of the framers on the protection of consumers,[53] their focus on electricity, and their neglect of software is easily understandable. If anything, the fact that Art. 2 PLD explicitly mentions electricity shows that the framers were concerned about non-tangible movables that could harm consumers in much the same way as defective corporeal artefacts could. This suggests the inclusion of software in the scope of the Product Liability Directive, per analogy to the inclusion of electricity or, even better, through a sufficiently broad interpretation of the concept of "movables" which includes non-corporeal objects.

---

51 Hans Claudius Taschner, *Produkthaftung* (Beck 1986) Art. 2 para 3.

52 Ibid, Art. 6 para 28; dissenting Hans Claudius Taschner in Hans Claudius Taschner, Edwin Frietsch, *Produkthaftungsgesetz und EG-Produkthaftungsrichtlinie* (2nd edn, CH Beck 1990) Art. 6 para 28; Edwin Frietsch, ibid § 2 ProdhaftG para 22.

53 Council Directive 85/374/EEC of 25 July 1985 on the approximation of the laws, regulations and administrative provisions of the Member States concerning liability for defective products [1985] OJ L210/29, recitals 1, 4.

5. The CJEU Decision on Printed Information

In a recent judgment, the CJEU had the chance to interpret the concept of movables, as used in Art. 2 of the Directive with a view not to software, but to information reproduced in a newspaper. In the underlying case from Austria, a newspaper had published health advice on the use of horseradish for alleviating rheumatic pain.[54] The advice was false in important respects, as it advised the application of the substance for hours instead of minutes. As a result, the claimant had suffered injury. She sued the publisher of the newspaper in damages under the Product Liability Directive. The CJEU did not concern itself with interpreting the concept of a "movable" as such but rejected the claim for the reason that the damage had been caused by a service, of which the product was "merely the medium".[55] The Court held that inaccurate health advice published in a printed newspaper fell outside the scope of the Product Liability Directive, even if it harmed the health of another person.[56]

In reaching this conclusion, the justices started from the premise that the liability regime of the Directive applied "only to movables which have been industrially produced or those which are used in the construction of immovables or are installed in immovables".[57] With respect, this conclusion needs some qualifications. It is true that mass production was a major driver of products liability law, both in the United States and in Europe. Recital 3 of the Product Liability Directive, which the Court cited, reflects this pedigree. However, technically speaking, the Directive is not limited to products that were industrially produced,[58] as evidenced by the simple fact that Art. 2 of the Directive, from the very beginning, included agricultural products. The CJEU itself held in the Veedfald case that a medical liquid prepared in a hospital for internal use in organ transplants qualified as a product – even though the liquid had certainly not been "industrially produced" in any meaningful sense.[59]

---

54 Case C-65/20 *VI v. Krone-Verlag* [2021] EU:C:2021:471, para 13 et seq.

55 Ibid, para 37.

56 Ibid, para 39.

57 Ibid, para 29.

58 Gerhard Wagner in *Münchener Kommentar zum Bürgerlichen Gesetzbuch: BGB* (8th edn, CH Beck 2020) § 2 ProdHaftG para 5; Simon Whittaker, *Liability for Products* (Oxford UP 2005) 476 seq; Jaques Flour, Jean-Luc Aubert, Eric Savaux, *Droit civil, Les obligations, 2. Le fait juridique* (14th edn, Sirey 2011) para 301; Francois Terré, Philippe Simler, Yves Lequette & Francois Chénedé, *Droit civil. Les obligations* (12th edn, Dalloz 2018) para 1221.

59 Case C-203/99 *Veedfald v Arhus Amtskommune* [2001] ECR I-3569, para 8.

The Court did not rest at the requirement of mass production. Rather, it contrasted liability for products, as defined in the Directive, with liability for services.[60] In the view of the justices, the concept of product defect was formulated with a view to the safety features of the product itself, and not to something not "inherent to the product itself".[61] With respect, it seems that this argument circumvents the question of whether false advice as to the treatment of pain or illness, given in a newspaper, is "inherent" to the paper or not.

6. *Products vs. Services*

Regardless of the criticism voiced above, there is much appeal to the approach of the CJEU to distinguish between products and services, and to limit the scope of the Product Liability Directive accordingly. As the Court said, the liability of service providers and the liability of manufacturers of products "constitute two distinct liability regimes" which must not be confused by incorporating services into the scope of the Directive covering products liability.[62] It is received wisdom that the Product Liability Directive is limited to just that – products – and does not impose liability on the providers of services.[63] This much is clear from Art. 2, but also from the legislative history as well as developments following the enactment of the Directive in 1985. Five years later, the Commission tabled a proposal for a council directive on the liability of service providers that was meant to supplement the Product Liability Directive, "based on the traditional distinction between service and the manufacture of goods".[64]

Interpreting Art. 2 of the Directive with a view to the distinction between products and services is a step forward, but does not resolve all problems. Rather, it shifts the analysis to this very distinction. What is it, then, that distinguishes products and services? The 1990 proposal of the European Commission for a Directive on the liability of service providers men-

60 Case C-65/20 *VI v. Krone-Verlag* [2021] EU:C:2021:471, para 27, 32 et seq.

61 Ibid, para 35.

62 Ibid, para 38.

63 Case C-495/10 *Centre hospitalier universitaire de Besancon v Dutrueux* [2011] ECR I-14174, para 39; cf. also Case C-203/99 *Veedfald v Arhus Amtskommune* [2001] ECR I-3569, para 17; Gert Brüggemeier, *Tort Law of the European Union* (Wolters Kluwer 2015) para 298.

64 Proposal for a Council Directive on the liability of suppliers of services, COM (90) 482 final [1991] OJ C12/8, recital 9.

tioned several characteristics of services, namely their "one-off" nature, the fact that services are often intangible, and that they "disappear" at the moment that damage is caused.[65] For purposes of the EU treaties, Art. 57 TFEU does not define services but uses a laundry list of heterogenous criteria, that shall be relevant only "in particular", namely the industrial character of the activity in question, its commercial character, and it being performed by craftsmen or professionals. From this list of criteria, the only element that may be helpful when distinguishing products from services is that services obviously involve "activities" rather than objects.

In thinking about the concept of services in European Union law, the Directive on services in the internal market comes to mind.[66] It applies to any service supplied by providers established in the internal market (Art. 2(1) of the Directive), but uses a very narrow definition of services that remains confined to the self-employed. Pursuant to Art. 4 (1) of the Directive, service "means any self-employed activity, normally provided for remuneration, as referred to in Art. 50 of the Treaty". Again, the only element in this definition that lends itself to generalization is the involvement of an "activity".

Finally, the contract law of the European Union might provide guidance when it comes to defining services. Any hopes in this direction result in disappointment. Large segments of EU contract law use the term "services" as an umbrella term for any contract concluded between a business and a consumer that does not qualify as a sales contract. Thus, the Directive on consumer rights defines the term "service contract" in opposition to the concept of a "sales contract", suggesting that any promise in exchange for money that does not involve a promise of the business to transfer ownership of goods qualifies as a service contract.[67] In other words, service contracts encompass all mutual contracts between businesses and consumers that do not qualify as sales contracts.

The framers of the DCFR aimed to move beyond this bloodless definition of service contracts when drafting Book IV.C. of the DCFR which deals with a variety of service contracts.[68] The result, however, is rather

---

65 Ibid, recital 6.

66 Directive 2006/123/EC of the European Parliament and of the Council of 12 December 2006 on services in the internal market, [2006] OJ L376/36.

67 Directive 2011/83/EU of the European Parliament and of the Council of 25 October 2011 on consumer rights [2011] OJ L304/64, Art. 2(6).

68 Marco B.M. Loos, 'Service Contracts' in Arthur S. Hartkamp, Martijn W. Hesselink, Ewoud Hondius, C Mak, Edgar du Perron (eds), *Towards a European Civil Code* (4th edn, Wolters Kluwer 2011) 756, 764.

disappointing, as Art. IV.C.-1:101(1)(a) DCVR offers the tautological definition that the Book on service contracts applies "to contracts under which one party, the service provider, undertakes to supply a service to the other party…". The only thing that is clear from the structure of the DCFR is that sales contracts, lease agreements, loan contracts and some other types of contracts fall outside the definition of a service, simply because they are regulated elsewhere in the DCFR. On the other hand, contracts that call for the production of a corporeal object, be it a building or a chattel, fall within the scope of legal rules on service contracts.[69]

The upshot of this brief review of European Union law dealing with "services" or contracts for services is brutal and short: One thing we know for sure is that sales contracts do not qualify as service contracts. This is so in spite of the fact that the seller undertakes to *do* something, namely to transfer ownership in a thing, a corporeal object. With the exception for sales contracts kept in mind, the crucial characteristic of services, as confirmed by the CJEU, is that they involve an *activity*.[70] In its jurisprudence under the Brussels I Regulation the Court has explicitly defined services as the carrying out of an activity in return for remuneration.[71] The service provider undertakes to *do* something for his or her client or, for that matter, to refrain from doing something he or she would otherwise do. In that sense, service contracts look to the promisor as a person and engage his or her activity, while a contract for sale or a lease contract look to the *object* that is the subject matter of the promise, i.e. the good that is sold or the apartment that is rented out.

The distinction between object-based rules and others that are activity-oriented seems to make the most of the juxtaposition of goods and services. However, even this insight must be handled with care, as legislative context and purpose remains decisive. As the CJEU has made clear beyond doubt in its jurisprudence on the allocation of jurisdiction for contract-based claims under the Brussels I regime, the concept of "services" does not have a uniform meaning, but must be interpreted differently depending on the legal context involved.[72]

---

69 Maurits Barendrecht, Chris Jansen, Marco Loos, Andrea Pinna, Rui Cascão, Stephanie van Gulijk, *Principles of European Law, Service Contracts* (Otto Schmidt/De Gruyter European law publishers 2007) 131.

70 Case C-533/07 *Falco Privatstiftung v Weller-Lindhorst* [2009] ECR I-3369, para 29.

71 Case C-533/07 *Falco Privatstiftung v Weller-Lindhorst* [2009] ECR I-3369, para 29; Case C-469/12 *Krejci Lager & Umschlagbetrieb GmbH v Olbrich Transport und Logistik GmbH* [2013] EU:C:2013:788, para 26.

72 Ibid, para 29, 38.

7. *Software between Good and Service*

The distinction between goods and services supplies the basis for answering the question whether software qualifies as a product, or rather: as a movable, under Art. 2 of the Product Liability Directive.[73] In light of the foregoing analysis of the meaning and scope of the concept of services in European Union law, the decisive question is whether software must be associated with objects, such as a cup, a table or a pair of glasses, or rather with activities, such as the treatment of a patient, the construction of a house, or the creation of a work of art. The answer will depend on the type of software under consideration.

In the early days of the computer, code was written by programmers for particular users, the hardware equipment these users had on hand, and the purposes and tasks they wanted their hardware to perform. Depending on the contractual relationship between the parties, the entity that had promised to "produce" the software may have remained in charge of it, in the sense that it remained in charge of maintenance and development. The user of the software had promised to pay royalties for use of the software on a month-by-month or other time-contingent basis. Such a relationship is far removed from the typical case of a sales transaction where an object changes hands, the price is paid, and that is it, at least for purposes of sales law. In the software example, the contract is not about an object, but about an activity, namely the activity to program, maintain, and develop the software in question.

With the advent of the personal computer in the late 1980s, software markets changed. Now, computers were mass produced and distributed to the public in much the same way as cars, radios and household appliances. A new computer that is bought from a dealer or from the OEM comes directly with standard software that was pre-installed by the manufacturer. If the user wanted to add more software, this could be bought in boxes containing floppy disks, CDs or DVDs. As the software was sold on a corporeal storage device one could settle with the view that it qualified as a movable, simply because the storage device was physical.

After the judgment of the CJEU in the Krone case, it is no longer possible to confuse the storage device with the information that is stored on it. The Court correctly distinguished between information and storage device in the case of the health advice provided in a newspaper, and the

73 Gerhard Wagner in *Münchener Kommentar zum Bürgerlichen Gesetzbuch: BGB* (8th edn, CH Beck 2020) § 823 para 25.

newspaper itself.[74] In the same way, it is necessary to distinguish between the software that was saved on the disk, CD or DVD, and these physical storage devices.[75]

Severing the link between software and storage device does not automatically lead to a classification of standard software as a service. Even if standard software is downloaded from the internet, it still represents an "object" that can and must be distinguished from the activity that created it, as well as the activity that made it available to the user. In today's life and economy, standard software is distributed, used and regarded as an object, albeit an incorporeal one. The buyer of a standard PC machine is in the same position vis-à-vis the hardware manufacturer as he or she is vis-à-vis the software manufacturer, be it Microsoft or another company. From the perspective of the buyer, it does not matter much that the hardware component is tangible and the software is not. He or she will regard the package of hard- and software as one integrated – "product"!

For purposes of the Product Liability Directive and its interpretation, the perspective of the buyer is the relevant one. After all, "protection of the consumer" is the central goal of the Directive.[76] In the eyes of the framers of the Directive, the consumer deserved protection from defective products put into the stream of commerce by any producer involved in the production process.[77] Liability of the producer is the mechanism for "a fair apportionment of the risks inherent in modern technological production".[78] In light of these aspirations, it is not an option to limit the scope of the Directive to physical objects (products) to the exclusion of non-physical ones (software). If this were the state of the law, the Product Liability Directive would lose its neutrality in the face of new technologies and develop into a liability regime for the old economy, with its steam engines, combustion engines, and abundance of hardware. Such an anachronistic interpretation of the scope of the Directive would fail to

---

74 Case C-65/20 *VI v. Krone-Verlag* [2021] EU:C:2021:471.

75 Gerhard Wagner in *Münchener Kommentar zum Bürgerlichen Gesetzbuch: BGB* (8th ed., CH Beck 2020) § 2 ProdHaftG para 22 et seq; dissenting Jürgen Oechsler in Staudinger Kommentar zum Bürgerlichen Gesetzbuch (Sellier/de Gruyter 2018) § 2 ProdHaftG para 65 seq.

76 Council Directive 85/374/EEC of 25 July 1985 on the approximation of the laws, regulations and administrative provisions of the Member States concerning liability for defective products [1985] OJ L210/29, recital 4.

77 Ibid.

78 Ibid, recital 3.

provide reasonable solutions to problems "peculiar to our age of increasing technicality", as the framers put it back in 1985.[79]

The failure of a narrow interpretation of Art. 2 Product Liability Directive, i.e. one that would exclude non-physical objects from its scope, is particularly astute in the case of embedded software, i.e. computer programs that operate hardware devices such as machines, components of cars, trains and airplanes, and household gadgets. Coupled with the rule of the CJEU judgment in Krone, that the information must be distinguished from the device it is stored on, the narrow view would lead to the conclusion that embedded software does not qualify as a product. As a consequence, the internet of things would remain outside the scope of the Directive, at least insofar as the harm is caused by defective software. And where IoT-devices fail, it would be for the consumer to prove that the defect was in the hardware, rather than the software that operated the product (Art. 4 PLD). This example illustrates the proposition, advanced above, that an interpretation of Art. 2 that restricts the scope of the Directive to movables of tangible quality, works to put the Directive out of step with today's technological developments and will render it obsolete in the near future.

8. *Categories of Software*

The above analysis suggests a nuanced treatment of software under the Product Liability Directive, namely one that distinguishes between standard software and bespoke software. Standard software displays all the features that the Product Liability Directive was designed to react to. It is a technological product that is mass-produced and then distributed to consumers and other customers in the same way as industrially produced hardware products. Standard software must be included in the scope of the Product Liability Directive, so that a broad range of IoT devices remain within the scope of the Directive. Thus, the manufacturer of standard software that is sold in a bundle with hardware can be held liable for defects under the PLD. The same result obtains where standard software is sold as a stand-alone product that is distributed independently from the respective hardware. Here, too, the software is offered not as a service, but as a product. The manufacturer of standard software does not offer future activities to the buyer. Rather, the software is offered as a non-tangible object, for the buyer to "take home" and use. For purposes of Art. 2 of the Directive,

79 Ibid.

standard software must be classified as a non-tangible movable, and not as a service.

With regard to bespoke software, the analysis must be different. Bespoke software refers to computer programs that are tailor-made for a specific customer and her needs. The fact alone that the software is neither mass-produced nor distributed to the general public does not stand in the way of classification as a product, as the scope of the Product Liability Directive is not so limited.[80] Still, the question remains whether bespoke software must be classified as a service because the would-be manufacturer offers to perform activities for the benefit of the would-be buyer and does not offer an, albeit intangible, product.

The classification of bespoke software as a product and a service will hinge on the circumstances of the case at hand. Where the provider develops the software and then operates it himself on behalf of the client, the contract is for services, and not for the delivery of an object. In that setting, the computer program should not qualify as a product under Art. 2 of the Directive, even if it is run on hardware owned or under the control of the client. Another way to look at the problem is to accept that, even here, the software must be classified as a product but to deny that it was ever "put into circulation", so that the manufacturer is exempt from liability under Art. 7(a) PLD. Unfortunately, this approach is foreclosed by the CJEU decision in Veedfald which held that a product is put into circulation even if it never leaves the sphere of the manufacturer but is used by her in the course of providing a medical service.[81] Of course, the same applies to the supply of digital services.

A more nuanced solution must be reached in cases where bespoke software was commissioned by a manufacturer which is then copied into digital products that are distributed to the general public. Pertinent examples may be found in the car industry, with a manufacturer contracting with a supplier for the programming of software according to specifications, and then installing the finished "product" (sic!) into the control boards of the cars or of discrete components. In this setting, the auto OEM is distributing software "products" to its customers, together with the tangible hardware. Still, the business that created the software is not liable under the Product Liability Directive. Without a doubt, the software business did not distribute the cars to the public, so it is not responsible for these

80 Supra IV.5.

81 Case C-203/99 *Veedfald v Arhus Amtskommune* [2001] ECR I-3569, para 11 seq, 18.

products. Moreover, it did not deliver a product to the car manufacturer, but instead rendered services.

V. Conclusion

At the time when the Product Liability Directive was designed, the computer industry was still in its infancy, at least when compared to what it looks like today. It is little wonder, then, that the framers of the Directive thought about products in terms of chattels, i.e. tangible items that are movable. Even back in 1985 there was some awareness of the existence of "products" that are non-tangible but which still pose serious threats to the interests of the consumer and other third parties. The most salient of these non-tangible items – electricity – was specifically addressed in Art. 2 and thus included into the scope of the Directive. Now the time has come to also include other non-tangible objects such as software.

Including software into the scope of Art. 2 PLD does not open the floodgates of liability and does not render Art. 2 limitless. Rather, the Product Liability Directive remains confined to objects, and does not reach services. The borderline between objects and services cannot be drawn in a naturalistic fashion because practically every object can be portrayed as the outcome of an activity. Union law differs widely in drawing the distinction between goods and services which suggests that it must be guided by the purpose of the norm in question. The purpose of protecting the consumer from the risk of mass production lies at the very core of the Product Liability Directive.

Against this background, standard software that is mass-produced and distributed to consumers together with hardware must be classified as an intangible object and thus as a product for purposes of Art. 2 PLD. The same applies to standard software that is distributed as a stand-alone product. The fact alone that software was developed according to the specifications of a particular customer does not foreclose the application of the Directive. Where the outcome of the efforts of the software developer was distributed to the public by a hardware manufacturer or otherwise, the application of the Directive is in order.

In conclusion, the Directive must not be cut off from technological development by confining it to the analogue products of the old industry. The Directive must be interpreted dynamically so as to keep pace with technological development. And the technological development of today is happening in the digital arena which is largely driven by software.

Liability for self-learning smart products

Georg Borges[1]

I. Change in AI systems as a challenge for product liability law

AI systems pose challenges to the law, not least in liability law. One of the characteristic features of AI systems is the ability to autonomously determine their own behaviour in response to the surroundings and depending on predefined goals. This is closely related to another aspect, namely the change of properties and capabilities of AI systems during operation. This possibility exists in particular for systems that acquire their capabilities through machine learning techniques.

Such changes in the capabilities of AI systems pose challenges for product liability law. The Product Liability Directive delimits responsibility for damage caused by products according to the moment they are placed on the market. The manufacturer's liability is limited to the causes of damage that existed when the specific product was placed on the market. Damaging properties of the product that develop only after it has been placed on the market do not trigger product liability. Defects caused by changes after the product has been placed on the market, therefore, pose a risk of liability gaps.

Therefore, it is of special interest whether the current product liability law adequately covers liability for changes to AI systems that occur after the system has been placed on the market, or if and which gaps exist in liability.

The question of liability for changes to AI systems occurring after they have been placed on the market arises against the background of a complex variety of possible circumstances. Changes to AI systems can occur regarding all components, spanning from hardware and software to information that the system accesses to control its behaviour.

From the perspective of product liability law, an important distinction must be made according to the originator of the modification: since only the producer is the addressee of product liability, changes made by other parties, in particular the user, do not give rise to liability in this respect.

1 Prof. Dr. Georg Borges, Professor of Civil Law, Saarland University.

In this context, it is also of special interest how changes brought about "by the machine itself" are to be classified in product liability law. This question arises in the case of AI systems that "continue to learn" after having been placed on the market – i.e. during operation – and thus change their capabilities.

Further distinctions are to be made according to the object and the extent of the change. In the case of changes to non-tangible components, the question arises whether and in which cases supply of such components can trigger liability after the product has been placed on the market. Updates to software are a classic example of this question, the latter of which is of the greatest practical importance for AI systems. This question is particularly difficult in relation to machine learning in AI systems. Here, it must be discussed whether learning is part of the manufacturing process, and who is to be regarded as the manufacturer.

With regard to the extent of the change, it must be clarified under which conditions a new product is created or whether it is merely a change to the existing product. If, for example in the case of a software update, only a – possibly minor – change is made, the question arises as to whether this creates a new product or how else an update is to be integrated into the systematics of product liability law.

The multitude of possible case groups cannot be fully examined within the scope of this article. Therefore, it shall focus on changes caused by machine learning processes. On the one hand, the significance of training for product liability in general (III. below) will be considered, and, on the other hand, liability for changes caused by the machine itself during operation (IV. below). Furthermore, alternative concepts shall be discussed (V.). First, however, it must be clarified to what extent AI systems, their components and machine learning are covered by product liability law (II.).

II. AI systems and their components in product liability law

1. AI systems

In the legal policy discussion on Artificial Intelligence in Europe, the term AI system has recently become very important. For example, this term was used by the EU Parliament in its resolution 2020/2014[2] in the proposal contained therein for a "Regulation on liability for the operation of Artificial Intelligence-systems". Above all, the term is a key concept in the Commission's proposal for an AI Act[3]. The term AI system is defined differently in both texts, but, apparently, is intended to describe the same subject matter. While Art. 3 lit. a) of the Parliament's proposed regulation defines an AI system as "a system that is either software-based or embedded in hardware devices, and that displays behaviour simulating intelligence by, inter alia, collecting and processing data, analysing and interpreting its environment, and by taking action, with some degree of autonomy, to achieve specific goals", Art. 3 para. 1 of the proposed AI Act describes AI systems as "software that is developed with one or more of the techniques and approaches listed in Annex I and can, for a given set of human-defined objectives, generate outputs such as content, predictions, recommendations, or decisions influencing the environments they interact with".

It is interesting for the issue at hand that both proposed regulations describe the AI system essentially as software, or at least as an intangible object that can be integrated into a machine, as is the case with autonomous vehicles.

The definitions of the proposed regulations thus take up the fact that AI systems are often, but not necessarily, embedded in hardware, i.e. a machine, and clarify that the proposed regulations also refer to non-embedded systems.

2. *AI systems as products within the meaning of product liability law*

From the perspective of the Product Liability Directive, which according to its Art. 2 refers to tangible objects only, a crucial question is whether a non-embedded "AI system" can be described as a product. In this respect, a

2 European Parliament resolution of 20 October 2020 with recommendations to the Commission on a civil liability regime for artificial intelligence (2020/2014(INL)). For an analysis of the proposed resolution see Wagner, "Liability for Artificial Intelligence: A Proposal of the European Parliament", in Eidenmüller and Wagner (eds), *Law by Algorithm* (Mohr Siebeck 2021), pp 127 et seq.

3 Proposal for a Regulation of the European Parliament and of the Council Laying Down Harmonized Rules on Artificial Intelligence (Artificial Intelligence Act) and amending Certain Union Legislative Acts of 21 April 2021, COM(2021) 206 final; see Ebert and Spiecker, "Der Kommissionsentwurf für eine KI-Verordnung der EU – Die EU als Trendsetter weltweiter KI-Regulierung" [2021], in Neue Zeitschrift für Verwaltungsrecht (NVwZ) 1188.

differentiation must be made: insofar as the AI system is embedded in a physical machine, the machine as a whole is a product in the sense of product liability law.[4] Liability thus also covers damage caused by defects of the AI system.[5]

However, there are also AI systems that are not embedded, but can be used in different running environments. Everyday examples include speech recognition software for installation on PCs, or "smart" keyboards that users can install on their smartphones.[6] Such AI systems can also be placed on the market in an unembodied form, for example via the internet, so that the long-standing discussion as to whether software constitutes a product within the meaning of product liability law also arises with regard to the classification of AI systems.

Whether and, if so, in which cases software constitutes a product has always been a matter of dispute, and the ECJ has not yet ruled on this. Different views are expressed in the literature.[7] According to one position, software is only to be regarded as an object if it is embodied, in particular if it is delivered on a physical data medium, but not if it is transmitted online.[8] The prevailing opinion in the literature today rightly regards computer programs as products, irrespective of whether they are stored on a data carrier or transmitted immaterially via the internet.[9]

---

4 Cf., for software in general, Borges, in Borges and Hilber (eds), *Beck'scher Online-Kommentar IT-Recht* (BeckOK IT-Recht) ([th] edn, Beck 2021) § 2 ProdHaftG mn. 23; Oechsler, in Staudinger (founder), *Kommentar zum Bürgerlichen Gesetzbuch* (new edn 2018, Sellier / de Gruyter 2018) § 2 ProdHaftG mn. 64; Redeker, *IT-Recht* (7th edn, Beck 2020) mn. 878; Wagner, in Säcker et al (eds), *Münchener Kommentar zum Bürgerlichen Gesetzbuch vol.* 7 (8th edn, Beck 2020) § 2 ProdHaftG mn. 6, 21.

5 The product error may stem from the application software as well as from the risk of the algorithms: Sommer, *Haftung für autonome Systeme* (Nomos 2020), p 231.

6 E.g. the keyboard application "SwiftKey" seehttps://www.microsoft.com/en-us/swif tkey.

7 For an overview of the discussion see e.g. Borges (n 4) § 2 ProdHaftG mn. 20 et seq; Förster, in Hau and Poseck (eds), *Beckscher Online-Kommentar zum BGB* (60th Edition, Beck 2021) § 2 ProdHaftG mn. 22; Heymann, "Haftung des Softwareimporteurs" [1990] in Computer und Recht (CR) 176; Rebin, in Gsell et al (eds), *beck-online.Grosskommentar zum Zivilrecht* (updated 01/10/2021, Beck) § 2 ProdHaftG mn. 49 et seq; Taeger, *Außervertragliche Haftung für fehlerhafte Computerprogramme* (Mohr Siebeck 1995), pp 89 et seq; Weitz, *Software als "Sache"* (LIT 1989), pp 111 et seqq .

8 Förster (n 7) § 2 ProdHaftG mn. 23; Oechsler (n 4) mn. 65 et seq.; Taschner and Frietsch, *Produkthaftungsgesetz und EG-Produkthaftungsrichtlinie* (2nd Edition, Beck 1990), mn. 22.

9 Borges (n 4) § 2 ProdHaftG mn. 26; Cahn, "Produkthaftung für verkörperte geistige Leistungen" [1996] in Neue Juristische Wochenschrift (NJW) 2899, 2904 ;

The application of product liability law cannot depend on whether the program was integrated into a machine by its manufacturer before it was placed on the market, or by the user afterwards.[10] As the application of product liability to embedded software, or software delivered on data carriers, is undisputed today, the differentiation according to the type of delivery seems to be inconsistent. Rather, the objectives of product liability suggest that product liability law should be applied to computer programs, irrespective of the way in which they are supplied by their manufacturer.[11] Excessive liability risks of software manufacturers are to be avoided by an appropriate interpretation of the term "defect" in Art. 6 of the Product Liability Directive (not every bug in a software program is a product defect[12]) and the liability exceptions (e.g. § 1 para. 2, 3 ProdHaftG).[13] This applies in particular to damage resulting from the interaction of the software with a machine not manufactured by the software manufacturer.[14]

As a result, an AI system, as defined in the two proposed regulations, is to be regarded as a product in the sense of product liability law.

3. *Machine learning and neural networks*

Machine learning is the field of Artificial Intelligence that has received the most attention in recent years. The focus of interest is on neural networks which, by "learning" or "training", acquire the ability to produce results (output), that can even greatly surpass the performance achievable by humans. The examples of the Alpha Go system, which was able to beat

---

Krause, in Soergel (founder), *Bürgerliches Gesetzbuch Schuldrecht 10* (13th edn, Kohlhammer 2005) § 2 ProdHaftG mn. 4; Rebin (n 7) ProdHaftG § 2 mn. 56 et seq; Wagner (n 3) § 2 ProdHaftG mn. 22.

10 Borges (n 4) § 2 ProdHaftG mn. 34 et seqq; Borges, "Kann ein Gegenstand nicht Sache und doch Sache sein? – Computerprogramme im Privatrecht" in Omlor (ed), *Weltbürgerliches Recht. Festschrift für Michael Martinek zum 70. Geburtstag* (Beck 2020), pp 45–59, 57.

11 Borges (n 4) § 2 ProdHaftG mn. 43; Rebin (n 7) ProdHaftG § 2 mn. 59; also Lehmann, "Produkt- und Produzentenhaftung für Software" [1992] in Neue Juristische Wochenschrift (NJW) 1721, 1724.

12 Borges (n 4) § 2 ProdHaftG mn. 37 et seq; Lehmann (n 11), 1721 (at footnote 4); regarding the utopia of bug-freedom of computer programms see Wiebe, "Produktsicherheitsrechtliche Pflicht zur Bereitstellung sicherheitsrelevanter Software-Updates" [2019] in Neue Juristische Wochenschrift (NJW) 625.

13 Borges (n 4) § 1 ProdHaftG mn. 38; Borges (n 10) p 57.

14 Borges (n 4) § 2 ProdHaftG mn. 42 et seq; Borges (n 10) pp 56 et seq.

the world champion in the board game Go, or Alpha Go zero, which was far better than Alpha Go, impressively demonstrate the performance of machine learning through neural networks.

The term machine learning refers to a series of programming techniques in which certain property or behaviour of a software is optimized based on sample data or empirical values from the past.[15] By this process, certain programme properties are determined by parameters. During the process of "learning", the programme executed to optimise these parameters using sample data.[16]

The algorithms used for learning can be described as abstract algorithms deriving a correct problem solution for a new input from data through the learning process. This applies in particular to so-called neural networks, which can approximately describe any mathematical function and thus any algorithm through the learning process,[17] as long as the network meets certain requirements for its complexity.

Artificial neural networks (also called multilayer perceptrons) are mathematical models that roughly resemble human brain functioning.[18] They consist of several (possibly hundreds or even thousands) so-called layers: an input layer, one or more hidden layers in the middle, and an output layer.[19] The number of layers determines the so-called depth of the network, which is where the term "deep learning" has been derived from.[20] The input data is "sent" step by step through each calculation layer, whereby a problem-invariant calculation operation (multiplication with a matrix) is carried out in each layer.[21] To illustrate neural networks, we often speak of neurons, the elements of the respective layer, and synapses, the connections between the neurons (and thus between the layers).[22] The strength of the connection, which is referred to as the weight, sometimes also as the synapse weight, is a component of the corresponding matrix of the respective layer and has decisive significance for the value that is given to the respective subsequent layer. Thus, a certain weighted combination

---

15 Alpaydin, *Maschinelles Lernen* (2nd Edition, De Gruyter 2019) p 3.
16 Alpaydin (n 15) p 3.
17 According to the theorem of universal approximation: Alpaydin (n 15) p 290.
18 Goodfellow et al, *Deep Learning Book* (MIT Press 2016) p 165.
19 Goodfellow et al (n 18) p 165.
20 Goodfellow et al (n 18) p 165.
21 Goodfellow et al (n 18) p 171.
22 Goswami, "Deep Learning – A State-of-the-Art Approach to Artificial Intelligence" in Bhattacharyya et al (eds), *Deep Learning. Research and Applications* (De Gruyter 2020) pp 1–21.

of outputs from neurons of the previous layer flows into a subsequent neuron.[23] Learning determines the weights and thus trains the network for a concrete problem solution.

The essential characteristic of machine learning is that the programmer must define the structure of the model (e.g. the architecture and the size of a neural network), and in particular provide (suitable) training data, but does not have to develop an explicit algorithm for the specific problem. This is automatically derived approximately in the learning process.

Within machine learning, a multitude of different methods are to be distinguished.[24] A rough distinction can be made between supervised and unsupervised learning.[25] In supervised learning, a general rule is learned on the basis of training data consisting of possible inputs and the desired corresponding model outputs. In unsupervised learning, on the other hand, the model learns the properties of the input space solely from exemplary input data, e.g. in the context of so-called clustering.[26]

For the topic of interest here, the distinction between "online" and "offline" learning methods[27] is important. In "offline" learning, the learning process is completed at a certain point on the basis of the data sets specified by the programmer, and the adjustment of the network parameters (weights) is then finalized. This procedure is typically used for products the properties of which should not change during operation. Similar to a classical, manually programmed algorithm, the properties of the programme are finally determined by the manufacturer.

With "online" learning, on the other hand, the learning process is carried out by adjusting the network parameters for each individual data

---

23 Alpaydin (n 15) pp 10 et seq.

24 See Alpaydin (n 15) pp 4–14; Baum, in Leupold et al, *Münchener Anwaltshandbuch IT-Recht* (4th Edition, Beck 2020), p 9 mn. 14 et seq; an overview of the different types is given by Niederée and Nejdl, in Ebers et al, *Künstliche Intelligenz und Robotik: Rechtshandbuch* (Beck 2020), § 2 mn. 39 et seqq; Russel and Norvig, *Artificial Intelligence* (4th Global Edition, Pearson 2022), pp 694 et seqq mainly distinguish between unsupervised, supervised and reinforcement learning; on the different forms of machine learning see also High-Level Expert Group on Artificial Intelligence, A Definition of AI: Main Capabilities and disciplines (2018), p 5, https://www.aepd.es/sites/default/files/2019-12/ai-definition.pdf.

25 Alpaydin (n 15) pp 10, 12; Niederée and Nejdl (n 24) § 2 mn. 40 et seq; for supervised as well as unsupervised learning see also Russel and Norvig (n 24) pp 694 et seq; Wagner, *Legal Tech und Legal Robots: Der Wandel im Rechtsmarkt durch neue Technologien und künstliche Intelligenz* (SpringerGabler 2018), p 63.

26 Alpaydin (n 15) p 12; for unsupervised learning see also Niederée and Nejdl (n 24) § 2 mn. 41 as well as Russel and Norvig (n 24), pp 694 et seq.

27 Alpaydin (n 15) p 12.

set. The latter makes it possible, for example, to continue training on the basis of user input even while the system is in operation, for example in the case of a speech recognition system adapting to the user.[28] There are some examples of systems that have a neural architecture and learn from user input. One example is auto-correction and auto-completion in word processing programs.[29] Microsoft also claims for its product "SwiftKey" that it learns from the user through Artificial Intelligence.[30]

III. Machine learning in the product liability

Machine learning, as described at the beginning, enables the production of AI systems with impressive capabilities, such as self-driving vehicles. Such AI systems can also cause damage, as the example of accidents caused by highly automated vehicles shows. In principle, product liability law is also applicable to such systems.

The special feature of machine learning, which is of interest from the perspective of product liability law, lies in the fact that the properties of the software are not explicitly programmed by humans, but are implicitly derived from training data used to adapt model parameters via machine learning (see II.3 above). This raises the question of how machine learning is to be classified in the systematics of product liability law.[31]

1. Machine learning as part of the manufacturing process

Insofar as software has been produced and marketed using machine learning methods, product liability law is applicable to it. If the software has a defect that is the cause of damage, the manufacturer of the software is liable for the damage.

---

28 For this example see Alpaydin (n 15) p 283.

29 An experimental architecture is given by Ghosh and Kristensson, “Neural Networks for Text Correction and Completion in Keyboard Decoding” <https://arxiv.org/pdf/1709.06429.pdf>.

30 <https://www.microsoft.com/en-us/swiftkey>.

31 On this: Baum (n 24) part 9.6.4 mn. 44; Müller-Hengstenberg and Kirn, ”Haftung des Betreibers von autonomen Softwareagents. Mögliche Auswirkungen der Entschließung des Europäischen Parlaments zur Haftung bei KI-Einsatz” [2021] Multimedia und Recht (MMR) 376, 379.

According to Art. 3 of the Product Liability Directive, the producer is the person who manufactures the product. Therefore, the crucial question is where the production process takes place in the case of software based on machine learning methods.

This question must be answered by recourse to the general principles of product liability law. The Product Liability Directive does not define the term "manufacture". Rather, it uses the term "producer" to determine the party liable. This is supposed to be the person who is responsible for the defect of the product. Since product liability focuses on the properties of the product, manufacture can be described as the process in which the product receives its properties.

This understanding is also reflected by the distinction between the production of a new product from work, and services being carried out on an existing product. Various aspects and groups of cases are being discussed. For example, filling and portioning activities are not considered to be the manufacture of a new product,[32] assembling, however, is.[33] In the case of product installation, a distinction is made as to whether the installation significantly influences the safety-relevant properties of the product[34] or whether it merely replaces the recipient's own work.[35]

As a guideline for delimitation, the guiding principle has been established that a manufacturer of a new product is one who makes safety-relevant changes to the product.[36] This shows that manufacturing is to be defined as the process in which a product receives (new) safety-relevant properties.[37]

---

32 OLG Düsseldorf NJW-RR 2001, 458; Borges (n 4) § 4 ProdHaftG mn. 8, 22; Oechsler (n 4) § 4 ProdHaftG mn. 28; Wagner (n 4) § 4 ProdhaftG mn. 25.

33 Borges (n 4) § 4 ProdHaftG mn. 2; Oechsler (n 4) § 4 ProdHaftG mn. 20; Förster (n 7) § 4 ProdHaftG mn. 9; Wilhelmi, in Erman (founder), *Bürgerliches Gesetzbuch* (16th Edition, Schmidt 2020) § 4 ProdHaftG mn. 2.

34 BGH NJW 2014, 2106, 2107 et seq; OLG Düsseldorf NJW-RR 2001, 458; Borges (n 4) § 4 ProdHaftG mn. 22; Oechsler (n 4) § 4 ProdHaftG mn. 12; Wagner (n 4) § 4 ProdHaftG mn. 11; Wilhelmi (n 33) § 4 ProdHaftG mn. 2.

35 Borges (n 4) § 4 ProdHaftG mn. 22; Förster (n 7) § 4 ProdHaftG mn. 7, 10; Oechsler (n 4) § 4 ProdHaftG mn. 23; Taschner and Frietsch (n 8) § 4 ProdHaftG mn. 26 et seq.

36 Borges (n 4) § 4 ProdHaftG mn. 10; Oechsler (n 4) § 4 ProdHaftG mn. 12, 21; Wagner (n 4) § 4 ProdHaftG mn. 13.

37 Cf. BGHZ 200, 242 mn. 16; Borges (n 4) ProdHaftG § 4 mn. 22; Förster (n 7) § 4 ProdHaftG mn. 7; Wagner (n 4) § 4 ProdHaftG mn. 11; arguing for an indication Oechsler (n 4) § 4 ProdHaftG mn. 22; Spickhoff, in Gsell et al (eds), *beck-online.Grosskommentar zum Zivilrecht* (updated 01/10/2021, Beck) § 4 ProdHaftG mn. 19.

Machine learning can be easily integrated into this concept. The functional capabilities of a machine or software are not least to be regarded as a property. Insofar as an AI system has functional capabilities that it has learned through machine learning techniques, these are properties of this system. Consequently, learning is part of the manufacturing process of the AI system.

The process of machine learning is also rightly called "training".[38] This term indicates that the learning process is initiated and controlled. Therefore, if training is part of the manufacturing process, then the one who initiates and controls training is the manufacturer of the AI system or the component it trains.[39]

2. *Majority of manufacturing processes through training of AI systems*

The learning process in machine learning of AI systems frequently takes place in stages, often induced by different actors. From the perspective of product liability law, the point of reference for the delimitation of the various stages of training is the moment of placing the product on the market. Merely the characteristics of the product at the time it is placed on the market are relevant for liability. This also applies to AI systems and their training. The relevant manufacturing process therefore ends at that time when the AI system or component is placed on the market.

With industry being based on the division of labour, an end product is regularly produced in a complex manufacturing process. Product liability law takes up this cascading manufacturing process by including the manufacturers of raw materials and partial products, who themselves can

---

38 Roughly, European Parliament, European Parliament resolution of 16 February 2017 with recommendations to the Commission on Civil Law Rules on Robotics, 2015/2103(INL) of 16/2/2017, P8_TA(2017)0051, mn. 56; Zech, "Künstliche Intelligenz und Haftungsfragen" [2019] Zeitschrift für die gesamte Privatrechtswissenschaft (ZfPW) 198, 209 et seq; Bliski and Schmid, "Verantwortungsfindung beim Einsatz maschinell lernender Systeme" [2019] Neue Juristische Online-Zeitschrift (NJOZ) 657, 657 et seq.

39 Leupold and Wiesner, in Leupold et al, *Münchener Anwaltshandbuch IT-Recht* (4th Edition, Beck 2020) part 9.6.4, mn. 44; Seehafer and Kohler, "Künstliche Intelligenz: Updates für das Produkthaftungsrecht? – Mögliche Anpassungen der europäischen Produkthaftungsrichtlinie für neue Technologien" [2020] Europäische Zeitschrift für Wirtschaftsrecht (EuZW) 213, 216; Wagner, "Produkthaftung für autonome Systeme" [2017] Archiv für Civilistische Praxis (AcP) 707, 719 et seq.

be the addressees of a claim for damages. Raw materials are parts that go into a product and are changed during the manufacturing process. Partial products are those which are integrated in a product without being changed themselves.

Insofar as the training of AI systems takes place in multiple stages, from the perspective of product liability law, there may be different manufacturing processes on each stage, in which a new manufacturing process follows after a partially trained system has been placed on the market.

As explained (above), changes to a product lead to the manufacturing of a new product if the product obtains new safety-relevant properties as a result of any such change. This standard must be used to determine under which conditions training of an AI system creates a new product in the sense of product liability law: if, as a result of training, the AI system exhibits new capabilities in a safety-relevant manner, a new product has been created.

With regard to the training of AI systems, therefore, it can be concluded that the training of AI systems often qualifies as the production of a new product. Anyone who trains an AI system and thus changes its functional properties in a safety-relevant way, becomes the manufacturer of a new product. However, product liability only applies if the new product is placed on the market; the mere self-use of the modified system does not trigger product liability.

Insofar as AI systems are trained several times in this way (change in safety-relevant capabilities), the AI system becomes the raw material for the resulting product. If the system is integrated into a machine, it becomes a component part of the machine.

3. *Operators of AI systems as manufacturers? Gap in product liability*

As just shown, the training of an AI system can lead to the creation of a new product. The manufacturer of this new product, and thus the addressee of product liability, is the person in whose organisational domain the training is carried out. According to this, not least the user or the operator of the AI system can also become the manufacturer if he continues to train the system whilst using it. However, this only applies if the user places the modified product on the market.

A similar principle has been enshrined/established/stipulated in the EU Commission's draft AI Act of April 2021. According to Art. 28 para. 2, the user of the AI system becomes the manufacturer if he changes the purpose or otherwise intervenes in the system. The draft AI law does not provide for civil liability, which is to be regulated in another European legal act.[40]

At the level of Member State law, such liability may already arise at present. In German law, it is already being discussed whether the future AI Act will be regarded as a protective law in the sense of of § 823 para. 2 of the German Civil Code (Bürgerliches Gesetzbuch – BGB) and, insofar as the question has been raised, it being answered in the affirmative.[41] However, liability under § 823 para. 2 BGB always presupposes fault, thus opening up the well-known liability gap in relation to the conduct of AI systems.[42]

From the perspective of European product liability law, a liability gap arises if the modified AI system is not placed on the market and nevertheless harms third parties. This is easy to imagine, as AI systems are often intended for use by third parties or get in contact with third parties. For example, a chatbot is typically operated for use by third parties, a highly automated vehicle gets in contact with other road users.

This liability gap could be closed de lege ferenda, in particular by introducing operator liability, which the Expert Group "Liability and New Technologies – New Technologies Formation" has called for in the case of AI systems with high risk potential.[43]

The European Parliament took up this ball in October 2020 and proposed in its resolution the introduction of operator liability for AI sys-

40 Annexes to the Communication from the Commission to the European Parliament, the Council the European Economic and Social Committee and the Committee of the Regions Fostering a European approach to Artificial Intelligence of 21.4.2021, COM(2021) 205 final, No. 9,p 33.

41 Cf. Grützmacher, "Die zivilrechtliche Haftung für KI nach dem Entwurf der geplanten KI-VO" [2021] in Computer und Recht (CR) 433, 437 et seq; Grützmacher and Füllsack, "Der Entwurf einer EU-KI-Verordnung" [2021] in IT-Rechtsberater (ITRB) 159, 163; Spindler, "Der Vorschlag der EU-Kommission für eine Verordnung zur Regulierung der Künstlichen Intelligenz (KI-VO-E)" [2021] in Computer und Recht (CR) 361, 362.

42 For this gap see Borges, "Rechtliche Rahmenbedingungen für autonome Systeme" [2018] in Neue Juristische Wochenschrift (NJW) 977, 981 et seq; Borges, "AI systems and product liability" in *Proceedings of the Eighteenth International Conference on Artificial Intelligence and Law* <https://doi.org/10.1145/3462757.3466099> (2021), pp 32, 35.

43 Report form the Expert Group on Liability and New Technologies – New Technologies Formation <https://www.europarl.europa.eu/meetdocs/2014_2019/plmrep/COMMITTEES/JURI/DV/2020/01-09/AI-report_EN.pdf> (2019), pp 39 et seq.

tems.[44] However, strict liability should only apply to so-called high-risk AI systems, and only if these are explicitly included in a list to be administered by the Commission.[45]

IV. Modification by the machine itself

1. Delimitations

The group of cases that is particularly interesting from a product liability perspective concerns changes in the capabilities of an AI system that develop through independent learning of the system itself.

The distinction from training AI systems is not a simple task as the boundaries between a "controlled" and a non-influenced process of machine learning are fluid. Systems can continue to learn during operation by interpreting user input or external influences as training data, or, as in "reinforcement learning", the subsequent behaviour of the environment can act as feedback for the autonomous learning process.[46] If this process is carried out in a targeted and, if necessary, supervised manner, training is present; if there is no such objective, one would probably speak of autonomous learning of the system.

Therefore, here may be cases in which the operator of an AI product, that continues to learn, doesn't do anything himself whilst the system continues to develop autonomously. As an extreme scenario, one can imagine that the operator is not even aware of the acquired product evolving. This can certainly happen, as the distinction between learning in the sense of a permanent change in function through learned behaviour, and mere reaction of the AI system to influences, is not apparent to laypersons. In such cases, one cannot speak of any "training" by the operator.

---

44 European Parliament resolution of 20 October 2020 with recommendations to the Commission on a civil liability regime for artificial intelligence (2020/2014(INL)).

45 See Art. 4 para. 1 and 2 of the proposed "Regulation on liability for the operation of Artificial Intelligence-systems", https://www.europarl.europa.eu/doceo/document/TA-9-2020-0276_EN.html.

46 For reinforcement learning as a method that does not rely on training data see Baum (n 24) part 9.1, mn. 34 et seq as well as Kevekordes, in Hoeren et al, *Handbuch Multimedia-Recht*, part 29.1 mn. 20 et seqq; being rather sketchy about "reinforcement learning" Erbguth and Molavi, "Künstliche Intelligenz und Deep Learning: Technische Grundlagen und ethische Einordnung" [2019] in IT-Rechtsberater (ITRB) 120.

Damage can be caused by such a further development initiated by the machine itself. As an example, one can again use the case of a chatbot that develops further without the operator's knowledge and that causes damage as a result of this process, for example through incorrect directions.

If a highly automated vehicle continues to learn during operation, which, admittedly, is not envisaged, it would also be conceivable that the vehicle learns incorrect behaviour, e.g. driving too fast or too short a distance, and causes an accident as a result. The learned characteristic, such as giving incorrect information or tailgating, could be identified as a defect of the AI system. From a product liability perspective, the question arises as to who is to be considered the manufacturer of the defective product in such cases and thus the addressee of possible liability.

A simple solution would be to always attribute the modification of the AI system to its operator and designate him as the manufacturer of the new system. However, this solution would not lead to liability under the current law, as the operator would not have put the system on the market. Irrespective of this, this solution does not seem justified, because ultimately product liability would then result in strict liability on the part of the operator, which is precisely what the Product Liability Directive does not aim to establish. Nor would such an allocation of liability risks to the operator be justified, since the operator cannot control this risk.[47]

2. *Changeability as a defect of AI systems?*

If an AI system continues to develop as intended, even after it has been placed on the market without control by third parties, i.e. again by the manufacturer or the operator, it is tempting to seek responsibility for any damage resulting from the modification of such AI systems in the determination of the product's modifiability.

Indeed, it can be assumed that one of the justified safety expectations of an AI system is that it does not change in an uncontrolled manner after being placed on the market in a way that increases the risk. For example, with regard to highly automated vehicles, the idea that an individual vehi-

47 Borges, "Haftung für selbstfahrende Autos" [2016] in Computer und Recht (CR) 272, 278; furthermore for the controllability of risk as basis of strict liability see Brüggemeier, *Deliktsrecht: Ein Hand- und Lehrbuch* (1st Edition, Nomos 1986), mn. 30; Hehl, *Das Verhältnis von Verschuldens- und Gefährdungshaftung* (Roderer 1999), p 90; Larenz, "Die Prinzipien der Schadenszurechnung – Ihr Zusammenspiel im modernen Schuldrecht" [1965] in Juristische Schulung (JuS) 373, 374.

cle "continues to learn" during operation is generally rejected, since safety cannot be guaranteed in the case of a vehicle that learns independently.[48]

It goes without saying that the question of whether the possibility of autonomous modification of an AI system is to be regarded as a defect can only be assessed in the light of the circumstances of the specific case. Therefore, it will not be possible to establish as a general guideline that the mere possibility of an AI system being modified through independent learning after it has been placed on the market is per se contrary to justified safety expectations, even in the case of systems with a recognisable risk potential, as long as the risks can be limited with sufficient certainty through monitoring. The dangerous nature of products – including the need for monitoring – is not per se a product defect.[49] This also applies to AI systems.

In such cases, however, there are increased requirements for instruction from a product liability perspective. It is true that the Product Liability Directive does not explicitly provide for an obligation to instruct the user. However, it is recognised to be a legitimate expectation of safety, that the user receives appropriate information together with the product regarding the risks of using the product and how to avoid them,[50] i.e. information with which he can control the risks arising from the product.

If it is not possible to control the risks, it must be assumed that the product is defective because it is dangerous. In this respect, the responsibility lies with the manufacturer of the AI system, not with its operator.

This leads to the conclusion that there are gaps in product liability law with regard to damage caused by AI systems that continue to learn during operation. Insofar as the mere possibility of further learning is not to be regarded as a product defect, changes to the system do not constitute a new "placing on the market", so that liability under product liability law cannot be assumed for either the manufacturer or the operator.

---

48 Cf. the strict requirements for software updates in vehicles in UN Regulation No 156 – Uniform provisions concerning the approval of vehicles with regards to software update and software updates management systems [2021/388], No. 7; Zech, "Künstliche Intelligenz und Haftungsfragen" [2019] in Zeitschrift für die gesamte Privatrechtswissenschaft (ZfPW) 198, 209.

49 BGH NJW 2009, 1669, 1670; Lorenz, "Grundwissen – Zivilrecht: Grundlagen der Gefährdungshaftung" [2021] in Juristische Schulung (JuS) 307, 309; Wagner (n 3) § 3 ProdHaftG mn. 7; Wilhelmi (n 33) § 3 ProdHaftG mn. 2.

50 Borges (n 3) § 3 ProdHaftG mn. 71; implicitly (product error by wrongful instruction about product risks) Goehl, in Gsell et al (eds), *beck-online.Grosskommentar zum Zivilrecht* (updated 01/10/2021, Beck) § 3 ProdHaftG mn. 74; Oechsler (n 4) § 3 ProdHaftG mn. 46; Wagner (n 3) § 3 ProdHaftG mn. 46.

V. *Alternative Concepts*

The identification of liability gaps in the operation of AI systems leads to the follow-up question of which concepts should be used to close the gaps. This is related to the more general question of how liability for AI systems should be regulated.

1. *Strict liability for AI systems*

A pivotal approach is the introduction of new, specific rules of strict liability for AI systems, which were proposed by the Expert Group, among others, particularly in relation to high-risk systems, and is being pursued by the EU Parliament within the framework of the proposed Regulation on liability for the operation of Artificial Intelligence systems in the form of strict liability for high-risk AI systems[51] (Art. 4 of the proposed Regulation).

One of the central questions in relation to the introduction of strict liability is who should be the addressee of liability. While the proposal of the EU Parliament, in line with the prevailing opinion in literature, refers to the operator of the AI system, it has been rightly pointed out by scholars that in some cases the manufacturer of the AI system is the appropriate addressee of strict liability, as he may be in a better position than the operator to control the risks associated with the operation of an AI system.[52] Specifically, this is argued for, for example, the manufacturer of highly automated vehicles,.[53]

Such elements of strict liability will, of course, always have a limited scope of application. This may be clearly seen, for example, in the legislative proposal by the EU Parliament, which aims at limiting strict liability to such systems that are explicitly named in the annex of the proposed regulation (cf. Art. 4 of the proposed regulation).

---

51 European Parliament resolution of 20 October 2020 with recommendations to the Commission on a civil liability regime for artificial intelligence (2020/2014(INL)).

52 Wagner, Robot Liability, in Lohsse, Schulze, Staudenmayer (eds), *Liability for Artificial Intelligence and the Internet of Things* (Hart Nomos 2019), pp 27–62, 40 et seq.

53 Borges (n 47) 274, 280; also Hinze, *Haftungsrisiken des automatisierten und autonomen Fahrens* (R&W 2021), 190 et seq.

2. *Obligations of manufacturers and operators of AI systems*

In the context of fault-based tort liability, which is known in all Member State legal systems, the obligation to compensate for damages presupposes the breach of a duty of care.

In relation to AI systems, due to the ability to act autonomously, duties relating to monitoring and verification of the systems are particularly relevant. Accordingly, the Expert Group, for example, explicitly proposed the introduction of duties to monitor AI systems in its final report. It is therefore of interest which obligations the manufacturer and the operator have in this respect.

a) *Obligation of the manufacturer to manage risks*

The specific risks of AI systems are addressed by the draft AI Act through the concept of comprehensive risk management (Art. 9 et seq. AI Act). The draft requires comprehensive risk management for so-called high-risk AI systems.[54] The need for risk management is justified in particular by the autonomy of AI systems, which control their own behaviour. With regard to changes to AI systems after they have been placed on the market, it is likely to be of significance that the obligation to manage risks does not end after the system has been placed on the market, but instead continues.

Basically, this concept is correct. Due to their ability to adapt their behaviour to the specific situation and to act accordingly, AI systems pose specific risks that require continuous monitoring, at least if there is a recognisable potential risk for third parties. Often, this can not be done by the user of the system, or at least not solely by the user.

Therefore, the manufacturer must be made responsible for risk management, even after the product has been placed on the market. Whether the concept of the AI Act, which exclusively addresses the manufacturer and pushes the operator into a consumer-like role (cf. Art. 28 AI Act), is convincing, cannot be discussed in the context of this article. In any case, a liability consequence should be attached to the breach of the duty to manage risk, if only to provide a sufficient incentive for proper compliance.

Whether such a liability consequence is to be regulated in product liability law or in the specific legal act announced by the EU Commission on liability for AI systems, is probably not decisive. It would be more impor-

54 Art. 9 of the proposed AI Act, COM(2021) 206.

tant to link the liability consequence with risk management under the AI Act. In German law, such a link could already arise de lege lata from § 823 para. 2 BGB, if the duty to manage risk is regarded as a protective law, as is already being advocated by scholars.

b) Monitoring obligations of the operator and manufacturer of AI systems

The Product Liability Directive does not regulate the obligations of the user of products, consequently also not those of the operator of AI systems.

There is no general operator's strict liability for machines in EU law, probably not in Member State law either, at least not in German law. In this respect, the rules of general tort law apply, from which monitoring obligations of the operators of AI systems can indeed be derived. For example, it is recognised in German law that the operator of a machine must monitor it in order to avoid damage to third parties.[55] Due to the great importance of monitoring AI systems, the Expert Group "Liability for new Technologies" has proposed the explicit regulation of an operator's duty to monitor.[56]

With regard to the producer's duty to monitor, a distinction must be made between a duty to monitor a specific product copy and a duty to monitor general product risks, with the latter of which being linked to the concept of a product monitoring duty.

The Product Liability Directive does not provide for a monitoring duty in relation to the specific product or a general product monitoring duty, but these duties can arise from general tort law of the Member States. German law provides for a product monitoring duty of the manufacturer within the scope of the so-called producer liability. According to this, the manufacturer must, among other things, collect information about possible risks of damage posed by his product and, in doing so, evaluate

55 Cf. for the supervisory duties of an operator Gless and Janal, "Hochautomatisiertes und autonomes Autofahren – Risiko und rechtliche Verantwortung" [2016] in Juristische Rundschau (JR) 561, 571; Leupold and Wiesner (n 39) part 9 mn. 83; Spindler, "Roboter, Automation, künstliche Intelligenz, selbst-steuernde Kfz – Braucht das Recht neue Haftungskategorien?" [2015] in Computer und Recht (CR) 766, 768; see also Horner and Kaulartz, "Haftung 4.0" [2016] in Computer und Recht (CR) 7, 8 et seq, who are in favour of an obligation to supervise an analogy to § 831 German Civil Code.

56 Expert Group on Liability and New Technologies – New Technologies Formation, Liability for New Technologies – Final Report, 2019, pp 44 et seq.

both the experience of competing products and scientific and technical literature.[57] He must also take note of and evaluate complaints from customers about damage and safety deficits.[58] If hazards become apparent, he may be obliged to warn the product users and, if necessary, to recall the products.

Such a product monitoring obligation is of particular importance in relation to AI systems, as harmful behaviour of AI systems may only become apparent in practice.[59] At the level of European law, a product monitoring obligation will possibly result from the risk management obligation under the future AI Act.

Undoubtedly, any such product monitoring obligation is also useful for products that are not to be classified as high-risk AI systems in the sense of the AI Act. Therefore, the revised product liability law should explicitly provide for a product monitoring obligation.

However, an obligation of the manufacturer to monitor specific product units is not being provided for in German tort law, either. To my knowledge, the introduction of such a unit-related monitoring duty of the manufacturer has not been suggested so far. In its final report, the Expert Group Liability for New Technologies also restrains themselves from introducing a monitoring obligation of the operator. This is convincing, as the law provides already for the operator's duty and competing monitoring duties of operator and manufacturer – unless the manufacturer changes roles resulting in him acting as operator, for example in the sense of the "backend operator" proposed by the Expert Group – are not necessary.

VI. Conclusion

Basically, the concept of product liability law is suitable to take into account the particularities of AI systems. However, clarifications are necessary, e.g. with regard to the applicability of product liability law to software and to function-changing modifications of machines.

---

57 Hager, in Staudinger (founder), *Kommentar zum Bürgerlichen Gesetzbuch* (new edn 2018, Sellier / de Gruyter 2018) § 823 BGB mn. <?> 21; Spindler, in Gsell et al (eds), *beck-online.Grosskommentar zum Zivilrecht* (updated 01/10/2021, Beck) § 823 BGB mn. 662; Wagner (n 3) § 823 BGB mn. 991.

58 BGH NJW 1994, 517, 519; Spindler (n 55) § 823 BGB mn. 662; Wagner (n 3) § 823 BGB mn. 990.

59 See also Expert Group (n 6) p 45.

There are also gaps in liability, especially for systems that modify their capabilities after having being placed on the market. These should be closed by means of strict liability, insofar as the systems have a particular risk potential.

Furthermore, there are gaps, at least at the level of European law, which are, with regard to the monitoring of machines, of particular importance for AI systems. A legal obligation for operators to monitor should be introduced here. At the level of product liability law, the obligation to monitor products should be regulated by law.

Product Liability for Beyond-Product Ecosystems – Is the Product Liability Directive ready to accommodate smart products?

Teresa Rodríguez de las Heras Ballell[1]

I. Smart Products in the Context of Product Liability Rules: the Problem

The European Union product liability regime pivots on two core elements: product and defect. Since its adoption in 1985, the Directive on liability for defective product (hereinafter, PLD)[2] provides for a definition, for the purposes of the Directive, of 'product'[3] – slightly amended in 1999 -[4] and determines accordingly its sphere of application. The meaning, and the

1 Associate Professor of Commercial Law, University Carlos III of Madrid. Sir Roy Goode UNIDROIT Scholar 2021–2022, UNIDROIT, Rome. Member of the Expert Group on liability and new technologies whose mission is to provide the Commission with expertise on the applicability of the Product Liability Directive to traditional products, new technologies and new societal challenges (Product Liability Directive formation) and assist the Commission in developing principles that can serve as guidelines for possible adaptations of applicable laws at EU and national level relating to new technologies (New Technologies formation). The present contribution expresses only the personal opinion of the author and does not necessarily represent the opinion of the Expert group.

2 Council Directive 85/374/EEC of 25 July 1985 on the approximation of the laws, regulations and administrative provisions of the Member States concerning liability for defective products, OJ L 210, 7.8.1985, p. 29–33.

3 Article 2
'For the purpose of this Directive 'product' means all movables, with the exception of primary agricultural products and game, even though incorporated into another movable or into an immovable. 'Primary agricultural products' means the products of the soil, of stock-farming and of fisheries, excluding products which have undergone initial processing. 'Product' includes electricity.'

4 Directive 1999/34/EC of the European Parliament and of the Council of 10 May 1999 amending Council Directive 85/374/EEC on the approximation of the laws, regulations and administrative provisions of the Member States concerning liability for defective products, OJ L 141, 4.6.1999, p. 20–21. The amendment entails removing the exclusion of primary agricultural products and game. The scope is then explicitly expanded upon the amendment of the definition in 1999.

extent of this central concept – product –[5] to cover upcoming market and technological developments is decisive in assessing the versatility of the rules and the full compliance of policy goals in the long term. Furthermore, the conception of product – its definition, the judicial interpretation, and its application – does pervade the entire defective product liability machinery and determines, directly or indirectly, the meaning, the extent, and the operation of other component parts (defect, producer, defences, causation, putting the product into circulation).

Hence, challenges posed by technology progress and market development cast over the core conceptual element of the defective product liability system, but also extend over other elements of the system. Smart products materialize the multi-faceted impact of technological advances[6] on the system devised by the PLD. Therefore, a holistic approach to assess the adequacy of the product liability system to smart products is needed.

The PDL has successfully reacted to the poundings of innovation waves in industrial production models and technology developments. Even more, the state and the expected progress of the scientific and technical knowledge are explicitly acknowledged and incorporated into the system – interestingly, with a function that is today critically questioned.[7] Despite the PLD seems to preserve its utility and ensure its efficacy in achieving the originally pursued goals, the rigidity of certain components may compromise its future effectiveness. The value of the PLD would significantly enhance if the main concepts underpinning the system are revisited and refined, revised or clarified where needed and to the extent that current trends claim.

The emergence and expanding penetration of smart products in the market are timely catalysts of this profound reflection for the review (or the re-reading) of the PDL through digital lenses. Smart products exceed the practical and conceptual perimeters of 'products' as conceived, devised, and constructed in 1985 – and expanded and updated in the

---

5 'For the purpose of this Directive, 'product' means all movables even if incorporated into another movable or into an immovable. 'Product' includes electricity.'

6 The thesis that the impact of the second generation of digital technologies is multi-faceted and multi-layered is previously formulated and elaborated on, *inter alia,* in Teresa Rodríguez de las Heras Ballell, 'The Layers of Digital Financial Innovation: Charting A Regulatory Response' [2020] XXV Fordham Journal of Corporate & Financial Law 381.

7 Seyyed Rohallah Ghasemzadeh, 'The Economic and Legal Bases of the Development Risk Defence in European Product Liability: A Critical Approach to Proponents' Bases of the Defence' [2019] 27(5) European Review of Private Law 1023.

subsequent years – still, and despite the clear aspiration of the PLD to produce adaptive rules, with a recognisable industrial and post-industrial flavour. Smart products embody all the distinctive characteristics of the digital economy and the most disruptive features of the second generation of the digital transformation.[8] The advent and the pervasive expansion of smart products in modern life means that 'products' transformed into data-based AI-driven complex ecosystems of interconnected devices. As a matter of fact, contemporary economy produces, relies, and is based on 'opened products' (more precisely, 'opened product ecosystems') that interact with the environment, grow so as new devices and components are incorporated, evolve upon being updated and upgraded, and constitute a undistinguishable melting of services and products. The conundrum is then whether the product liability regime can embrace these 'Beyond-Product Ecosystems'.

The aim of this Paper is to unveil the challenges that smart products pose to the PLD and to assess the versatility of its core concepts and rules to accommodate them into the system without compromising its effectiveness and preserving its goals. This assessment will be based on the analysis of four elements: product, defect, causation, and defences. They constitute characterizing angles of the conception, and the operation of the product liability regime. The primary focus will be the concept of product and its evolution. As a consequence, the definition and the extent of defect, the determination of the causal link, and the admissibility of defences will be reconsidered accordingly. Thus, reflections on these four perspectives should provide relevant lessons and sufficient guidance for a general assessment. In conducting the analysis, an original conceptualization of smart products is proposed in this Paper: Beyond-Product ecosystems.

II. Beyond-Product Ecosystems: The Challenging Features

The stylized definition of 'product' in Article 2 PLD covers all movables, including those incorporated into, affixed, or associated to another movable or an immovable.[9] It is a broad and malleable definition that

---

8 As described in Teresa Rodríguez de las Heras Ballell, 'Legal challenges of artificial intelligence: modelling the disruptive features of emerging technologies and assessing their possible legal impact [2019] 1 Uniform Law Review 1.

9 Interestingly, the acknowledgment as products of accessions, fixtures, implements, or components in the definition is a convenient and clarifying drafting solution, as comparative law approaches differ in the legal treatment of such incorporated or

effectively encompasses the varied typology of products stemmed from industry and market innovation. It is indeed comprehensive and reasonably future proof, but still somehow corseted by an industrial logic. Therefore, smart products challenge not only the concept of product in the PDL, but also and fundamentally the foundations of the distinction of products# and services,[10] assets and data,[11] objects and subjects, in the modern economy, and consequently in the formulation and the application of legal rules. That is precisely the reason why smart products invite a dauntless revisiting of the conceptual basis and the policy vectors underpinning the PLD.

---

associated parts and their legal nature (legal individuality, movable or immovable by accession, etc). Therefore, the decision to avoid that dogmatic and legal issue for the purposes of the PDL has the actual effect of, not only providing certainty in the demarcation of the scope of the Directive, but also expanding the potential material scope of the defective product liability. In the field of secured transactions, in particular, the legal status of accessories, fixtures, or immovable-associated movables is crucial and has been at length debated – Marek Dubovec, 'Accessions and Non-Accessions under the Cape Town Convention: Special Focus on MAC Equipment' [2017] 6 Cape Town Convention Journal 52; Teresa Rodríguez de las Heras Ballell, 'Right of Accession, Ownership of Property, and Extension of Security Interests: Concepts, Conflicts, and Rules' [2016] III Philippines Journal of Legal Education 1; Teresa Rodríguez de las Heras Ballell; Megumi Hara, 'MAC Protocol and Treaty Design: Examination of the Delimitation of Scope and Mechanism of Amendment' [2017] 6 Cape Town Convention Journal 10; Teresa Rodríguez de las Heras Ballell, 'The interaction between the MAC Protocol to the Cape Town Convention and domestic law' [2020] 35/2 Butterworths Journal of International Banking and Financial Law 112; Benjamin Von Bodungen, & Charles W. Mooney, 'Immovable-Associated Equipment under the Draft Mac Protocol: A Sui Generis Challenge for the Cape Town Convention' [2017] 37 Cape Town Convention Journal 37, U of Penn, Inst for Law & Econ Research Paper No. 20–07, Available at SSRN: https://ssrn.com/abstract=3481481.

10 Janja Hojnik, 'Technology neutral EU law: digital goods within the traditional goods/services distinction' [2017] 25/1 International Journal of Law and Information Technology 63.

11 The applicability of the DPL to software has intensely discussed at length by scholars. Their reflections and views are of great value for the purposes of this Paper, even if the main thesis is that smart products pose challenges beyond this fundamental, traditional discussion. Michael Gemignani, 'Product liability and software' [1980–1981] 8 Rutgers Computer & Technology Law Journal 173; Sarah Green & Djakhongir Saidov, 'Software as goods' [2007] J Bus Law 161; Andrew Scott, 'Software as "Goods": Nullum simile est idem' [1987] 3(4) Computer Law & Practice 133; Jane Stapleton, 'Software, information and the concept of product' [1989] 9 Tel Aviv University Studies in Law 147; Lori A. Weber, 'Bad bytes: the application of strict products liability to computer software' [2012] 66(2) St. John's Law Review 469.

As proposed in this Paper, smart products defy legacy product liability system because they blur the line distinguishing products from services,[12] overflow the contours of products as single units to transform them into complex ecosystems, and evolve throughout its life cycle being updated and upgraded, being fed by data and interacting with the environment as if they were, metaphorically, *quasi* 'living beings'.[13] These are the disruptive dimensions of smart products that perfectly capture the specific characteristics of emerging digital technologies[14] guiding the reflection

---

12 Under the tendency towards a 'servitization of business' – Sandra Vandermerwe & Juan Rada, 'Servitization of business: adding value by adding services' [1988] 6(4) European Management Journal 314 -, the conceptualization and the distinction of products and services have been long debated in the management and business literature. L. Araujo & M. Spring, 'Services, products and the institutional structure of production' [2006] 35(7) Industrial Marketing Management 797; J. Gadrey, 'The characterization of goods and services: An alternative approach' [2000] 46(3) Review of Income and Wealth 369; Glenn Parry and others, 'Goods, Products and Services' in M Macintyre and others (eds), *Service Design and Delivery* (Springer 2011) 18; P. Hill, 'Tangibles, intangibles and services: a new taxonomy for the classification of output' [1999] 32(2) Canadian Journal of Economics-Revue Canadienne D Economique 426–446; J.M. Rathmell, 'What is meant by services?' [1966] 30(4) Journal of Marketing 32.
The characterization as goods or services is also of paramount importance for legal purposes (taxation, consumer protection, conformity, liability). ECJ case law has addressed this relevance distinction for different purposes of the EU internal market law – Case 7/68, Commission v Italy (Art), ECLI:EU:C:1968:46; Case C-2/90, Commission v Belgium (Wallonian waste), ECLI:EU:C:1992:310; Case 155/73, Giuseppe Sacchi, ECLI:EU:C:1974:40, paras 6–7; Case 52/79, Debauve, ECLI:EU:C:1980:83; Case 6/64, Flaminio Costa v ENEL, ECLI:EU:C:1964:66; Case C-393/92, Commune d'Almelo and others v NV Energiebedrijf Ijsselmij, ECLI:EU:C:1994:171; Case C-158/94, Commission v Italy, ECLI:EU:C:1997:500, paras 14–20; Case C-97/98, Jägerskiöld, ECLI:EU:C:1999:515.

13 An idea previously developed for understanding the particularities of software for the purposes of liability rules as they interact with the digital environment, are subject to the user's performance, and depend upon updates and upgrades. Then, the metaphor that software act as *quasi* 'living beings' were put forward. Teresa Rodríguez de las Heras Ballell, 'La responsabilidad por *software* defectuoso en la contratación mercantil' [2006] 10 Revista Aranzadi de Derecho y Nuevas Tecnologías 83.

14 Commission Staff Working Document, *Liability for emerging digital technologies* – Accompanying the document Communication from the Commission to the European Parliament, the European Council, the Council, the European Economic and Social Committee and the Committee of the Regions, *Artificial intelligence for Europe*, SWD(2018) 137 final.

exercise led by the European Union to assess the adequacy of liability legal frameworks[15] and its ability to accommodate digital innovation.[16]

Complexity, opacity, increasing autonomy, openness, vulnerability, and data dependency are distinctive features of emerging digital technologies (AI and IoT powered systems). They are present in the constellation of emerging digital technologies with different intensity. As a matter of fact, complexity, opacity or autonomy are matter-of-scale factors. A legal scrutiny of these distinctive features reveals that in certain cases these characteristics are actually game changers, entailing a profound redefinition of existing rules and principles, while in others they simply shake the pillars of the legal system without compromising their stability and durability. In this Paper, it is sustained that some of the characteristics of smart products show potential to reverse certain assumptions of the PDL and claim innovative, better-suited solutions.

1. *Complexity: The Ecosystem is the Product and the Product is an Ecosystem*

The most conspicuous and illustrative characteristic of smart products is complexity. Naturally, complexity is not a singular feature of smart products as traditional products do show notable, even high, degrees of complexity. A wide array of pre-digital products such as industrial equipment can be significantly complex. Complexity manifests in the plurality of component parts, in a technically sophisticated functioning, or in the need of highly trained users for their operation. Smart products' complexity goes beyond these manifestations. Smart products are 'ecosystems', where the ecosystem as a complex unit of interconnected devices becomes 'the product' in its use and operation by the user. It might be argued contrari-

---

15 R*eport on Liability for Artificial Intelligence and other emerging technologies* prepared by the *Expert Group on Liability and new Technologies. New Technologies formation*, 2019 – at https://op.europa.eu/en/publication-detail/-/publication/1c5e30be-1197-11ea-8c1f-01aa75ed71a1/language-en. Report from the Commission to the European Parliament, the Council and the European Economic and Social Committee, *Report on the safety and liability implications of Artificial Intelligence, the Internet of Things and robotics*, COM(2020) 64 final, Brussels, 19.2.2020

16 A challenge that defies all legal harmonization efforts both at a regional and at an international level, as addressed in Teresa Rodríguez de las Heras Ballell, 'Embracing Technological Disruption in International Transactions: Challenges for Legal Harmonization' in *National, International, Trasnational: Harmonischer Dreiklang Im Recht, Festschrift Für Herbert Kronke, Zum. 70 Geburstag* (Bielefeld, Giesekin Verlag 2020) 1223.

wise that such an ecosystem might simply be understood as a collection or combination of products or even as a complex product with multiple components and parts. Accordingly, the current definition of 'product' as per Article 2 PLD would, arguably, smoothly embrace smart products with minor frictions. However, the thesis of 'beyond-product ecosystems' in this Paper encapsulates a more disruptive approach and leads to a more radical consequence: the ecosystem is the product.

Several factors and illustrations may better convey the actual relevance of this statement.

A smart home system serves as a revealing example. The system operates on the basis of a combination of interconnected devices and components that are integrated or can be removed from the system in different moments and that can be, in general terms, configured under a diversity of models (number of devices, types of components, types of services) selected and personalized by the user on a voluntary basis, but also determined and constrained by a variety of reasons of technical nature (availability, interoperability, interconnectivity, geolocation), market or business character (market distribution, exclusivity agreements, cooperation arrangements, price) or legal and regulatory consideration (standards, limitations, regulatory requirements). The value and the utility of the system for the user stem from the system as a unit. Mostly, isolated single components or devices, outside the smart home system, are either useless (a disconnected device to control A/C) or simply satisfy a different purpose for the user – a normal fridge versus a smart fridge connected with the smart home hub and enabled to initiate online shopping.

Yet, a new addition to the smart home system does increase the global value of the ecosystem – as well as the potential risk – exceeding the individual value that the single device can separately provide the user with. New devices and components of the smart home system can be integrated into the ecosystem under very diverse forms producing 'different unique products' that do not necessarily correspond to any previous factory design and that have not been even considered throughout the manufacturing process. However, for the user, the ecosystem itself becomes 'the product'.

Such a holistic, integrating approach is also adopted by companies as a business and marketing strategy. The graphically named 'super devices'[17] are designed to enhance user experience in contexts with multiple devices used for different purposes and in varied scenarios. Siloed systems, inter-

17 As marketed by Huawei, see https://consumer.huawei.com/sa-en/offer/huawei-super-device/.

connectivity complications, and technical underperformance force users to a fragmented, low-standard experience. The aim of these 'super products' is said to be providing a single system that integrates all hardware and resources to unify the varied needs of all types of different devices, to enable flexible deployment as needed, and to freely leverage the capabilities of its component devices based on the user's real-time needs. Beyond the technical description and the marketing goals, this line of products reinforces the idea that products become complex ecosystems that integrate devices (old stand-alone products) to provide a single, versatile product experience to user. These interconnected devices are not mere components of a compound product, as a last intent to subsume these smart products to the current wording of Article 2 PLD might suggest, they are at the same time products susceptible of distinct and separate use and parts of the 'super product'.

It is our understanding that such technological advancements and market realities endorse the proposal to revisit the concept of product under the PLD and signal the need to assess the suitability of legacy legal solutions. Recent trends in product innovation should guide the understanding of products in the contemporary economy and inspire the evaluation of the current legal framework to ensure its future-proof resilience.

2. *Opacity, vulnerability,...and increasing autonomy*

Complexity of smart products (as ecosystems) is not only structural, but also operational. As the illustration of the smart home system reveals, the line between product and service is blurred. The 'smart quality' of a smart product is greatly based on the added-value services that the system adds on the non-smart use of a non-connected device. Not surprisingly, it is not unreasonable to question whether the paramountcy of the service is even prevailing over the importance of the product. Services that are delivered by the operation of algorithm/AI-driven solutions embedded in the 'product ecosystem'. The algorithm/AI-based solutions, fed by large amounts of data collected from different sources, drive actions to be performed by (devices of) the system, deliver services, and take certain decisions. That attributes to smart products other disruptive properties of digital emerging technologies: opacity, vulnerability, and increasing autonomy.

These features obscure the possibilities of discovering the effective cause/s upon the causing of damages (opacity), complicate the identification of the causal link (autonomy), magnify the damaging impact (vulnerability), and even raise the question whether unpredictable deviations from the expected performance of the autonomous decision-making system amounts to be a defect.

Despite a general mono-causal, human-centric conception, situations with multiple actors involved in causing damages and multiple causes likely to concur in the causation are not unfamiliar to traditional liability legal systems. Solutions are provided for by legacy systems. Nevertheless, the higher uncertainty, the excessive weight of the burden of proof on the victim, or an undesired and ineffective allocation of risks and incentives among participating actors invite further consideration.

Thus, *inter alia*, the *European Parliament resolution of 20 October 2020 with recommendations to the Commission on a civil liability regime for artificial intelligence*[18] aims to devise a predictable, effective, and more operational two-layer liability system (fault-based and list-based strict liability) for damages caused by AI systems pivoting on the figure of the operator – defined on the basis of two elements: control and benefit. The system proposed in the Resolution does neither interfere nor replace the defective product liability; therefore, it simply refers to the PLD the categorization of the AI system as product under the Directive and the attribution of the liability as far the producer is concerned.[19] In sum, the questions are reverted to the defective liability system and have to be addressed within the logical framework of the PLD and in conformity with its functions and purposes.

The Expert Group on New Technologies and Liability, New Technologies formation, had already identified in the *Report on Liability for Artificial Intelligence and other emerging technologies* (pp. 27–29) the main challenges for certain components of the defective-product-liability machinery, along with the very concept of product: defect, causation, and defences.

---

18 20 October 2020, 2020/2014(INL).

19 Recital 9:
'(9) Council Directive 85/374/EEC(3) ('the Product Liability Directive') has proven for over 30 years to be an effective means of getting compensation for damage triggered by a defective product. Hence, it should also be used with regard to civil liability claims of a party who suffers harm or damage against the producer of a defective AI-system. In line with the better regulation principles of the Union, any necessary legislative adjustments should be discussed during the necessary review of that Directive. The existing fault-based liability law of the Member States also offers in most cases a sufficient level of protection for persons that suffer harm or damage caused by an interfering third person, as that interference regularly constitutes a fault-based action, where the third-party uses the AI system to cause harm. Consequently, this Regulation should focus on claims against the operator of an AI-system.'

It is also our understanding that opacity, autonomy, and complexity challenge the equilibrium of interests underlying the current distribution of the burden of proof in the PLD (Article 4). The injured party will encounter significant difficulties in proving the defect and the causal relationship between defect and damage in the face of highly opaque, complex AI-driven decision-making. Mere transparency ('opening the black box') might not succeed in enhancing the position of the victim due to the complexity of the underlying algorithmic bases if they are not enlightened by an effective explanation of the reasons, the decision-making path, and the possible critical deviations or biases. Likewise, the efforts to collect relevant evidence, trace actions throughout the causation chain, and gather data might be fruitless, dissuasive, or unaffordable without the cooperation of the actors involved in the operation of the technological ecosystem.

In acknowledging the asymmetry that the above-described disruptive features are likely to provoke in detriment of the injured party, the legal logic underpinning the defective product liability regime should be revisited. Shifting, alleviating, or lowering the standard of the burden of proof in favour of the weaker party are reasonable responses to re-equilibrate the imbalance. In addition, the Expert Group has also put forward proposals to crystalize duties on the producer/operator aimed to ease the burden of proof and re-allocate the costs on the party who is better placed to adopt the needed measures. For example, the duty on producers to equip technology with logging solutions – (logging by design) [20]-[23] of the Report – is precisely intended to ensure the available of information instrumental to the discovery of the causes and give the victim the opportunity to reasonably access the needed information. Logging duties would operate in conjunction with a scheme of rebuttable presumption aimed to discourage the producer from failing to fulfil the duty or to provide the information upon request.

3. *Openness: Smart Products as quasi 'living beings'*

There are two other characteristics of smart products that are particularly disconcerting and challenging for the traditional product liability logic: data-dependency and openness.

The ability of the smart product to perform actions and take decisions primary depends upon static and dynamic data processed by the system: personalized settings by the user, direct instructions, data collected by connected IoT devices, predictions, data provided by authorized oracles or by third parties. Smart products are then highly data-dependant. Consequently, the availability, accuracy, sufficiency, and reliability of the data inputted into the system are critical performance factors for the smart product. The defective functioning of the smart product may be caused by 'defective information' (false or inaccurate information).[20] That impacts on the applicable liability rules, but does also affect the traditional role of the producer in controlling the product. In fact, the role of the producer dilutes in a multitude of other actors contributing to the design, functioning, and use of the smart product (Report, p. 28). The product is not a 'finished product', at least in the classical meaning. On the contrary, it is an 'opened, unfinished product' that is fed by multiple data flows, personalized by the user, and trained in the course of its operation on the basis of the self-learning capabilities (machine learning, deep learning).

Furthermore, unlike traditional products, smart products are enriched by updates, additions, and upgrades throughout its life cycle and after circulation. Updates and upgrades may be delivered unharmoniously in relation to the different interconnected devices. Respective producers can react asymmetrically in providing updates, releasing security patches or solving vulnerabilities. And the proactive cooperation of the user or the operator may be required to complete or render effective the implementation. All these considerations challenge the adequacy of the 'put-into-circulation' moment in a smart products' universe. This factor is relevant for assessing defectiveness in the light of the safety expectations of the average consumer[21] and in relation to certain defences and limitations of liability. Putting the product into circulation does not draw the end line of the producer's oversight and his/her interaction with the product. That relates to the reasonableness of the later-defect defence, and the adequacy of a development risks defence in a world of 'opened smart products'.

III. Commercial and Technological Units: the Proposal

The increasingly high complexity embedded in smart products, pictured as ecosystems, as expounded above (*supra* II) triggers an evident practical

20 On the liability applicable to the damages (including pure economic loss) caused by incorrect and false information, previously in Teresa Rodríguez de las Heras Ballell, 'El tercero de confianza en el suministro de información. Propuesta de un modelo contractual para la sociedad de la información' [2010] LXIII Anuario de Derecho Civil 1245.

21 Piotr Machnikowski (ed), *European Product Liability: An Analysis of the State of the Art in the Era of New Technologies* (Intersentia 2016).

problem of legal relevance. Multiple actors could contribute to the causation of the damage. A plurality of actual or potential tortfeasors is certainly not a new problem for tort law that indeed provides for solutions.[22] However, the thesis in this Paper is that there are special factors in smart products that force the resistance of traditional rules and solutions and may require a more radical approach. The proposal that smart products are and operate as ecosystems is not a pure factual description, but, as previously explained, it intends to be a conceptual proposition: the ecosystem itself becomes 'the product'. This conceptual proposition is linked to the formulation of better-suited legal solution for complex ecosystems: the concept of commercial and technological units and its consequences in the context of liability rules, as proposed by the Expert Group on New Technologies and Liability, New Technologies formation, in the *Report on Liability for Artificial Intelligence and other emerging technologies* [29]-[30]. In advocating for this solution, the Expert Group takes into consideration several factors.

The multitude of actors participating in the design and the evolving operation of a 'beyond-product ecosystem' could act without prior coordination or planned intervention, the contribution could be occasional or spontaneous, and the participation of some actors could be totally unknown or even unforeseen by the main operators (data provider, hacker, non-interoperable system, inexperienced user). Hence, in some circumstances, flawed functioning, harmful outcomes, or damage to the operation of the system could be provoked by the lack of inter-operability among the components, the interaction with other unexpected components or software, wrong data, or inexpert or inadequate use by the user. In such scenarios, the damage cannot be easily attributed to a specific component, a well-defined cause, or a single actor. The damage derives from the ecosystem as a whole, specially from the perspective of the injured party.

Far from being the classical mono-causal conception of causing harm, frequently, the damage results from a conjunction of interwoven effective causes and has been collectively triggered by multiple actors. This situati-

---

22 Bernhard A. Koch, 'Proportional Liability for Causal Uncertainty', in Martin-Casals/ Papayannis, *Uncertain Causation in Tort Law* (Cambridge University Press 2015); W. V. Horton Rodgers (ed.), *Unification of Tort Law: Multiple Tortfeasors* (Kluwer Law International, 2004); Bénédicte Winiger et al. (eds.), *Digest of European Tort law I: Essential Cases on Natural Causation* (Verlag Österreich 2007); Bénédict Winiger, 'Multiple Tortfeasors', in Lubos Tichý (ed.), *Causation in Law* (University of Karlowa 2007).

on is not unfamiliar to current legal systems either. Rules dealing with damages caused by multiple causes are indeed presently provided for in all jurisdictions, as acknowledged above. Nonetheless, unlike traditional products, once circulated by the original manufacturer and without the latter's participation, subsequent actors can intervene in the marketing, the use, or the upkeep of sophisticated technological products without the participation of the original producer. Accordingly, in the cycle of production and use of the product, subsequent activities, tasks, and causes can interfere and contribute in the likeliness of the damage being caused. That multi-layer process implies the overlapping and convergence of many sources of damage – software updates, personalizing options by the end user, self-learning actions, and data collection.

The perturbing effects of observing how significantly smart products differ from traditional products has a two-fold impact. On the side of the injured party, the victim encounters difficulties in identifying the party to sue, may be forced to assume higher procedural costs, and takes the risks of being undercompensated or finally unprotected if he fails to sue the right party or cannot identify whom to sue. An opportunistic design of complex internal structures or unknow arrangements among the participants in the ecosystem may entail the dilution of responsibility and the obscuration of causal links for the victim. On the side of the participating actors, parties are, however, exposed to judicial actions without having the opportunity to adopt the effective measures to prevent the damage or mitigate the risk as they are integrated in a complex ecosystem with no control over the full operation. That means that incentives are misplaced and the liability system fails to fulfil its goals. The defence of the component producer might be relevant (Article 7 (f) PLD), but that would mean to assume that each interconnected device is a component of the main product and has been designed to fit into the product or as per the instruction given by the manufacturer. Under the concept of 'beyond-product ecosystem' such an assumption is contradictory and inaccurate, so the defence needs to be put under consideration.

Given all above, the proposal of the Expert Groups works as follows. The existence of a commercial and technological unit for the purposes of the product liability is to be assessed on the basis of several factors: coordinated marketing actions, technical interdependency, interoperability, and the degree of specificity or exclusivity in the combination and the joint operation of the devices within the ecosystem. The legal consequence is that where the victim can demonstrate that at least one element of that unit has caused the damage, without the need to single out which element in particular or to which extent,[23] all members of the unit as potential tortfeasors should be jointly and severally liable vis-à-vis the victim. Naturally, participants into a technological unit can and are encouraged to make contractual arrangements to gain efficiency and provide predictability in the redress stage. The solution is designed to protect victims and ensure that they are not undercompensated or unprotected due to the complexity, and opacity of the ecosystem.

In evaluating the proposal, it might be discussed the suitability and predictability of the factors that defines a technological unit. On the one hand, a prior contractual agreement among the participants might be a clear signal of the existence of a technological unit and would mean that parties have incentives to anticipate the liability distribution among them and act accordingly. But it might not be assumed that a contractual relationship is always possible or necessarily visible or recognisable by third parties. As it has been explained previously, ecosystems can grow and evolve under different conditioning factors and by effect of customizing actions of the end user or other intermediate participants in the supply chain. Then, on the other hand, a technological unit might be identified where other factors such as the subject to the control of the main operator, common standards, coordinated marketing, close interoperability, exclusivity agreements, or belonging to a platform concur, as proposed in the Report.

Whereas the option for the solidarity effectively addresses and solves the external relationships between the victim/s and the multiple tortfeasors integrated in a commercial and technological unit, the internal relationship among joint and several tortfeasors must be also carefully tackled. The most effective solution seems to keep the rule of several liability among tortfeasors that is typically ascertained in proportion to their contribution to the causing of the damage. This rule protects the tortfeasors against excessive claim that could asphyxiate small actors and innovative start ups, but it allocates the burden of full compensation and the uncertainty in the reimbursement level on the payor (the tortfeasor who paid the full compensation on the basis of the jointly-and-severally-liability rule). It has also the drawback of entailing a multitude of judicial proceedings initiated by the payor against each tortfeasor for the corresponding proportion. Certainly, the rule of several liability does simply postpone to a second

---

23 Bernhard A. Koch, 'Proportional Liability for Causal Uncertainty', in Martin-Casals/ Papayannis, *Uncertain Causation in Tort Law* (Cambridge University Press 2015.

stage the complexity and the uncertainty on the identification of relevant causes in technological ecosystem, as previously expounded in detail. But the solidary rule in the outer sphere vis-à-vis the injured party achieves the full satisfaction of the compensation function of the liability rules. In the inner sphere of the 'beyond-product ecosystem' parties are incentivized to reach agreements and distribution liabilities on a consensual basis. Otherwise, liability of other tortfeasors towards the one who has paid damages, within the commercial and technological unit, to the victim is normally several. There is no reason to deviate from these principles in the context of 'beyond-product ecosystem' and as a natural complement of the commercial and technological unit's doctrine.

The Paper aims to show the challenges that smart products signify for the core concepts and the main solutions of the product liability regime as crystallized in the PLD and to assess their versatility to accommodate the idea of 'product-as-ecosystem' (beyond-product ecosystems) without undermining the effectiveness in pursuing its goals. The analysis has gone through the role, the extent, and the meaning of four main elements of the PDL machinery: product, defect, causation, and defences. With a primary focus on the concept of product and its evolution, the proposal is to reconsider entirely the concept of finished product and complex products with multiple components, as the PDL assumes, and to accept the ambitious idea that smart products are ecosystems (opened, evolving, and complex ecosystems). Consequently, the ecosystem is the product, and the product becomes an ecosystem (beyond-product ecosystem). Thus, the definition and the extent of defect, the determination of the causal link, and the admissibility of defences have to be reconsidered accordingly. These reflections of the Paper aspire to contribute to the fundamental debate on the adaptability of the PDL to embrace and effectively accommodate smart products.

Discussion Panel

Liability for AI

Introductory Statement of Axel Voss, Member of the European Parliament (MEP)

Axel Voss[1]

Every technical and technological innovation – including the rapid progress in the development of "artificial intelligence" (AI) – leads to both risks and opportunities. Despite the enormous opportunities that AI offers for all areas of our lives, the question of liability plays a major role in our legal system.

It is key for legislators to minimize the risks and create the conditions for a European AI industry that will be able to compete in the global market. Therefore, the liability law must provide legal certainty.

I. Why we need European liability

1) The political dimension

On the issue of regulating liability for AI, legislative competence lies primarily with the EU Member States. However, the increasingly borderless and global dimension of digitalization no longer fits with our national civil law. The European digital single market will become completely fragmented if we do not harmonize civil law issues with digital relevance at European level. I therefore hope that the realization that digitalization requires central systems in terms of efficiency and economic growth instead of fragmented legal systems will also catch on among the Member States. In other words: If we want to succeed in a European AI development, we need a European Digital Single Market and thus a European regulation.

---

1 Member of the European Parliament (MEP), Christian Democratic Union of Germany, European People's Party Group (EPP Group)

2) The legal dimension

Any AI (its development, application, impact) is already subject to liability according to the respective national character. However, the 27 Member States have provided different requirements, distinctions and connecting factors to existing forms of contract. This not only ignores the European single market but also means an unnecessarily high legal burden and thus a high legal risk for both developers and users.

We therefore need a horizontal legal framework for all AI systems. It is crucial that it ideally takes the form of an EU Regulation so that everywhere the same standards will be applied. This framework should be supplemented by sector-specific regulations for the broad range of possible AI applications.

II. Closing legal gaps

Due to the complexity, connectivity, opacity, vulnerability and autonomy of AI systems, new specific liability rules are needed to avoid a situation where a person who suffers harm is left without compensation, for example, if he or she cannot prove the fault of the operator of the AI system. In particular, cases in which many unaware third parties are affected, such as when an AI operates in public spaces must be covered as they would otherwise have no liability claims against the operator due to the absence of a contract or fault.

III. What principles should guide a European regulation on AI liability?

1) Our aims

- Full harmonization
- Adherence to the existing legal standards of the liability regimes, but at the same time we must be open to future international standards
- Not preventing the development of AI systems
- Legal clarity and legal certainty

2) *Adjustments to the law*

The liability regulations must be in line with the Product Liability Directive, the General Data Protection Regulation, the Consumer Protection Regulations, the Medical Devices Directive and the anti-discrimination regulations as special legal regulations.

IV. Which AI systems are affected?

According to the ideas of the European Parliament (EP), only so-called high-risk AI systems should fall under a strict liability regime. There must be a balanced definition of what AI is and which systems can be considered as high-risk. In order not to increase the threshhold on AI, the EP assumes that only systems that are capable of causing any damage at all to life, limb, health and property are covered and that it is not foreseeable who the potential injured party would be, i.e. that there is a kind of general risk.

V. Legal consequences of a high-risk AI system

High-risk AI systems should be subject to a strict liability regime, while other AI systems can continue to be subject to fault-based liability. Liability for high-risk AI systems should correspond to strict liability and – like the operation of a motor vehicle – entail an insurance obligation. In order not to demand innovation-deterring insurance sums here, the EP has focused on the approach and amount similar to car insurance. This should not be an unreasonable requirement or risk, neither for insurance companies nor for developers or operators.

In the EP´s draft, the respective operator of the AI system is to be liable towards the injured party; questions of joint liability as well as of internal compensation for damages between software/hardware developers and the manufacturer are related to contractual and tort law rights.

VI. Assignment to high-risk AI systems

What constitutes high-risk AI systems should be exhaustively listed in an annex to the regulation so that there is legal certainty for everyone. To adapt the list to the rapid technological developments as quickly as possible, the Commission should permanently adjust it within the framework of the so-called "delegated acts" in consultation with a panel of experts.

Introductory Statement

Evelyne Gebhhardt, Member of the European Parliament (MEP)

Evelyne Gebhardt[*]

Smart devices have long entered our daily lives. They are part of our routines, collect and record data of our habits and use these to assist us in a variety of ways. Smart products play our favorite music, remind us when our fridge runs out of milk, they even monitor our medicine intake or watch our children. Smart products, also known as the internet of things (IoT) are certainly of benefit for consumers. We should however not underestimate their risks. A smart fire alarm might lose connection and not warn against a blaze. There could be a flaw in your home security system, which would consequently fail to impede a burglary. A smart toy might be hacked and could in turn put children in danger.

The list is endless and current product liability law fails to provide answers. Now, what is clear is that we need to rethink concepts like product, defect or damage considering these new challenges. How do you allocate responsibility for damage? What kind of damages deserve compensation? What about insurance? How do you make sure the party that bears the risk also holds the responsibility?

Moreover, we need to look at novel forms of contracting to address situations where smart and autonomous products interact without human intervention, for instance, a smart fridge ordering products online or a shopping order done based on a voice-enabled smart assistance tool such as Amazon Alexa or Google Assistant. To what extent are such contracts binding on the parties? Who is responsible in case of errors if something goes wrong with an order initiated by a smart product or an incorrect voice transmission? Contract law needs to be adapted to cover these situations. We need strong safeguards to ensure that contracts in the digital economy preserve the rights of our consumers and citizens.

While AI endeavors to improve our lives in many sectors it also causes risks from the development stage on to the moment when products and

---

* Member of the European Parliament (MEP), Social Democratic Party of Germany, Party of European Socialists.

services reach the market. Liability law needs to be updated in order to prevent consumers from being the ones bearing the burden of proving the causal relationship between a potential damage and the underlying defect. Liability should lie on the party controlling the risks of the operation. This refers to the person continuously defining the features of the relevant technology and providing essential and ongoing backend support. We need to avoid that the normal consumer ends up paying for a defect he or she has no knowledge about nor control over. For the normal consumer it is impossible to understand, let alone to prove, the causal relationship between a defect and a damage in an AI system and the legal framework needs to take account of this. It is worth considering to what extent it is appropriate that the natural or legal person operating the AI technology also holds some degree of responsibility. Nevertheless, that degree of responsibility should always be that which can reasonably be expected depending on the person's circumstances. This could entail the installation of updates, for instance.

It is however advisable to distinguish between sophisticated and less sophisticated users. While an update obligation can be expected to be performed by a hospital deploying an AI technology, a vulnerable consumer operating an AI technology might not even be able to install those updates.

Assigning liability to one or the other person is relevant because the kind of damage a self-learning device can cause is probably much more present, diverse, and different than that of an analogue product. One of the particularities of IoT relates to the fact that, while a smart product might apparently seem harmless, it can very well cause severe damage. As a matter of fact, data hijacking, data breaches or device theft are just some examples of dangers to users of smart products. And there is more, a software might also pose problems not because of an attack or manipulation by a third party but because the purpose it was designed for is questionable. Let's take the example of discriminatory practices in credit concession through credit scoring or discrimination within recruitment processes. These kinds of practices should be prohibited as a matter of principle and while this escapes the remits of product liability law, the latter needs to be designed to take account of these kinds of circumstances.

Indeed, we must distinguish an ex-ante control phase and an ex-post liability phase. The purpose of the ex-ante control phase is controlling which kind of technologies can be put on the market. The ex-post liability phase aims to compensate the victim, placing the victim in the position in which he or she would have been had the tort not been committed.

This phase should follow a precautionary approach to the development and use of AI as well as a more gradual establishment of risks and corresponding legal requirements. This includes a right of information about the use of AI and automated decision-making as well as preventive impact assessments in order to allow the banning of highly dangerous technologies. While it makes sense to have this gradual distinction in the ex-ante phase for the purpose of certifying, controlling, and prohibiting technologies, it is not advisable to include a risk distinction in the liability phase. This is so because alleged low risk technologies may very well cause severe harm. Let´s take the example of an AI driven grass cutter that loses connection and drives over a toddler. The kind of damage a technology can cause on users is unrelated to the risk categorization that took place during the regulatory phase.

As we said, AI and automated decision-making bears the potential to create harm in a much more far-reaching manner than analogue products. It is especially so with regards to immaterial harm. While analogue products may as well cause immaterial damages and most Member States' national legislations provide for compensation against non-material damages, the likeliness that smart products or services cause immaterial harm is considerably higher. Thus, it is even more important that the law envisages compensation against immaterial harm caused by AI technologies. Currently Member States foresee compensation against violations of a variety of personality rights. These include violations to the right to life, physical and mental health, reputation, honor, health (pain and suffering), dignity, name, privacy of personal and family life, freedom, worsening of social position among others. It is not surprising that AI driven products or services entail a much higher risk to cause immaterial harm to these rights than analogue products. This is so because AI driven technologies are susceptible of being cyberattacked or manipulated by third parties (hackers, malicious programs) and because of the special characteristics of these technologies. These technologies can be placed to take decisions that affect consumers (credit concession, recruitment). They can gather sensitive information about consumers (tastes, habits) and can exploit these in an abusive manner with a view to maximizing counter performance from consumers (personalized advertising). The purpose and functioning of these technologies might be in accordance with current laws and standards of consumer protection and non-discrimination. They might even be legitimate from an ethical point of view but the purpose they were designed for might change via updates or self-learning. Such changes could transform a legally or ethically sound technology into an illegal or ethically questionable technology.

Overall, it becomes obvious that self-learning technologies entail much higher risks susceptible of causing severe immaterial harm than analogue products. The special characteristics of smart products and machine learning, its complexity, opacity, vulnerability, the capacity of being modified through updates as well as the capacity for self-learning, stress the need to modernize product liability law. Product liability law and AI-specific legislative acts need to constitute a sort of safety net in case something goes wrong despite the before mentioned ex-ante control. Citizens and consumers must be adequately protected and we need to avoid those persons who suffer harm to their person or property end up without compensation. Where the ex-ante phase failed or where unintended new events arise, we need to ensure a compensation.

But we should not only look at liability. We should not only care about ex-post compensation. As legislators, we should first and foremost care about what we want to permit. Where are the limits of what is acceptable? Is it proportionate to supply public spaces with facial recognition systems for the sake of security?

We should not strive for a societal model that enables enterprises to gather sensitive information about consumers in order to maximize benefits. We have accepted business models that are very questionable from an ethical point of view. We got used to giving our data the category of economical counter performance. We pay with our data in order to be able to communicate with our family and friends on social media. Is it really worth it? Are we aware about the degree of commercial surveillance we are subject to? Do we talk about real consent if there is no informed choice, alternative nor opt out? We got used to enterprises applying different prices depending on the kind of information they gathered about us. Targeted advertising and manipulative choice architecture lead to less consumer choice, not only regarding products but also regarding information. The Cambridge Analytica scandal has highlighted the dangers of online manipulation. Nevertheless, not much has happened since then to meaningfully change these business models. We accept them for the sake of convenience.

While new technologies can create efficiencies from an economical point of view and while they can improve our lives in many ways, certain practices should undoubtedly be prohibited. While security of course matters, facial recognition in public spaces is not exempt from risks. If systems are fed with biased data that erroneously link certain behaviors, mimics and body language to behavior classified as suspicious from a criminal point of view, innocent persons can be categorized as suspects.

We need to prohibit the use of self-learning algorithms enabling businesses to gain a comprehensive insight about consumer's personal circumstances and behavior patterns, allowing them to tailor their advertising and contract terms to specific profiles thus exploiting consumer's willingness to purchase goods and services. We need to prohibit scoring systems that decide whether a specific consumer can purchase a product or take up a service. We need to ban commercial tracking and profiling of consumers. We have to prohibit the mixing of data from different services and not make this prohibition dependent on consumer consent as the design makes it often too hard if not impossible to refuse consent. We need to comprehensively regulate emerging digital technologies to forbid an unfair or abusive use of such systems.

Unfair practices of big online platforms affect individuals but as well society and democracy. It is not only about the economic implications to consumers: higher prices, lower quality, less choice, but also about fundamental rights, individuals, society, and democracy. Big platforms that control the access to goods and services, also called "gatekeepers" already expanded into a position where they control access to essential services in areas such as information infrastructure (search engines), communication infrastructure (social networks) and trading infrastructure (online marketplaces). The power and mode of operation of these online platforms could extend further to public services, such as healthcare and education. Already now, they provide services of general interest, citizens, business, and workers depend on. The COVID-19 pandemic exacerbated this dependency.

The infrastructure that platforms have built is not neutral. It is a means to exercise power. They collect data and control the behavior of users in a way that further increases the power of platform owners. Therefore, their power needs to be balanced. We need consumer protection by default and a ban of dark patterns. We need to prohibit abusive defaults such as tying or bundling practices. Platforms need to be held responsible. Interoperability, data protection, data portability and transparency are key. Many of the services provided by gatekeeper platforms are essential infrastructure. Citizens, business, and workers depend on them. The COVID-19 crisis exacerbated this dependency even further. Digital markets must be deconcentrated to allow alternative business models and civil society to flourish. We need to ensure that emerging digital technologies are not used to the detriment of consumers and citizens.

How should ‘smart products’ be handled in contractual and (product) liability law?

Susanne Dehmel, Bitkom e.V.[1]

„Smart products” are characterized by the fact that they consist not only of material objects (hardware) but also of software, with the software assuming a control function and thus enabling automated, and in some cases even autonomous, functioning of the smart product. The smarter the product, i.e. the more artificial intelligence (maybe even based on machine learning) is contained in a material object, the louder the calls for additional regulation.

Liability rules must strike a delicate balance between providing legal certainty to the users of smart products about the risk they take in the course of their business, encouragement to prevent damage, surety that injured parties are compensated on the one hand and promoting innovation on the other hand. To maintain this balance, a nuanced approach to liability regulation, based on clear definitions and an honest look at the existing regulatory framework is necessary.

1 Member of the Executive Board at Bitkom e.V., Bitkom represents more than 2,700 companies of the digital economy, including 1,900 direct members. Through IT- and communication services alone, our members generate a domestic annual turnover of 190 billion Euros, including 50 billion Euros in exports. The members of Bitkom employ more than 2 million people in Germany. Among these members are 1,000 small and medium-sized businesses, over 500 startups and almost all global players. They offer a wide range of software technologies, IT-services, and telecommunications or internet services, produce hardware and consumer electronics, operate in the digital media sector or are in other ways affiliated with the digital economy. 80 percent of the members’ headquarters are located in Germany with an additional 8 percent both in the EU and the USA, as well as 4 percent in other regions of the world. Bitkom promotes the digital transformation of the German economy, as well as of German society at large, enabling citizens to benefit from digitalisation. A strong European digital policy and a fully integrated digital single market are at the heart of Bitkom’s concerns, as well as establishing Germany as a key driver of digital change in Europe and globally.

I. What is Artificial Intelligence?

Artificial intelligence (AI) systems include rule-based systems (expert systems) and learning systems. What all currently used types of AI have in common is that they operate within the limits of the respective programming and within the scope of a narrowly defined task area. They do not dictate to themselves the results to be achieved and the evaluation procedures for the analysis of input data. Purpose of use, target and analysis specifications are programmed by humans and are unchangeable. Because of these limitations, current AI systems are commonly referred to as "weak AI." Systems with "strong AI", which could independently perform any mental task that humans are also capable of, independently leave the scope of action set by their developer, and independently adopt any mental target, are currently purely visionary. Systems of "strong AI" will probably not exist in several decades (if at all).

Presently and in the foreseeable future only "weak" AI systems or assistance systems are deployed. These AI systems either provide recommendations to prepare a final human decision or follow learning and decision-making processes in a human-defined frame and within pre-defined limits. Their application is therefore principally not connected with an increased risk. On the contrary, by avoiding human errors (e.g. delayed reaction, overlooking essential data/information, subjectivity), AI systems can reduce human errors and thus the risk of damages. To promote and make full use of these opportunities, legislators should not burden operators and manufacturers of AI systems with additional liability risks that exceed the liability risks of other technologies. In particular, regulations of AI systems aiming at mitigating the risks of complexity, autonomy or connectivity of a system would lead to excessive regulation, because these qualities are not specific characteristics of all AI Systems.

II. Current regulation of Artificial Intelligence

The current law has a dense network of various regulations for the manufacture and use of technical products. On the one hand, the law imposes conformity requirements, particularly with regard to product safety, which a product must meet in order to be approved for sale in the EU. On the other hand, various liability provisions apply to damage that occurs during the operation of technical products despite these conformity requirements.

Although conformity requirements and liability regulations have not been formulated specifically for AI applications, they must be observed by manufacturers, operators and users of AI applications without exceptions. Manufacturers are liable to their contractual partners under warranty for the freedom from defects of their AI products and to injured users of an AI application under product and producer liability. Additional requirements for manufacturers are set out in product safety law, which is designed to prevent violations of legal rights. The operator of an AI system is liable for ensuring that data protection violations, discrimination, personal injury or property damage do not occur when the system is used. If the operator uses the AI system to fulfill its contractual obligations, contractual liability claims are added, which may be exacerbated by professional liability. The user is also liable under tort law for his own fault. In addition, contributory negligence must be taken into account when assessing possible damages.

Current law bases its liability obligations not least on the danger to important legal assets. The greater the potential danger and the higher the ranking of the endangered legal asset, the more severe the liability and the more bases for claims and liable parties are potentially available to the injured party. If, for example, the timely performance of a contract is impaired, the party injured as a result can assert claims for default against the contracting party alone. If, on the other hand, the passenger is injured in a car accident, liability claims can be made against the driver on the basis of contractual and fault liability against the other party involved in the accident on the basis of fault liability, against the vehicle manufacturer on the basis of product liability, and against the owners of the vehicles involved in the accident or their insurers on the basis of strict liability. This graduated liability also becomes clear in the case of producer liability. Accordingly, the more dangerous the product and the more likely it is that damage will occur, the higher the due diligence requirements for the manufacturer. The AI Act, which will regulate artificial intelligence and that is currently in the process of being drafted at EU level, will continue this risk-based approach. Where necessary, the new AI proposal will address specific risks according to possible damages and the environment in which the technology is implemented.

Furthermore, the current liability law correctly follows a technology-neutral approach. This means that liability is based on the damage to a legal asset, without regard to the specific technology involved in causing the damage. Legislators should not deviate from this approach by introducing special liability rules for AI and thereby disadvantaging AI technology. Liability law must guarantee reliable compensation for damage that has occurred, regardless of which technology contributed to the occurrence of the damage.

III. Revision of the Product Liability Directive

The existing liability framework in the EU consists of the Product Liability Directive 85/374/EEC (PLD) and national liability rules. In order to ensure that this framework is fit for the digital age and flexible enough to still strike the aforementioned delicate balance of interests surrounding liability, certain proposed changes and additions to the PLD are subject to discussion.

1. Proposed extension of the product definition

Whether software and AI applications should be considered products in this sense is a matter of debate. For the sake of clarification, but also to expand the definition of the term "product", it is proposed to explicitly include CI applications as well as digital content and services in the scope of the PLD.

One argument against extending the established concept of product to software, especially if it includes AI, is that there have not been any liability gaps in the deployment and use of such systems to date and that the applicable product liability law has proven its effectiveness. It is already recognized by case law that a manufacturer is liable under the applicable principles of product liability if the damage was caused by the malfunction of control software (embedded software) integrated into the product.

An argument against the qualification of stand-alone software as a product is that significant dangers, e.g. security vulnerabilities, depend not only on the original manufacturer of the stand-alone software, but also substantially on the user/operator. In particular, the manufacturer of the software can hardly foresee or control with which other software components the operator/user will connect the software. Furthermore, applying product liability to stand-alone software would impose unacceptable liability risks on the creators of open source software, which could lead to this type of software no longer being offered.

Finally, the requirement to include services in the concept of product and thus in the scope of application of product liability law has so far not been sufficiently substantiated and jeopardizes the necessary balance of interests. In particular, it is not clear how damage to uninvolved third parties can occur outside the contractual relationship for a service. If the customer of a service is harmed, he or she can already obtain sufficient compensation for this under current contract law.

2. *Proposed prolongation of responsibility*

Under current product liability law, the manufacturer is responsible for defects that have their cause before the product is placed on the market. It is proposed that liability be extended to include defects that arise only after the product has been placed on the market in the course of use (e.g., due to cyberattacks or updates). In this respect, the manufacturer would in future be subject to an obligation derived from product liability to keep an AI system up to date after it has been placed on the market (update obligation) and to make these updates available to all users – irrespective of existing maintenance contracts.

An update obligation for providers of digital products has already been introduced by Art. 7(3) of Directive (EU) 2019/771, but – rightfully so – limited to contractual relationships. Only if a contractual relationship exists and the software manufacturer has data on the software customers, is it possible for him to install updates to the necessary extent on the customers' devices. In addition, software updates serve to maintain the functionality of the program and thus to preserve the user value. This interest in equivalence is protected by contract law. Product liability, on the other hand, serves to protect third parties not involved in a contractual relationship in the integrity of their legal interests. However, this does not necessarily require software updates, but a danger to the legal interests of third parties could be ensured, for example, by warnings, recall or – especially in the case of machine learning systems -by switching off the learning function.

In addition, it must be kept in mind that the maintenance of software requires considerable effort on the part of the manufacturer. The more complex and specific the software is, the greater is the effort needed. For this reason, software maintenance services are regularly provided in business transactions between companies only on the basis of special contractual arrangements and in return for payment. Within the scope of software maintenance, the specific operating environment of a software product, the interaction with other hardware and software components, and current technical progress as well as current cyber security threats can be taken into account appropriately and on a customer-specific basis. A similar update obligation based on product liability would not only deprive manufacturers of an important business segment, but such an obligation would simply not be feasible for them in terms of the necessary customer individualization. A legal obligation to guarantee that updates are free of errors that goes even further would further increase costs and would no longer be calculable for manufacturers. Ultimately, the manufacturer of software, and in particular of AI systems, can only be expected to accept strict liability to the extent that he has direct and immediate influence on the course of events. However, such controllability of the course of events is only given on the basis of a contract or until a product is placed on the market.

3. *Proposed extension of the scope of application to non-material damages*

Under the current rules of product liability, compensation is only payable if a person is killed, injured, their health impaired or if a privately used item is damaged. In some cases, there are calls for the obligation to pay compensation to be extended to include immaterial damage such as data loss or data protection violations or infringements of informational self-determination.

Product liability is subject to comparatively low requirements in order to provide adequate protection primarily for consumers, irrespective of existing contracts. To compensate for this, damages can only be claimed in the event of infringements of particularly important legal interests. This balance shouldn't be eliminated by an unrestricted expansion of the protected legal interests. Infringements of data privacy and personal rights with the aid of digital tools are already sanctioned outside of product liability in data privacy law, anti-discrimination law and tort liability. There are therefore no gaps in protection in this respect. It would not make sense to double the already severe sanctions for companies. A necessary risk-oriented approach to liability also means that there should not be multiple liability for any damage under the same conditions.

IV. *Striking the delicate balance*

Neither humans nor AI, which are created by humans, can be expected to act error-free. As things stand, this is technically impossible to achieve. Accordingly, a sanction must not affect the manufacturer or operator of an AI system merely if a status of being error-free is not achieved. However, AI systems cannot be said to have a special propensity for danger that goes beyond previously known technologies. Rather the opposite is true: by avoiding human errors (e.g., delayed response, subjectivity) AI can reduce human errors of judgment and thus risks of harm. If these possibilities are to be realized, producers and operators of AI must not be burdened with liability risks that go beyond the liability risks associated with other technologies.

Especially with the national implementation of the Digital Content Directive (Directive (EU) 2019/770) and the Sale of Goods Directive (Directive (EU) 2019/771), new requirements to provide updates for smart devices will protect the consumer for longer period of times and give users additional rights.

There is currently no need for horizontal and stricter liability rules, maybe even with compulsory liability insurance for operators of high-risk systems with artificial intelligence, as the risks of such systems (e.g., autonomous motor vehicles, drones, smart medical devices) are already, and often very highly regulated, by sector-specific rules (national traffic and aviation laws). Neither in liability law nor in market access control does it make sense to create new regulations that only apply to applications with artificial intelligence. Liability is and should be based on the scope of applications and typical risk potential of a device, not on the technology used.

Smart liability for smart products

Introductory Statement of Jutta Gurkmann, Federation of German Consumer Organisations (vzbv)

Jutta Gurkmann[1]

According to a representative Bitkom-survey of 2020[2], almost one in four German households is already using smart technology for lighting, 18 % for their alarm system, 16 % for video surveillance and 15 % for heating. The main reasons for use are higher levels of convenience (72 %), security (65 %) and energy efficiency (52 %).[3] 49 percent of consumers who do not use connected devices are discouraged by the lack of data protection, while 47 percent fear cyber-attacks and other disruptions caused by criminals.[4]

These figures show the need for a new legislation, not leaving consumers with the risk of bearing the costs for damage caused by smart products. From the consumers' perspective, smart products need a comprehensive and coherent regulation which at least should take into consideration product liability, sales law and AI regulation.

The regulation in force determining when manufacturers are liable for damage caused by faulty products is based on a directive passed in 1985. At that time, there were no digital voice assistants or devices connected to the internet. Consequently, the legal situation today is not at all adapted to the products offered nowadays. When we look at the current product liability regulation it is at least difficult to say whether software and therefore smart products are included. The new directive should therefore clearly comprise software in whatever form it might be placed at the disposal.

Presently, liability is limited to personal and property damages. As smart products work with large quantities of data, moral prejudices for

1 Jutta Gurkmann, Head of the Consumer Affairs Department at the Federation of German Consumer Organisations (vzbv).

2 https://www.bitkom.org/sites/default/files/2020-09/200922_studienbericht_smart-home.pdf (p. 7)

3 https://www.bitkom.org/sites/default/files/2020-09/200922_studienbericht_smart-home.pdf (p. 9)

4 https://www.vzbv.de/sites/default/files/downloads/2020/01/10/2019_vzbv_factsheet_smart_product_liability.pdf

privacy breaches or financial losses as a result of identity theft are very likely. Liability should therefore be extended to immaterial and also to financial damages. Just as within the directive on certain aspects concerning contracts for the supply of digital content and digital services, there should be an obligation for the supply of updates.

As consumers could never localise the source of a defect when a problem with a smart product occurs, the producer should bear the burden of proof as long as the product is used for the designated purpose. This impossibility is also the reason why different producers of networked devices should have joint liability.

But not only producers should be liable for their products: with the ongoing boom in the e-commerce sector, online marketplaces play an increasingly important role for the supply of goods. At the same time, they are under no obligation to check whether producers from outside the EU comply with the EU product safety regulation. That's why platforms offering the sale of goods from producers outside the EU should firstly be obliged to ensure that the producer complies with EU law and secondly be fully liable if the producer is not available in case a problem occurs.

With regard to the possibilities the Sales of goods Directive offers, vzbv asks for a prolongation of the legal guarantee for durable goods. A synchronisation of the legal guarantee and the obligation to supply updates would be reasonable. Since the seller or the supplier might in many cases not be able to install updates on the sold devices, the obligation should be extended to the producer.

Furthermore, vzbv asks for a differenciation between the different types of updates (function-conserving, function-modifying, security, content, ...). Consumers must get all necessary information (including the implications for the consumers' rights) to be able to decide whether they want to install the update.

Introductory Statement

Gerhard Schomburg[1]

On the subject of the panel, how 'smart products' should be handled in law, I actually cannot submit concrete proposals. As a federal official I am very much depending on the composition of the government and its political agenda. The current legislative period is almost through, we will have elections in September and then we will get a new coalition with a new political agenda. Therefore, I want to stick to some questions that seem to be obvious looking at the present and the upcoming legal situation:

I. Scope of the obligation to supply updates for 'smart products'

According to our new rules for the transformation of the Sales of goods Directive and the Digital Content Directive into German law the obligation to supply updates only applies to contracts between businesses and consumers (B2C). This is in line with the Directives and complies with the coalition agreement of CDU/CSU and SPD that provides for a one-to-one transposition of EU-Rules. But we have missed the chance to adjust the law to the requirements of 'smart products' for B2B-contracts too. From January 2022 on, the business that sells a 'smart product' to a consumer will have a legal obligation to supply updates to the consumer. But the businesses in the supply chain up to the producer of the 'smart product' are obliged to supply updates only if this is agreed contractually. We are intending to watch how the obligation to provide updates will work in its small scope and, where appropriate, widen the scope to B2B-contracts.

1 Dr. Gerhard Schomburg, Ministerial Councilor, Federal Ministry of Justice and Consumer Protection.

II. Extension of the obligations of the producer?

According to the Sales of goods Directive and the Digital Content Directive the seller or any other business which supplies the 'smart product' to the consumer is the addressee of the new obligation to supply updates. In practice the seller, or other contractual partner of the consumer, regularly will not be able to supply the update. Mostly only the producer of the 'smart product' will have the necessary technical knowledge to do this.

In view of this, a discussion has begun whether the obligations of the producers should be extended. In that regard we see with great interest that the EU-Commission announces in her 'Circular Electronics Initiative' measures to ensure that electronic devices are designed for durability, maintenance, reuse, and recycling, and that consumers have a 'right to repair' them including software updates. Beyond that we should not preclude further measures in civil law: In my ministry we are currently preparing to tender a study to consider whether it is useful to widen the non-contractual liability by giving the consumer who has bought a defective good a right to repair or replacement against the producer. In Germany this concept is discussed under the heading of "gewährleistungsähnliche Herstellerhaftung". We want to know how great the advantages of such a direct claim would be for consumers and which economic implications this would have for the producers and the sellers in the supply chain.

Last but not least the liability for damage caused by defective products must cover the new challenges of smart products. We appreciate that this question is currently under investigation by the Commission. Where necessary the Product Liability Directive should be revised in order to ensure its application to all new digital products and to ensure its consistency to all aspects of these items able to cause damage to the consumer. We welcome that the Commission has announced a proposal on that.

One Specific Problem from a Tort Law Perspective

Introductory Statement of Professor Bernhard A. Koch, University of Innsbruck

Bernhard A. Koch[1]

In addition to what has already been said in this conference, e.g. the question of whether, and if so, to what extent the Product Liability Directive (PLD) in its current form can adequately respond to harm caused by smart products, I would like to highlight one particular challenge as food for thought.

As we have heard, tangible smart products as such clearly fall within the scope of the PLD even if their defectiveness is due to a flawed algorithm pre-installed in the gadget. However, we have also heard how difficult it is to properly apply the PLD considering continuous updates to such digital content, putting a big question mark on the future relevance of the PLD's magic moment when the product was put into circulation.

I believe that a rather significant additional complication arises from the connectedness of smart products and the possibility for the user to adjust the smart content to her individual needs. If this remains within the framework set by the developer of the product's firmware, it may be unproblematic, as any choices made by the user are (or at least should be) foreseen by the manufacturer.

However, if it is in the very nature of the product being connected to other gadgets or systems, it gets more complicated. Take the example of a smart home system that is based on a generic standard like Zigbee. The user first needs a hub but is then typically free to add further components which do not necessarily have to be from the same manufacturer. Let's say I buy the Philips Hue Bridge, because I start my home automation with a lighting system. I add some light strips from IKEA, connect them to Amazon's Alexa, I then use smart sockets of some no-name producer sold in a local hardware store in order to steer other electronic devices with the system. I also add a smoke detector from yet another manufacturer that inter alia turns my balcony lights to flashing red in case of fire. Since the

1 Professor of Civil Law, University of Innsbruck.

features of Philips' own app are rather limited for what I want to do, I install an alternative app on my smartphone instead developed by a further independent company. To sum it up – I have just created an ecosystem of the kind Teresa Rodríguez was speaking of earlier.

While I am at a conference in Münster, one of the many components goes haywire, the system is constantly turned on and off, which eventually causes one of the lighting elements to overheat and ultimately start a fire that not only burns down my own apartment, but also spreads to the neighbour and causes harm to her inventory or even to herself.

Even if I were able to identify the defective component that started the whole mess (which I doubt as it will usually have melted like everything else), I still may not necessarily know exactly how to properly allocate that risk. After all, the gateway should have had its own built-in protection against chaotic on-and-off commands, my app should have informed me that something is wrong (which would have given me the opportunity to intervene), and maybe my smoke detector should have gone off and alerted the neighbour in time, but it just didn't.

The point is – apart from finding an appropriate liability solution for each individual product in that conglomerate, we need to keep in mind the big picture of allocating risks, which do not necessarily come from a singular product in an isolated environment. With smart products interconnected by default, this is even more true.

The most significant challenge in practice – before we even get to the question whether the manufacturer shall be strictly liable or only accountable for fault (even if the latter is presumed) – will be identifying the cause (or rather causes) of a harmful event. This is, of course, primarily a task for the technical experts, those who have to dig through the remains of my smart home system, which will probably be nothing more than a huge, melted lump of plastic and wires. So, I fear quite often these experts will come back shrugging shoulders.

How shall we deal with the remaining uncertainty regarding causation? In practise, this is closely related to the domestic laws of procedure which – at least at present – are beyond reach for harmonisation. The different standards of proof within the EU can lead to entirely different results in such complex scenarios – for example, shall we proceed from the assumption that the hub was flawed, even if the experts came to the conclusion that there is only a 51 % probability for such a scenario? Even if all components were subject to the same liability regime, harmony at the level of substantive law will not lead to identical results as long as this question is answered differently from jurisdiction to jurisdiction.

The laws of evidence sometimes provide unique answers to exceptional challenges, as seen in the *Sanofi Pasteur* case four years ago (C-621/15). The CJEU – as you recall – greenlighted the French approach to dealing with uncertain causation in such circumstances, arguing that it did not go so far as to entirely overthrow the burden of proof provided in Art 4 of the PLD. The public outcry against the court's press release (which, though, did not fully reflect the technicalities of this case and therefore led to misunderstandings) is the best evidence that something may still be wrong here.

Similar differences between European legal systems exist at the level of substantive law when it comes to problems of alternative causation, for example. Let's say it can be proven with a probability exceeding the standard of proof that it was one (and only one) of two lightstrips that triggered the fire, but not which one. Too bad they were produced by different manufacturers. It is a pity that European legal systems do not agree when it comes to alternative causality, with some denying liability for both possible causes altogether, others foreseeing joint and several liability, and yet others offering different solutions.

Shall we "resolve" this problem by taking a step back and channel liability for the entire combination of components onto the owner (in my example, me)? This would obviously relieve my neighbour of the burden of proving which component was the actual cause and therefore of the question which manufacturer she should sue. However, this certainly cannot happen on the basis of fault – I bought commercially available appliances marketed as suitable for this combination, I did nothing wrong when connecting each individual component, and I did not forget to install all updates to the respective firmware as soon as they were released. So, shall I be strictly liable for anything I have in my apartment? Nothing has fallen out of my dwelling, it hasn't collapsed, so the traditional bases of liability known from Roman times do not help. Are household appliances like lightstrips as dangerous as the general clauses of strict (or at least stricter) liability had in mind? Each component was of course a "thing" within the meaning of the *gardien* liability, but do we need or want to extend this concept to all other member states, and if so, only with respect to smart goods?

We could of course build upon an idea already used in the PLD – am I, as the homeowner, in this case comparable to a supplier and therefore liable as a producer if I cannot tell my neighbour the true manufacturer of the defective component "within a reasonable time"? This would clearly require legislative action, even though the argument as such sounds plausible. But do we want to take that step?

As Teresa said, we have addressed some of these problems of complex ecosystems in the Expert Group, but there is clearly no one-size-fits-all answer to each of these problems, certainly not in a comparative perspective. As a panellist, I am in the fortunate position of not having to answer the questions that I have raised in order to stimulate the discussion that follows, but I think we should at least also be aware of those levels of complexity when designing legal responses to the challenges of smart products.

Introductory statement

Jean-Sébastien Borghetti[1]

Two questions at least can be raised on the issue of how smart products should be handled in product liability law.

The first one is whether smart products require liability rules which make not only the providers, but also the users of such products liable for harm caused by these products. In most legal systems, the general rule is that users of products are not liable for damage caused by these products, unless they were at fault. There are some exceptions, however. French law, for example, has a "liability for things" regime, which is basically a strict liability regime for damage caused by the thing used by the defendant, regardless of his fault. Do smart products have a specificity that would justify switching from the traditional fault-based liability to strict liability of users? I do not think so, for at least two reasons. One is that smart products are not necessarily and per se more dangerous than ordinary products (should we call them dumb products?). The second is that this would mean a drastic change in national liability laws.

The second question is whether liability of products providers, as it now exists for example in the European Product Liability Directive (PLD), is adapted to smart products. Here again, I do not think so, for at least two reasons. The first one, which has little to do with smart products, is that the channeling of liability on producers and importers, as is currently the case with the PLD, is not a good solution for plaintiffs. Even leaving aside the difficulty to identify the producer, which may become even greater with smart products, reaching to the producer or the importer is often very difficult for the plaintiff. It is indeed remarkable that there seems to be very few product liability claims against importers into the EU of non-EU products, even though these products cause accidents, just like products manufactured in the EU, about which there are many claims. This, I think, is an indication that the channeling of liability on producers and importers is not a good solution for plaintiffs. It would be much better to make professional providers of products liable for harm caused by the defective products they sell. This idea is becoming fashionable with the

1 Professor of Civil Law, Paris II Panthéon-Assas University.

rise of platforms, but such liability existed in some countries before the PLD was adopted and could apply more broadly than to just platforms.

A second reason why product liability in its current state is ill-adapted is that the notion of "defect" is difficult to apply to smart products, and more generally to artificial intelligence (AI). It will probably be very difficult to prove the defectiveness of an AI. To go past this obstacle, two solutions at least can be contemplated: one is a reversal of the burden of proof of defect; the second one is a switch to truly strict liability, i.e., basically purely causal liability, but this is rather extreme and could be justified only for certain types of products, such as those incorporating "high risk AI" as is suggested by the recent European Parliament proposal on civil liability for AI.